Delinquency and Dropout

Delinquency and Dropout

Delbert S. Elliott
University of Colorado

Harwin L. Voss
University of Kentucky

P. 95

Lexington Books
D.C. Heath and Company
Lexington, Massachusetts
Toronto   London

Library of Congress Cataloging in Publication Data

Elliott, Delbert S.
　　Delinquency and dropout.

　　1. Juvenile delinquency—United States. 2. Dropouts. I. Voss, Harwin
L., joint author. II. Title.
HV9104.E44　　　364.36'0973　　　73-19727
ISBM 0-699-91934-9

Published simultaneously in Canada.

Printed in the United States of America.

International Standard Book Number: 0-669-91934-9

Library of Congress Catalog Card Number: 73-19727

To
The High School Class of 1967,
Sweetwater Union High School District
and Ravenswood High School

Contents

List of Figures

List of Tables

Preface

The work on this project began in September 1962 with a pilot study on the relationship between delinquency and dropout in two local high schools. In February 1963, a grant from the National Institute of Mental Health was received, and the initial phase of the research began. The study was conducted in several junior and senior high schools in southern California and in one high school in northern California. The data-gathering phase of the study covered the five-year period between February 1963 and September 1967. During that time, a massive amount of information on the 2,617 subjects was accumulated.

The initial grant request was developed by Delbert S. Elliott with the assistance of Aubrey Wendling. Harwin L. Voss joined the research team at the time the grant request was submitted. All three investigators participated jointly in the development of interview schedules and questionnaires and in the data collection. Responsibility for data processing, analysis, and writing was assumed by the authors, and this volume represents our collaboration.

We wish to express our appreciation to the administrators, faculty, and staff of the schools in the Sweetwater Union High School District and Ravenswood High School in the Sequoia Union High School District. They graciously gave their time and patiently responded to our many demands and interruptions. In particular, we would like to thank Mr. Joseph Rindone, Superintendent; Mr. Harry Ruby, Assistant Superintendent; Mr. Ward Donnely, Pupil Accounting Officer; and Mr. Malcolm Taylor, Principal. Throughout the trials and tribulations of this extended investigation they maintained their interest and support.

For their comments and advice on the study, we would like to thank Donald R. Cressey, Clarence Schrag, and Lyle W. Shannon. We would also like to thank Richard Jessor for his helpful suggestions on an earlier draft of the manuscript. Special thanks are due to Carol Voss for her invaluable assistance. Finally, we owe our lasting gratitude to Elinor Kastelic who supervised the laborious tasks of coding, editing, and processing the data.

Delinquency and Dropout

1

The Problem and Objectives

For many years concern with the condition of youth centered largely on delinquency, but within the last decade dropout has also been seen as a critical social problem. While there is general agreement that delinquency constitutes a serious problem of youth, the view that dropping out of school also comprises a contemporary social problem requires explanation. In contrast with delinquency—where the behavior of juveniles is deemed improper—there is nothing inherent in the act of leaving school to explain a societal definition of dropouts as problematic. Termination of one's education short of high school graduation formerly was a common practice in this country. Today, however, it occurs in a social context quite unlike the situation earlier in this century when there were no negative consequences, other than possible limitation on the chances of upward social mobility resulting from not completing high school. The modern dropout encounters a different world than did his counterpart in the 1920s who found ready employment in the mills, factories, or mines. In that earlier era, a "dropout" found a job, married, and raised a family; without great difficulty he became a conventional citizen. Technological changes, however, have drastically reduced the range and number of jobs available today for the person with less than a high school education. There is no longer a ready-made place for the dropout in the community's economic system. Not only have many unskilled jobs been eliminated, but a high school diploma has become a credential needed for entry into many jobs.

Further, many persons perceive a linkage between dropping out of school and other social problems, particularly unemployment and delinquency. The usual view is that, lacking jobs, dropouts become involved in delinquency. Unfortunately, this causal relation has been assumed, rather than documented. Nevertheless, it is generally agreed that dropout does entail undesirable consequences. As early as 1957, a causal connection between dropout, unemployment, and delinquency was claimed by the Committee on the Judiciary of the United States Senate:

Special attention was given to the problem of the "dropout" student, the child who leaves school at an early age and is not able to obtain a job. This child often drifts from job to job, then to no job, and, in too many cases, sets a foot on the road to delinquency. . . . Many of these children, often referred to as the school dropouts, are potential delinquents who receive little in the way of special services needed to solve the problems which caused them to drop out of school. [242, pp. 8, 12-13]

3

Dropouts have also been linked to the rioting and civil disorders of the late 1960s. The National Advisory Commission on Civil Disorders reported that their survey of riot cities revealed "that the typical riot participant was a high school dropout" [157, p. 425]. For most adults dropping out of school is associated with "getting into trouble," whether it be delinquency, civil disobedience, drug use, or involvement in the counter culture.

Without question the rates of officially recorded delinquency have increased in recent decades, and these higher rates have been linked directly with dropout by law enforcement officials, sociologists, and educators. For example, Schreiber, Director of the School Dropout Project of the National Education Association, claims that there is a definite connection between delinquency and dropout [198, 199]. Asserting that the exact nature of the relationship has not as yet been determined, he concludes that the adjudicated delinquent is quite likely to be a dropout. On the basis of juvenile court records, the rate of delinquency in the total population is about 3 percent, whereas the rate of delinquency in the dropout subpopulation is 30 to 35 percent. The available evidence would seem to support the idea that there is a causal relation between dropout and delinquency.

Historically, the explanation for quitting school was considered obvious—it was adequately expressed in the stereotype of the dropout as "dumb," "dull," or "mentally retarded." This explanation also provided the causal link between dropout and delinquency, because mental retardation was regarded as a major variable in the etiology of delinquency. Recent studies have, however, discredited both propositions. Most dropouts have the necessary intellectual ability to complete a high school curriculum; further, delinquents as a group appear to be indistinguishable from nondelinquents with respect to I.Q. and achievement test scores [24; 62; 96; 229]. It is apparent that limited intellectual capacity is an important variable in the explanation of some dropouts, but other variables are necessary to account for the majority of dropouts who appear to be intellectually capable [252].

The initial task in this research was the development of a systematic theory sufficiently comprehensive to account for delinquency and dropout among intellectually capable students. While in the area of delinquency there is a rich body of theory, there is a paucity of theorizing concerning dropout. In the development of our theoretical scheme, we relied heavily upon the seminal works of Sutherland [228] and Merton [148; 149], as well as the more recent theoretical refinements of Cohen [34] and Cloward and Ohlin [33]. We are particularly indebted to Cloward and Ohlin's effort to integrate the theoretical traditions of differential association and anomie; the theory that we have developed to explain delinquent behavior and dropout is essentially a modification and extension of their formulation. Nevertheless, this research should not be construed as a test of Cloward and Ohlin's formulation. Whereas they explicitly limited the scope of their theory to gang delinquency among urban, lower-class males, we attempt to account for involvement in delinquency of youth, both male and female, from all social classes.

/We propose that the crucial conditions for delinquency are real or anticipated failure, extrapunitiveness, normlessness, and extensive exposure to delinquent persons or groups./ A similar set of variables and causal sequences provide a parallel explanation of high school dropouts: dropout involves failure to achieve valued goals, intropunitiveness, social isolation, and exposure to pro-dropout influences. Our research reflects an attempt to relate these conditions as they are found in the community, school, and home to delinquent behavior and dropout. /The guiding proposition for this study is that both delinquent behavior and dropping out are alternative responses to failure, alienation, and selective exposure to these forms of behavior. Because of the central place occupied by the school in the lives of young people, we believe it to be the most important context in the generation of delinquent behavior. Further, we expect delinquency to lead to dropout\\ [60]. Although the relationship is complicated by such factors as official labeling as a delinquent and the inability to secure employment, movement out of the school context should reduce school-related frustration and alienation and thereby lead to a decreasing involvement in delinquency.

The major purpose of this investigation was to evaluate the adequacy of our theoretical scheme. If our objective had been to estimate precisely the delinquency and dropout rates in a community, a probability sample would have been essential. Convinced that variable representation is more important than proportionate representation, we have employed a purposive sampling technique to obtain the combinations of variable values required to evaluate our theory. The effect of this decision is that generalization of the relationships observed in this study to other populations cannot be made with a known degree of accuracy.

In this research, a type of cluster sample was used in which the basic sampling unit was a school, rather than a person. We sampled only in the purposive selection of 8 schools to guarantee inclusion of students with a wide range of social, economic, and racial or ethnic characteristics. All of the schools were located within 2 metropolitan areas; 7 of the schools were located in southern California, the other in the northern part of the state. All students who entered these schools as ninth graders in September 1963 comprised the target population. From the available pool of 2,663 students, we encountered 5 student refusals and did not obtain parental permission to interview 41 others. Thus, the study population consisted of 2,617 students.

The research design was longitudinal. Initial observations were obtained when the study population entered the ninth grade, and additional observations were obtained annually until the usual date for graduation from high school for the cohort. Limitation of the study population to a single academic class "controls" the effects of age or maturation. We attempted to make personal contact with each respondent in the original cohort during each of the 4 annual data-gathering phases. Included in this effort were those students who dropped out as well as those who transferred to another school.

While completion of a longitudinal study involves considerable expense and presents a number of special data-gathering problems, the nature of our problem required use of this type of design, if we were to assess postulated cause-effect relationships. The first observations were calculated to precede dropout and extensive involvement in delinquent behavior in order to permit accurate determination of the temporal order of events. As is often the case with research in the behavioral sciences, neither the independent nor dependent variables could be manipulated artificially; it was essential to take repeated measurements through time and to relate previous measurements to subsequent differences while controlling for those factors known to be relevant. A longitudinal design permits a more adequate test of expected relationships than a cross-sectional design. On the other hand, a fundamental problem in longitudinal studies involves the loss of subjects over the course of the project. To minimize case attrition because of residential mobility, we developed rather elaborate tracking techniques.

In this study we have attempted to overcome three basic difficulties characteristic of previous empirical research about delinquency and dropout. One limitation of the available research is that few studies have been directed by any systematic theory; the findings presented in the current body of literature are largely descriptive rather than explanatory. Correlations between delinquency, dropout, and certain other variables and attributes are reported in an atheoretical context. Yet, without relevant theory these correlations, regardless of their magnitude, do not offer an explanation of the phenomena under investigation [37].

This volume reflects the authors' conviction that sound insight and understanding of the phenomena of delinquency and dropout require that research be embedded in systematic theory, because theory not only specifies the nature of the propositions to be examined but also functions to direct the research effort at each phase of its execution. Theory also provides an essential element in the effort to make causal inferences from empirical data. In this work we utilize theory to account not only for delinquency, but also to explain why a student drops out. Contemporary delinquency theory is extended to comprehend the phenomenon of dropout among capable students, and the interrelationship between delinquency and dropout is explicated.

Another limitation of much of the accumulated research is one of inadequate conceptualization of delinquency and dropout. The distinction between behavior in violation of legal statutes and the process whereby suspected offenders are labeled as delinquents is rarely made in delinquency research. Yet, the question of how one comes to engage in behavior classified as delinquent is conceptually distinct from the question of how one is labeled as a delinquent person. Typically, theories of delinquency have been designed to account for the occurrence of delinquent acts, but in most tests of these theories investigators have employed official contact with a law enforcement agency to distinguish between delinquent and nondelinquent persons. Failure to make a distinction between delinquent behavior and the delinquent person has limited the utility of much of the research in delinquency.

While *dropout* may be viewed as an act or as a label applied to persons, most of the research thus far has dealt with the persons to whom the term could be applied. However, there are no clear or consistent rules for assigning this label. Some investigators consider only those who leave school voluntarily as dropouts, whereas others include all persons who fail to graduate for any reason other than death or severe physical disability. An important limitation of many studies involves cohort attrition. Lacking adequate funds to pursue mobile families, many researchers eliminate from their sample students who move out of the district in which the study is inaugurated. In areas of high mobility, attrition in the sample is a serious problem, and the result is that the study is refocused as an analysis of the school's "holding power" because the investigator does not know the status of mobile students.

Awareness of conceptual problems is a first step toward their resolution. We paid considerable attention to the problems involved in defining delinquency and dropout clearly. Self-reported delinquency items were embedded in the questionnaires administered to students in the first and fourth years of the study. In addition, official delinquency data were collected from law enforcement agencies in cities where the respondents resided. In the analysis we distinguish between actual delinquent behavior and delinquency as a label attached to persons. Because of student movement in and out of school during the course of the study, a single definition of dropout is inadequate, but at this point definition as one who does not graduate from high school is sufficient.

The third and most important limitation of existing research on delinquency and dropout is the almost exclusive reliance on cross-sectional designs. A tremendous volume of research has been conducted, but investigators have rarely used a longitudinal design. Efforts have been made in recent years to develop strategies to permit the derivation of causal inferences from data gathered at one point in time, but few strong causal arguments about delinquency or dropout have been formulated [14]. A longitudinal study provides for the collection of theoretically relevant data prior to the occurrence of dropout or the inception of delinquent behavior. Because of the difficulty involved in establishing the temporal order of variables, causal inferences are difficult to derive from cross-sectional data. Data gathered at one point in time generally preclude insight into developmental sequences or processes that lead to delinquent behavior or dropout. As in a cross-sectional study, we examine the relationship between initial or first-year scores on a variable and subsequent delinquent behavior or dropout. However, the availability of data gathered at different points in time permits assessment of the direction and amount of change in these scores during the course of the study and enables us to derive causal inferences.

In our research we attempted to deal with each of the basic limitations of previous studies. First, a systematic theory encompassing delinquency and dropout was developed to account for the incidence of delinquent behavior and dropout, as well as to explain the nature of their interrelationship. Second, we established precise definitions of the phenomena under investigation. Third, a longitudinal study design was utilized to afford maximum support for causal inferences. Having completed the research, we are now in a position to evaluate the theory in light of the empirical data.

Our goals cannot be described as modest; at some points it will be obvious that we did not completely succeed in our effort. Specifically, the advantages of a longitudinal research design are partially offset by its unique problems. Many of the statistical tools available to researchers are appropriate in cross-sectional analyses; with the exception of cautions concerning contamination effects, guidelines for the analysis of longitudinal data in the literature are, at best, inadequate. Nevertheless, we are convinced that these kinds of data are necessary for adequate testing of theoretical propositions.

2 The Conceptual Framework

Few theories have had greater impact on delinquency research and action programs than Cloward and Ohlin's formulation in *Delinquency and Opportunity* [33]. Cloward and Ohlin attempt to integrate the theory of anomie, as stated by Durkheim and Merton, with Sutherland's theory of differential association.[1] They locate the motivational stimulus for delinquency in the structural conditions that give rise to anomie, whereas it is in the exposure to delinquent subcultures that delinquent behavior is learned and positively reinforced as an alternative means to achieve cultural goals. This formulation provides the general foundation for our explanation of delinquency and dropout. While the major thrust of Cloward and Ohlin's work concerned the emergence, maintenance, and content of specific delinquent subcultures, we have focused upon those aspects of their formulation that deal with the genesis of delinquent behavior. From their discussion of how specific conditions and processes lead to delinquent behavior and the emergence of subcultural norms, we have developed an explanation of delinquent behavior and dropout. Although Cloward and Ohlin had different objectives, we propose that implicit in their formulation is an explanation of delinquent behavior in terms of the following four variables: (1) aspiration-opportunity disjunction, (2) external attribution of blame, (3) alienation or normlessness, and (4) access and exposure to delinquent groups.

Critical analyses of their position and relevant empirical research have accumulated over the past decade, and we have attempted to take these developments into account. Unfortunately, few investigators have examined any of the complex conditional relationships suggested by the theorists, and only Jessor [110] and his co-workers have attempted a multivariate analysis. The available evidence pertains almost exclusively to the postulated relationship between aspirations, opportunities, and delinquency; to our knowledge no one has examined the temporal sequences or the causal order of the major variables. Although considerable evidence has been accumulated on the two-variable relationships between delinquency and goal-success disjunction, punitiveness, alienation, and exposure, there has been little systematic effort to evaluate this theoretical position. Our review of the available evidence leads us to question the salience of the particular goal-opportunity disjunctions identified by Cloward and Ohlin as the instigating forces for delinquency, as well as their limitation of the theory of differential opportunity to lower-class youth.

In subsequent pages we present a general theoretical explanation of delinquency and dropout that constitutes a modification and elaboration of Cloward and Ohlin's formulation. We suggest that failure to achieve valued goals, when attributed to injustices or inequities in the social system, leads to normlessness. Juveniles who experience this form of alienation and who have access to delinquent groups are most likely to engage in delinquent behavior. As previously mentioned, the critical conditions for delinquency are real or anticipated failure, extrapunitiveness, normlessness, and extensive exposure to delinquent persons or groups. A similar set of variables and causal sequences provides a parallel explanation of high school dropouts. The motivational stimulus to drop out is found in an individual's failure to achieve desired goals. If the individual attributes this failure to his own inadequacy, he may protect himself from further loss of self-esteem by dropping out. Dropout involves failure to achieve valued goals, intropunitiveness, social isolation, and exposure to dropout. We propose to relate these conditions, as they are found in the community, school, and home to delinquent behavior and dropout. Further, these conditions are not unique to the lower class; rather, they tend to be found among youth of both sexes and from all social classes. On the basis of official data and self reports, researchers have consistently reported a lower delinquency rate for females than males, but this does not mean that different etiological processes are involved. Similarly, studies of self-reported delinquency offer little evidence to support the contention that delinquent behavior is heavily concentrated in the lower class. Whereas Cloward and Ohlin explicitly limit the scope of their theory to gang delinquency among urban, lower-class males, we attempt to account for the involvement in delinquency of all youth, regardless of sex or social class. Consequently, our research should not be construed as a systematic test of Cloward and Ohlin's theory. Reliance on the work of Cloward and Ohlin in the development of our formulation offers a distinct advantage—attention is focused upon psychologically normal responses to structural strains and inconsistencies in the social order. Delinquency is not attributed to personal pathology, inadequate socialization, or abnormal personality configurations. On the contrary, it is viewed as purposive behavior, oriented toward conventional social goals and involving the means most readily accessible for their realization.[2] In our formulation, delinquency and dropout are viewed as alternative adaptations to failure. The adoption of one alternative as opposed to the other depends upon the individual's explanation of failure, type of alienation, and exposure to delinquent or dropout influence. The total scheme is presented in Figure 2-1.

Defining Delinquent Behavior and Dropout

All too often a theory of delinquency is developed without specification of the phenomenon to be explained; researchers have often employed a measure of

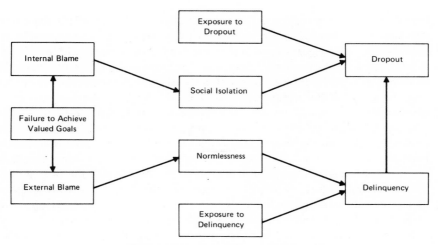

Figure 2-1. General Theoretical Scheme

delinquency that had little or no correspondence with their conceptualization of delinquency. Traditionally, theories of delinquency have been designed to account for the occurrence of delinquent acts, but in most tests of these theories investigators have employed official contact with a law enforcement agency as the criterion of delinquency and, consequently, a classification of persons as delinquent or nondelinquent. Careful attention to the conceptualization of delinquency will not solve all of the problems in the field, but it will remove one important source of ambiguity. Specifically, failure to make the conceptual distinction between delinquent behavior and delinquent persons has limited the utility of much of the research in delinquency. The availability of official records that designate a population of delinquents has led many researchers to test etiological theories of delinquent behavior on the basis of a classification of delinquent persons. Cohen cautions, "In order to build a sociology of deviant behavior, we must always keep as our point of reference deviant behavior, not kinds of people" [35, p. 463].

Problems of definition and measurement plague investigators interested in delinquency and dropout. These difficulties are related because the problems in measurement are partially a result of conceptual difficulties.[3] There is little agreement concerning the appropriate unit of analysis in delinquency research; a review of the literature reveals that attention has primarily been focused on behavior, persons, or groups, although at times delinquency has been viewed as a social problem [251]. The situation with respect to dropout is similar with one exception—dropout has rarely been conceptualized as a group phenomenon.

In the first definition of delinquency, primary concern is with a type of behavior or a class of behavioral acts that is consistent with Cohen's concept of deviance as "behavior which violates institutionalized expectations—that is, expectations which are shared and recognized as legitimate within a social system" [35, p. 462]. Hirschi states that "delinquency is defined by acts, the detection of which is thought to result in punishment of the person committing them by agents of the larger society" [103, p. 47]. Similarly, Cloward and Ohlin propose that the delinquent act "is behavior that violates basic norms of the society, and, when officially known, it evokes a judgment by agents of criminal justice that such norms have been violated" [33, p. 3]. These definitions do not enumerate the specific acts that are to be considered delinquent although a specific class of acts or behavior is implied as the appropriate unit of analysis.[4]

In using the second concept of delinquency, other theorists and investigators focus their attention on delinquency as a quality or attribute of persons. This usage is involved in role definitions of delinquency and is implicit in research based on official records. Utilizing police, court, or institutional records, investigators frequently employ official contact with law enforcement agencies as the criterion of delinquency. In the process, the assumption that there are only two kinds of children—delinquent and nondelinquent—is unwittingly introduced. In a strict legal sense, a juvenile is adjudicated as a delinquent in court proceedings. If one is legally declared a "delinquent child" and this is known to others, it is likely that one will be invested with the social role of a delinquent [37]. Recently, some sociologists have examined the process whereby a juvenile is labeled as a delinquent person; societal reaction to deviant acts is said to produce deviant persons. With reference to delinquency, the person is endowed with the social role of a delinquent. According to Becker, "We are not so much interested in the person who commits a deviant act once as in the person who sustains a pattern of deviance over a long period of time, who makes of deviance a way of life, who organizes his identity around a pattern of deviant behavior" [9, p. 30].

The third use of the term delinquency is in reference to specific groups, gangs, or subcultures. While such usage parallels the emphasis on delinquent persons, the characterization is applied to the group as a whole. To some investigators, delinquent gangs are groups that sustain a pattern of delinquency over a period of time, make a delinquent adaptation to their immediate environment, and organize their group identity around their delinquent activities [33; 34; 38; 72; 261]. Others define groups or gangs as delinquent on the basis of the frequency or seriousness of delinquent activity on the part of members or the proportion of members having official delinquency records [114; 115; 209; 217]. Finally, writers at times consider delinquency a social problem; they take vaguely defined, but presumably undesirable, patterns of behavior and conditions as the referent of delinquency and virtually ignore the nature of the behavior involved.

If our purpose were to make a direct or systematic evaluation of Cloward and

Ohlin's theory of differential opportunity, we obviously would have to adopt a group-oriented definition of delinquency. However, since attention in this study is focused on delinquent behavior, we attempt to develop and test an explanatory framework to account for the occurrence of such behavior. Like most sociologists, we are also interested in the concepts of delinquent persons and delinquent groups, and we will examine the utility of a "persons" measure. Nevertheless, we are primarily concerned with behavior, including the delinquent acts of persons regarded socially as nondelinquents, as well as those acts committed by persons socially defined as delinquents. Attention to what is being done, rather than who is doing it, avoids the many problems associated with the characterization of persons as delinquent on the basis of a relatively few acts—that is, we are interested in the occurrence of delinquent acts whether or not they involve the enactment of a delinquent role [110]. For those who adopt a role definition, once one is classified as a delinquent person, his "delinquent behavior is nothing more than an epiphenomenal outgrowth of the assumption of a delinquent role" [103, p. 49; see 240]. We do not deny the importance of societal reaction, but it is our belief that one cannot treat delinquent acts as nonproblematic. An adequate understanding of the etiology of delinquent behavior is a necessary prerequisite to an understanding of the process in which persons are characterized as delinquent, because a delinquent act is the initial occurrence in this process.

Many of the issues involved in the characterization of behavior as deviant have been discussed extensively in the literature [9; 32; 35; 36; 103; 110; 150]. There is general consensus that: (1) deviance is not an intrinsic characteristic of any specific act but involves a social evaluation of behavior with reference to some normative standard; (2) the characterization of behavior as deviant requires that departure from normative standards be substantial—behavior beyond the tolerance limits of the group is seen as conduct requiring attention; (3) behavior characterized as deviant is acquired through normal learning processes and, from the actor's perspective, is purposive or instrumental action; and (4) the distinction between conforming and deviant acts is not found in the goals to which the actor is oriented, but deviant and conforming behavior are viewed as alternative means to achieve similar goals.

Delinquent behavior may be viewed as a special subclass of deviant behavior, but it is not simply the deviant acts of youth. While deviance includes all acts that are treated as violations of prevailing normative standards, delinquent behavior includes only those acts that constitute a violation of the specific set of proscriptive norms established in legal statutes [74]. In this study the unit of analysis is a specific kind of act—a delinquent act. As it refers to those specific acts proscribed by the legal code, the term delinquent has a special meaning with reference to a class of behavior. Cloward and Ohlin observe that "delinquent acts are distinguished from other deviant acts by the very fact that they result, or are likely to result, in the initiation of official proceedings by agents of criminal justice. The norms which are challenged by acts of delinquency are backed by official sanctions" [33, p. 4]. The point of reference for an operational definition of delinquency must be the legal code, not the conduct norms of particular social groups. The significance of the proscriptions in the legal code is that there is some probability of official response to behavior that violates the statutes. Although official action does not necessarily occur when a delinquent act is detected, it is largely restricted to these acts. In this research delinquency is defined as behavior that violates the legal codes as they apply to juveniles; delinquent behavior, then, is illegal behavior. This form of norm-violating behavior takes on special meaning because: (1) there is generally broad community consensus supporting these norms [110]; and (2) virtually all persons are aware that these specific proscriptions are enforced by official sanctions, and the risk of detection and punitive action are important considerations in their occurrence. The official response to delinquent acts may vary from community to community and within communities with changes in police and court policy. Such variations undoubtedly affect the probability of detection for particular acts, and the risk may vary in different locales. Nevertheless, the risk of official action is restricted to acts in violation of the statutes.

In contrast, dropping out of school is not a delinquent act, although in many segments of American society it is viewed as a type of deviance. Cervantes observes, "In view of society's educational expectations for modern youth and dropout youth's inability to get a job while 'just waiting around for something to happen,' the very state of being a dropout has all but become by definition a condition of semidelinquency" [25, p. 197]. While dropout may also be viewed as a unit of behavior, most of the research thus far has dealt with persons to whom the term dropout could be applied. There are no clear or consistent rules for assigning this label, and the use of various definitions makes it difficult to compare the findings of different studies.[5] Because students rarely drop out of school more than once or twice, a behavioral definition is not particularly useful. Thus, we tentatively adopted the following definition: "A dropout is a pupil who leaves school, for any reason except death, before graduation or completion of a program of studies and without transferring to another school" [173, p. 13].

Many studies of school dropouts have been conducted and many facts accumulated, but there have been few efforts to develop a theoretical perspective that would allow integration of these data. The facts about dropouts are contradictory and confusing, and our general understanding of this phenomenon is limited. After reviewing the research on the intelligence, reading achievement, grade retardation, academic grades, age, and social class of school dropouts, we discovered that much of the confusion is attributable to the conception, either implicit or explicit, that students who drop out of school are a homogeneous group; there is a stereotype of dropouts as "dummies" or persons lacking the ability to complete high school. Variations on this theme stress the dropout's difficulties with reading, poor grades, and grade retardation. If there is an exception, it is an emphasis on problems of health or economic pressures that might lead a student to drop out. Yet, the evidence suggests that differences in the ability of high school graduates and dropouts are minimal.[6] Thus, the facts are inconsistent with the "dummy" stereotype. In an effort to impose some order on the empirical data, we distinguished three major types of dropouts: involuntary, educationally handicapped, and intellectually capable [62; 252].

Individuals who leave school as a result of some personal crisis constitute involuntary dropouts. Each year, as a result of illness or accident, a limited number of students are physically disabled and forced to withdraw from school. For others, the death of a parent, particularly the father, requires an immediate entry into the world of work. Regardless of the specific reason, involuntary dropouts leave school because of external circumstances over which they have no control. There are some students who claim physical health or economic problems as the reason for dropping out when, in fact, they are unable to do the required work; thus for typological clarity, only intellectually capable students are considered as involuntary dropouts. Although the number of involuntary dropouts is limited, it is important to distinguish this type of dropout, for their academic and social characteristics might confound any analysis, if included with the other types.

Educationally handicapped dropouts are not capable of doing the work required for promotion to higher grades and completion of high school. Two types contribute to this category: students with limited innate ability and students who have the potential ability, but lack requisite skills. In general, dropouts with limited ability may be identified by their low scores on achievement and intelligence tests and low grade point averages. In some cases of school retardation, however, students may have average or high intelligence if tested with a nonverbal I.Q. test. Their low reading ability results in low achievement scores, low grades, and possibly even grade retardation. Many dropouts of this type are officially labeled *uneducable* and dropped from school by administrative authority.

In contrast, capable dropouts have the requisite ability to do passing or even superior work. The key to identifying the capable dropout is adequate reading ability and an average or high intelligence level. In some instances, grades are also average or high, but typically they are low. Gordon has shown that nonacademic criteria affect students' grades [87]. Low grades may be attributed to poor citizenship, irregular attendance or truancy, behavioral problems in school, failure to complete assignments, or simply a lack of motivation; however, intelligence and reading test scores reveal that the student has the ability to complete high school.

When dropouts are discussed as a social problem, the implicit reference is to capable dropouts; concern is expressed that their potentialities are not realized and thus constitute a societal waste. It is this type of dropout that we attempt to explain. The available data indicate that at least one-half and perhaps as many as three-fourths of all dropouts have the necessary ability to graduate from high school [124; 142; 241]. Because they are, by definition, intellectually capable, it is not possible to identify the students who are likely to drop out through examination of scores on intelligence and reading tests, grades, or other information available in school records. Explanation of these dropouts requires an analysis of the structures and processes characteristic of the school in order to identify sources of strain and tension.

Explaining Delinquent Behavior
and Dropout

Commenting on their indebtedness to Durkheim, Cloward and Ohlin recognize that industrial societies tend to make a virtue of "position discontent" [33, pp. 81-2]. To obtain a rough correlation between talent and ultimate position, success goals may be defined as accessible to everyone, as is the case in the United States. The result is one of the paradoxes of social life—those structures and processes established to produce order and survival of the industrial system may also be sources of disorder and deviance. Thus, the initial premise in Cloward and Ohlin's explanation of delinquency is that instigating forces for delinquent activity are located in the basic structure of society and in the normal functioning of the social order. Specifically, it is in the societal regulation of goals and approved ways of striving for these goals that the theorists find pressures for deviance. Their development of this position is based on Merton's essay on social structure and anomie [148; 149].

Cloward and Ohlin propose that pressures toward delinquent behavior originate in the perceived discrepancy between culturally prescribed goals and anticipated possibilities of achieving them by socially approved means. They further postulate that the disparity between aspirations and perceived opportunities increases as one descends the class structure with the greatest pressures for delinquency to be found among lower-class youth. Cloward and Ohlin view the means-goals discrepancy as the precipitating cause of delinquent behavior:

The disparity between what lower-class youth are led to want and what is actually available to them is the source of a major problem of adjustment. Adolescents who form delinquent subcultures, we suggest, have internalized an emphasis upon conventional goals. Faced with limitations on legitimate avenues of access to these goals, and unable to revise their aspirations downward, they experience intense frustrations; the exploration of nonconformist alternatives may be the result. [33, p. 86]

This hypothesis asserts that anticipation of failure to achieve one's aspirations through conventional means produces intense frustration, which in turn may lead to the exploration of nonconforming alternative means.

Aspirations and Opportunities

The absolute level of aspirations is not, in itself, viewed as especially problematic. Rather, Cloward and Ohlin are concerned with relative aspirations or "the height to which people aspire in relation to the point from which they start" [33, p. 89]. Consequently, their position does not require an assumption that a sizable proportion of lower-class youth have high aspirations: "it is sufficient to show that a *significant number* of lower-class members aspire beyond their means if it can also be demonstrated that these same persons contribute disproportionately to the ranks of delinquent subcultures" [33, p. 88]. In contrast with earlier theorists, such as Merton, Cloward and Ohlin treat both aspirations and perceived opportunities as variables. The goal-opportunity disjunction is equated with levels of aspirations "beyond one's means." The significant feature of their proposition is that the relative discrepancy between aspirations and opportunities is greatest among lower-class youth, even though their absolute aspirations are lower than among persons in the middle and upper classes.

It is a desire for improvement of one's economic position that Cloward and Ohlin link to delinquent behavior. Restricted access to conventional means for improving one's economic status exerts pressure on lower-class youth to employ delinquent means to achieve this conventional goal. Education and occupation are the primary avenues of legitimate opportunity. Access to general success goals, including improvement in one's economic position, is facilitated by advanced levels of education and entry into certain occupational roles. Likewise, limited educational attainment and entry into low-status occupational positions severely restrict the chances of improving one's economic position. Consequently, the major barrier to the achievement of success goals by lower-class youth is limited access to educational opportunities. Citing extensive research on class differentials in access to educational facilities, Cloward and Ohlin conclude that the limited economic resources of persons in the lower class are responsible for their failure to take advantage of available educational opportunities [33]. Further, the objective reality of limited opportunities in the lower class has resulted in a belief among lower-class persons that they cannot expect much in the way of educational opportunities. Prestigious, highly paid occupations either require advanced educational training or sizable economic resources. There are a few exceptions—entertainment and sports are open to those with little education and limited economic resources and are considered legitimate avenues to success. However, relatively few succeed in these pursuits. Faced with limited access to educational and occupational opportunities, many lower-class youth see no legitimate path to an improvement in their economic position, and they are under considerable pressure to resolve this inconsistency. One solution is to revise their aspirations downward. Another is to adopt unconventional means that offer some hope of achieving their goal.

A final observation relevant to the hypothesis regarding goal-opportunity disjunction concerns the subjective belief that one will fail or is failing in his efforts to improve his economic status. Cloward and Ohlin take the position that one need not actually experience failure; anticipation of failure has the same effect [33]. At this point the theorists' hypothesis regarding the conditions precipitating delinquent behavior may be restated in more specific terms: *The perception on the part of lower-class youth that they are isolated from socially approved ways of improving their economic position motivates them to explore delinquent means for achievement of this goal.*[7] Delinquent activity is viewed as a consequence of position discontent, anticipated failure, and low expectations for realization of one's aspirations through conventional means. While all lower-class youth are confronted with limitations in view of their social position, not all of them are aware of the goal-opportunity disjunction described by Cloward and Ohlin. Presumably, it is this difference in response to the realities of lower-class life that explains, in part, the differential involvement of lower-class youth in delinquent activity. Although the theorists focus on the types of delinquent subculture found in lower-class areas of large cities, their proposition appears to have broader applicability; we consider it important in any attempt to explain the selective occurrence of delinquent behavior within the lower class, as well as its general distribution in the class structure.

In rejecting Merton's premise that all youth strive for the same lofty success goals, Cloward and Ohlin made a major conceptual modification of anomie theory. With an emphasis upon the relative discrepancy between aspirations and opportunities, objective limitations in opportunities cease to be crucial in accounting for pressures toward deviance. If one accepts the assertion of Veblen [245] and Durkheim [55] that man's aspirations, particularly his economic aspirations, are unlimited, then there is reason to expect that middle-class youth also aspire beyond what is actually available to them. It is, therefore, possible that middle-class youth may also experience goal-opportunity disjunction, perhaps as frequently as lower-class youth. Although their objective opportunities are greater than those of lower-class youth, the aspirations of middle-class juveniles are also likely to be greater. This interpretation is consistent with Durkheim's observation that poverty operates to restrict aspirations as "the less one has the less he is tempted to extend the range of his needs indefinitely" [55, p. 254].

Aspiration-Opportunity Disjunctions

Several investigators have related educational and occupational disjunctions to delinquency. In a study of delinquent and nondelinquent Negro boys in three Chicago neighborhoods, Spergel found evidence of educational and occupational disjunction: higher proportions of the delinquents who wanted to graduate from college and enter high status occupations did not anticipate achievement of these goals [225]. Employing similar discrepancy measures, Elliott also found support for the disjunction hypothesis [59]. Delinquents reported greater disparity between educational aspirations and expectations than nondelinquents; the delinquents' average educational disjunction was one grade level, while there was essentially no discrepancy for nondelinquents. An even greater difference was observed for occupational disjunctions; 60 percent of the delinquents in comparison with 33 percent of the nondelinquents aspired to managerial and professional occupations, but did not expect to enter such occupations.

To assess the importance of position discontent, Short ranked 6 race-class-gang status groups according to three measures [214]. These rankings were then compared with rankings based upon the mean number of offenses known to the police and the mean number of self-reported offenses. The rank orderings, based on fathers' occupational level and boys' occupational aspirations and expectations, were quite different from the ordering established with the two delinquency measures. In contrast, a measure reflecting the disparity between the boys' occupational aspirations and expectations produced an ordering quite similar to the delinquency rankings. However, Short, Rivera, and Tennyson observed that the correlation between individual opportunity scores and delinquent behavior is low [219]. With respect to educational aspirations, Short [214] observed the highest rates of police contact among boys who perceive educational opportunities as closed, which is consistent with Cloward and Ohlin's hypothesis. However, among the boys who perceive educational opportunities as closed, higher rates of delinquency were found for boys with *low* aspirations; this finding is clearly at odds with the hypothesis concerning aspiration-opportunity disjunction.[8] Short found no difference in delinquency rates between high and low aspirers who perceive opportunities as open. Consequently, delinquency did not vary inversely with aspirations, but with expectations. Short concludes that "high educational and occupational aspirations in this instance seem clearly not to pressure the boys toward deviance, despite limitations, perceived and objective, in opportunities for achievement of those aspirations" [214, p. 115].

Employing a measure of educational discrepancy similar to the one used by Spergel, Elliott, and Short, Hirschi found that 47 percent of his subjects with some educational disjunction and 43 percent of the students with no disjunction reported one or more delinquent acts [103]. Of the respondents with some disjunction, 22 percent had a record of one or more officially recorded delinquent acts as did 17 percent of the students with no disjunction.[9] The differences in delinquency involvement are minimal, and Hirschi concludes that "those boys whose aspirations exceed their expectations are no more likely to be delinquent than those boys whose aspirations and expectations are identical" [103, p. 173]. His data on occupational disjunctions and delinquency show slight differences; the average number of self-reported delinquent acts for youth with some disparity is .81 and .75 for students with no disparity.[10] However, the highest rate of delinquency was observed among students aspiring to and expecting manual jobs, and delinquency varied inversely with aspiration level, regardless of expectations [103]. Thus, Hirschi reached a somewhat different conclusion than did Short.

Liska [130] reviewed four studies, including Short's [214] and Spergel's [225], of discrepancies in aspirations and opportunities in relation to delinquency. He concludes that the data generally support the disjunction hypothesis in the sense that delinquency is higher in the high aspiration-high expectancy category than in the high aspiration-low expectancy category. However, a comparison of subjects in the high-high and low-low categories reveals that in all four studies persons in the latter category have consistently higher rates of delinquency. Because the discrepancy hypothesis suggests that there would be low rates in both of these categories, this finding does not support the hypothesis. Liska concludes that delinquency differentials appear to be "a simple inverse function of educational and occupational expectations" [130, p. 105].

Nevertheless, the results of a number of studies imply that goal-opportunity disjunction may produce motivation for delinquency among youth from all socio-economic classes. Mizruchi reports that middle-class respondents experienced greater stress than lower-class respondents when confronted with limited opportunities to realize their occupational aspirations. According to Mizruchi, "There is a tendency for the middle classes to experience the effects of anomie associated with striving toward occupational goals to a degree that was not anticipated in Merton's hypothesis. When occupational achievement is perceived as blocked, the middle classes tend to become more demoralized than do the lower classes" [154, p. 127]. Not only does he suggest that the strain of occupational failure is greater in the middle class, but he also implies that this type of failure may be more frequent in the middle class because "the achievement goals of the middle classes are, by their very nature more difficult to reach than the concrete success goals of the lower classes" [154, pp. 130-1]. Runciman found that manual workers and their wives were consistently less likely to feel deprived or dissatisfied with their income than were white-collar workers and their wives [191]. Empey compared the preferred and anticipated occupations of high school seniors; students from *all* socio-economic strata "anticipated having occupations somewhat lower than their preferred ones," and the magnitude of the discrepancy did not vary appreciably with father's status [63, p. 708]. Lower-class seniors "were only slightly more inclined to think that their chances of entering their preferred occupations were less than those of seniors on strata above them," and the difference was not statistically significant [63, p. 708]. Wendling and Elliott report on class differences in educational aspirations and expectations of parents for their high-school-aged children [257]. Both aspirations and expectations vary by class, and a significantly higher proportion of middle-class than lower-class mothers desire and expect their children to graduate from college. However, in terms of the discrepancy between such aspirations and expectations a higher proportion of middle- than lower-class mothers anticipate their child's failure to realize parental aspirations. There is also evidence that middle-class delinquents are as likely to anticipate occupational and educational failure as are lower-class delinquents [60; 168].

In view of the contradictory evidence about the hypothesis that anticipated failure to achieve educational and occupational goals is associated with delinquency, two points may be made in defense of the hypothesis. First, in all of the studies a cross-sectional design was employed, and comparisons were made between juveniles already delinquent and those "not yet" delinquent, or the prior delinquencies of subjects currently with goal disjunction were compared to those without. These data must be interpreted cautiously because in every case the time order of the aspiration-opportunity disjunction and delinquency is the reverse of the postulated causal sequence. None of the investigators have examined the relationship between perception of failure at one point in time and subsequent rates of delinquency. Failure to find major differences in delinquency in the *histories* of subjects currently anticipating success or failure is scarcely an adequate basis for rejection of the causal sequence. Recognition of this limitation of cross-sectional studies does not resolve the apparent inconsistencies in the available data, but it does provide grounds for arguing against premature rejection of the hypothesis. Second, a weak two-variable relationship between educational and occupational disjunctions and delinquency is not necessarily unfavorable evidence. The proposition is not that all persons anticipating failure will become delinquent; other conditional variables are involved, and they may account for the modest association. For these reasons, testing of the relationship between educational and occupational disjunctions and subsequent delinquency with longitudinal data is warranted.

Nevertheless, the low proportions of youth perceiving any disparity in their aspirations and expectations raise questions about the amount of delinquency attributable to such disjunctions. In fact, some investigators have questioned whether long-range educational and occupational goals are salient for youth [16; 59; 117; 214; 227]. Douvan and Adelson provide some empirical evidence that future educational and occupational goals have little relevance for teenage girls' present orientations [52]. Kobrin and his co-investigators recognize that status concerns are not confined to the abstract realm of social class and mobility; they argue that concern with status in interpersonal relations is an immediate problem and of greater importance. While some delinquent groups may be oriented toward adult achievement criteria, apparently others are oriented primarily toward adolescent status criteria [117]. In fact, we believe that delinquency is more highly related to youth values than to adult values and is associated primarily with an orientation toward school rather than work [127].

The empirical evidence also leads us to question whether anticipated failure to achieve long-range goals is a cause or an effect of delinquency. The available data are consistent with either interpretation; given the temporal ordering of the variables, the "effect" interpretation may be favored. The argument is that participation in delinquent groups or gangs diminishes the fitness of boys for adult roles and effectively hinders conventional opportunities [16]. Liu and Fahey provide some empirical support for this position in their study of occupational aspirations and opportunities [131].

It is our view that Cloward and Ohlin have too narrowly restricted the types of goals toward which youth are oriented and that there are other cultural goals impinging upon youth. Cloward and Ohlin appear to have followed Merton's lead in emphasizing adult economic goals; yet Merton explicitly argues that limited access to any culturally valued goal can create pressures for deviance [149]. We propose, therefore, to elaborate on the types of aspiration-opportunity discrepancies that might lead to normlessness and delinquency. Specifically, we intend to identify culturally prescribed goals in each of three general social contexts—the community, school, and home—that are involved in the socialization of youth. These contexts involve different institutional settings; each contains specific goal prescriptions, opportunity structures, and normative standards. The definitions of success in the general community differ from those found in the school, particularly in the informal peer culture; in the home, other success criteria are employed. In part, the psychic strains of adolescence may be attributed to difficulties in coordinating the requirements of the adult culture and the home with the demands of the youth culture. Because youth are simultaneously enmeshed in all three contexts, it is appropriate to examine aspiration-opportunity disjunctions in each and to assess the relative importance of success or failure in each context for delinquent behavior.

The Community Context. Educational and occupational achievement are the primary avenues of upward social mobility in the community, and general goals, such as prestige, power, wealth, and security, are largely dependent upon these avenues to success. Because Cloward and Ohlin confine their attention to long-range goals, they are forced to argue that anticipation of failure to achieve desirable adult roles and statuses at some time in the future, not immediate problems, motivates youth toward delinquency [17]. From our perspective, the salient feature of the community context is that it prescribes future goals for youth and a set of success criteria that are employed by adults when evaluating youth; these evaluations typically involve an assessment of the youth's potential adult status. To the extent that youth are oriented toward long-range goals and adult evaluations, anticipated failure to achieve these goals should be conducive to delinquency. For the community context we will focus upon perceived access to educational and occupational goals and thereby examine Cloward and Ohlin's original hypothesis regarding limited opportunity.

The School Context. For analytic purposes we view the school context as comprised of two subsystems: the formal system that embodies the "official" values of the adult community and is charged with the responsibility of training youth for future adult roles, and the informal system that incorporates the youth culture with its own set of values, goals, and norms. Definitions of success in the formal system are linked to a single goal—academic achievement; in the informal system, they reflect emphases of the youth culture.

There is substantial evidence that the adolescent world is increasingly becoming a world apart, with its own fashions, terminology, values, goals, and norms, all of which are poorly understood by adults [39; 40; 87; 89; 163; 201; 223; 239]. The emergence of this youth culture is usually traced to the increasing specialization and higher levels of training required in our technical, urban society and to the extended period of compulsory formal education. The effect of extended contacts among adolescents and relative isolation from the larger society is development of a distinctive subculture. One element of this youth culture is resistance to adult expectations and authority. Gordon reports that a student's status in the school is a composite of academic achievement, participation in student organizations and activities, and position in the informal sociometric network [87]. However, achievement in social activities is the most important determinant of one's status, while academic achievement is the least influential. Gordon concludes that the behavior of adolescents is oriented primarily toward those roles and activities that give them status in the informal peer system, even though such behavior often results in conflict with teachers and school administrators. Within the peer social system, the significance of intellectual pursuits is minimized; relatively greater value is placed on social skills, athletic ability, physical appearance, participation in extracurricular activities, and membership in high-status groups [39; 52]. The trend away from adult values and toward peer values increases as students proceed through junior high school [4]. Although some writers disagree, there is consensus that the basic values of the youth culture are qualitatively distinct from those of the formal academic institution and the general community [57; 64; 108]. It is this youth culture with its emphasis upon interpersonal social skills and participation in school-related organizations and activities that we equate with the informal system of the school.

The youth culture has an institutional focus—that is, the teenage social system is primarily concerned with status within the school as determined by achievement in school-related activities. However, Stinchcombe [226], Sugarman [227], and Polk and Pink [169] call attention to a different type of youth culture. It flourishes outside the school and is not oriented toward the school and its activities; rather, it is characterized by a thorough-going alienation from school. Polk and Pink suggest that this particular species of youth culture emerges in reaction to failure in both the formal and informal systems in the school [169]. The existence of this type of subculture has particular relevance for our theoretical conceptualization because it directly links failure in the context of the school to collective expressions of alienation from the school and involvement in norm-violating behavior.

Failure to achieve desired goals in either the formal academic system or the informal peer culture may result in frustrating, demoralizing, and humiliating experiences at school. Students who fail in these areas tend to be shunned and excluded by other students, teachers, and by the school system in general [79; 120; 197; 246]. In the face of such experiences it is likely that an individual would seek some type of adaptation. Failure may precipitate a negative attitude toward school and unsuccessful students may band together for mutual support. One adaptation to school failure may be the collective generation of alternative standards of conduct condoning and perhaps encouraging delinquent behavior.

There is ample evidence that failure in the formal system of the school, as reflected in grades and achievement tests, is associated with delinquency [79; 83; 96; 99; 103; 120; 168; 175; 238; 256]. Less work has been done on the association between failure to achieve peer culture goals and delinquency, but the available data provide some support for this relationship [103; 176; 196; 238; 260]. There is also evidence linking failure in the peer culture to low self esteem [39; 185]. Toby and Toby examined the relationship of academic and peer status to a measure of association with delinquent companions and concluded that academic status was more important for delinquency in the context of the school [238]. However, academic failure may lead to peer group failure. Vinter and Sarri report that those who receive low grades are also denied, as a direct consequence, a wide variety of privileges and opportunities at school; they lose esteem among their classmates and are excluded from participation in extracurricular activities [246]. As a result, the slow student is often the target of derision. In addition, academic failure often precipitates negative parental reactions and direct attempts to limit peer-oriented activities [178].

It is generally acknowledged that social class is related to academic success, but the school context tends to be an equalizing medium in which the significance of class background is minimized [28; 39; 87; 123; 168; 239]. This is particularly true with respect to the informal youth culture that operates to limit the importance of academic success and high ambition. According to Turner, the youth culture "tends to dull the discriminations of both stratification of origin and stratification of destination" [239, p. 222]. While class is generally related to academic success, its effect on school performance is less direct than suggested by Hollingshead [105; see also 28; 168; 239]. Polk and Halferty report that rates of delinquency are high among both middle- and lower-class youth whose academic performance is low [167]. Stinchcombe observes that among the academically unsuccessful, middle-class boys are the most rebellious [226]. For middle-class youth, academic failure represents not only a limitation on upward social mobility but may also initiate downward mobility and loss of status. These studies suggest that among youth who are failing academically there may be greater pressure for delinquency among middle-class than lower-class youth.

The Home Context. A persistent image of the delinquent is one of an adolescent from an unhappy or broken home. Hirschi claims it is well documented in delinquency research that delinquents are more likely to be estranged from their parents than nondelinquents [103]. While the use of familial variables in the explanation of delinquency has been largely confined to social control or psychiatric perspectives, the relevant data are also consistent with a "strain" perspective—that is, delinquency may be a response to the adolescent's perceived failure to satisfy basic social and psychological needs or to achieve a meaningful position within this social context. Such an interpretation may be preferable to explanations involving "internal controls" or "internalization of norms" because the latter do not adequately account for the increase in delinquent behavior during early adolescence nor its decline in late adolescence. This limitation is avoided in an explanation that focuses upon the child's development and the changes in roles and statuses within the family through time. Efforts to achieve independence from parental control occur during the period of adolescence; desiring greater freedom, the adolescent threatens the parent-child relationship previously established. In spite of the efforts teenagers exert to change patterns of family relationships, presumably all youth desire parental affection and acceptance. If parent-child conflicts are not resolved, at least partially, they may result in a rejection of parental values and norms and an attempt to find acceptance in peer groups subscribing to different norms and standards. Our concern is not merely with the failure of the adolescent to meet particular parental expectations, but extends to the broader implications of such failures for the adolescent's status within the family. Because the juvenile's perceptions are highly important, failure in the family may be measured in terms of the adolescent's perception of his acceptance and his satisfaction with interpersonal relationships in the home.

There is a substantial body of research supporting the position that parental rejection of the adolescent is associated with delinquency [5; 50; 77; 110; 140; 160; 184; 222; 237; 255]. Also, youth who experience parental rejection are less likely to internalize the normative standards and values of their parents [7; 160].[11] There is no a priori reason to assume that failure to find love and acceptance in the home is a problem unique to lower-class youth; nor is there consistent empirical data that there is a relationship between external explanations of failure, normlessness, and social class [20; 110; 126; 230; 259]. Again, this suggests that our explanation of delinquency and dropout may appropriately be stated with reference to all youth, and not simply lower-class juveniles.

There is reason to expect that failure in one context may be related to failure in another and that the effects of failure may be cumulative. We hypothesize that youth who experience failure in more than one context will have higher rates of delinquency than subjects who only experience failure in one setting.

Further, we suggest that the school is the most critical context—delinquency is primarily a response to school failure. There are several reasons for this assertion. First, failure in school presents an immediate problem for youth.[12] The research of Kobrin, Puntil, and Peluso implies that immediate problems are more salient than long-range goals, and anticipated failure to achieve such goals may be an effect, rather than a cause of delinquency [117]. Second, adolescents are primarily oriented toward the school and their status within it. Among others, Coleman provides evidence that during the adolescent years, peer influence becomes dominant with peer recognition and status serving as major goals for youth [39]. Third, like the home, the school is a compulsory context; Goodman refers to it as the "universal trap" in which participation is required even in the face of repeated failure [86]. Failure in this context has broader consequences and greater visibility than failure at home [128]. It influences the adolescent's status with his peers and teachers, and often precipitates negative parental reaction as well. School failures are typically thrown together through a tracking system or assignment to "slow learner" or "trouble-maker" classes for purposes of special treatment or control. The effect of these institutional labeling practices is to increase common identity and produce group reinforcement for shared feelings of rejection and alienation. The structure of the school often unwittingly provides the setting required for the emergence and maintenance of collective adaptations [33; 34; 127]. Fourth, those who are failing are confronted with the problem of survival in a context in which they regularly experience rejection and humiliation. If they cannot withdraw, the delinquent subculture offers a possible solution. It provides alternative means to formal educational goals, for example, through organized cheating and intimidation of teachers; it also provides an alternative set of informal status criteria that "unpopular" youth can more readily meet. Psychologically it is attractive: it provides a form of protection from the denigration of teachers and students. Finally, the view that delinquency is a response to failure in school is consistent with the maturational reform of delinquents; it offers an explanation for the decline in delinquency with the onset of adulthood. The "reformation" of delinquents occurs after the age of 17 or at the time when youth finish their compulsory education, marry, enter college, or the world of work [12; 54; 137; 141]. For most youth the strains of competition in school are resolved with high school graduation; this may account for maturational reform.[13] In addition to maturational reform, there appear to be temporary declines in delinquency during the summer months [60; 120]. Kvaraceus also reports that delinquent activity reaches its peak in the hours immediately after school and diminishes during the weekend. These findings are consistent with the hypothesis that the school is the most important social context and that delinquent behavior is related to failure within the peer status system.

Our extension of the goal disjunction hypothesis to the school and home affords additional bases for testing the general proposition that limited access to culturally valued goals is conducive to delinquency. This relationship is viewed as conditional upon other variables; external attribution of blame, normlessness, and exposure to delinquency are each considered to be context specific. Alienation attributed to school failure is primarily alienation *from the school*, and it is likely to result in increased exposure to delinquent influences *in the school*, where group adaptations to failure have already emerged. While the type of goal-opportunity disjunction varies by context, we are not suggesting that the explanation for failure or the form of alienation varies. For each context, failure to achieve valued goals, when attributed to injustices in the social system, leads to normlessness.

Viewing delinquency and dropout as alternative responses to the strains generated by failure to achieve valued goals, we hypothesize that dropout is precipitated by aspiration-opportunity disjunctions. Again, the relevant goals may be either long-range educational and occupational goals, formal academic goals, peer culture goals, or acceptance within the family. While failure to achieve any one of these goals may be conducive to dropout, we hypothesize that dropout is primarily a response to school failure. Specifically, it is failure to achieve the goals of the youth culture, rather than academic goals, that motivates most capable dropouts to leave school. Cervantes observes, "The problem of the dropout is less an academic problem than a disciplinary problem. The problem of discipline is a problem of peers and positive interests" [25, p. 67]. Lichter and his co-workers also emphasize the significance of the peer culture; in their study, capable dropouts uniformly had unsuccessful school experiences, and most of them encountered difficulties in more than one area of school life [128]. Liddle reports that dropouts generally were dissatisfied about their relationships with their classmates [129]. They attributed their dropping out to limited peer acceptance in school; in particular, the dropouts perceived themselves at odds with the elite groups in the school. According to Amble, male graduates were typically well-liked and sought out by other students, whereas male dropouts were rejected or merely tolerated by classmates [3]. Similar findings have been reported by other investigators [23; 56; 194]. It is also well-established that dropouts do not participate in the extracurricular activities of the high school [13; 88; 224; 235]. Livingston found that this one factor accounted for more than one-third of the variance between dropout and graduate categories [132]. These findings strongly indicate that dropout is a response to rejection and failure in the informal peer system.

Most researchers emphasize the frustrations dropouts experience in school, but Cervantes proposes that the home is equally important [25]. He reports that four out of five dropouts believe that their families never understood or accepted them and that they also anticipated failure in their efforts to achieve educational goals.

The Process of Alienation

A disparity between aspirations and opportunities is conducive to delinquent behavior, but failure to achieve one's aspirations through conventional means is not directly linked to delinquency; rather, it is an important source of alienation from conventional norms. Pressures for goal attainment make one vulnerable to alternative nonconforming means, but they are not adequate, in themselves, to account for the actual adoption of delinquent means. Individuals must also be freed from the constraints of the normative order and from allegiance to the conventional opportunity structure; the validity of conventional norms must be questioned and judged as inappropriate [33].

Yet, the thwarting of one's aspirations does not necessarily lead to alienation from conventional norms. How one interprets failure is important. "The most significant step in the withdrawal of sentiments supporting the legitimacy of conventional norms is the attribution of the cause of failure to the social order rather than to oneself, for the way in which a person explains his failure largely determines what he will do about it" [33, p. 111]. Individuals who perceive their failure as a consequence of limited access to the opportunity structure can point to the existence of unjust or arbitrary institutional arrangements [33]. They have reason to criticize and attack the social order, and they may become alienated from the dominant normative system. A sense of injustice may arise when there is a discrepancy between the formal, institutionally established criteria of evaluation and the informal operative criteria. Persons capable of meeting the formal criteria may discover that informal ones, such as race, religion, social class, or family, may be invoked when there is a surplus of eligible candidates. In addition to the covert use of ideologically repudiated criteria, highly visible forms of racial discrimination may lead unsuccessful members of minority groups to attribute their difficulties to the social order [33]. The explanation of failure is a conditional variable in the relationship between the aspiration-opportunity disjunction and delinquent behavior. It explains why some lower-class youth experiencing or anticipating failure in their efforts to improve their status become alienated from conventional norms and adopt delinquent means while others do not.

The explanation of failure in terms of inequities in the social structure also provides an essential condition for collective adaptations. According to Cloward and Ohlin, youngsters motivated by a sense of injustice tentatively withdraw attributions of legitimacy from conventional norms. Their initial violations are minor, but they bring the individual into conflict with members of the conventional community. Facing a hostile response the individual needs encouragement and reassurance; hence, he is motivated to seek support from peers, particularly persons who have experienced similar difficulties. Without support for his deviant acts the individual will find it difficult to justify his defiance of the established social order [33]. As the conflict between the individual and the community intensifies, "the process of alienation is accelerated, and . . . he becomes increasingly dependent on the support of others in his position. The gang of peers forms a new social world in which the legitimacy of his delinquent conduct is strongly reinforced" [33, p. 127]. Collective adaptations require communication among alienated youth. On this point Cohen's perspective is adopted: "The crucial condition for the emergence of new cultural forms is the existence, *in effective interaction with one another, of a number of actors with similar problems of adjustment*" [34, p. 59]. It is in the context of the group that deviant solutions to the common adjustment problem emerge.

The community's response to exploratory delinquent acts is also important, but we do not accept the view that alienation and deviance are direct consequences of the community's response to the "innocent" misconduct of children. Instead, we assign an active role to delinquent youth. The beginnings of the process of alienation lie in the orientation of certain youth to the social structure, not in the societal response to their acts. Failure and the process of alienation precede extensive involvement in delinquent behavior. The prior development of a collective belief structure provides a rationalization for delinquency and helps to neutralize possible guilt feelings [231]. External attribution of blame results in a collective withdrawal of sentiments of legitimacy from official norms, but this does not necessarily challenge the moral validity of these norms. An individual "may believe that law-abiding conduct is morally right but inappropriate or impossible in a particular situation" [33, p. 137]. Together, the prior justification for delinquent behavior and the emphasis upon its expediency, rather than its moral validity, serve to neutralize the guilt feelings that are likely to arise from delinquent behavior.

Not all persons who fail or anticipate failure attribute their problem to the social order.[14] If personal inadequacy—lack of discipline, effort, or intelligence—is considered the source of failure, then the outcome is pressure either to change oneself or to develop techniques to protect oneself from a feeling of personal inadequacy. An internal explanation of failure implies acceptance of the legitimacy of conventional norms, not alienation from them. Apart from developing greater personal competence, there are two possible adaptations for persons who attribute blame internally: the individual may lower his aspirations and engage in a form of passive compliance to the norms, or he may withdraw from efforts to achieve presumably unattainable goals. In the context of the school, students who adopt the first solution are referred to as "low achievers" or "poorly motivated" students, whereas students who adopt the latter solution are referred to as truants and dropouts. Dropping out of school is one alternative for youth who are failing to achieve valued goals and who assume personal responsibility for this problem.

Alienation has been defined in various ways, and two specific subtypes—normlessness and social isolation—are relevant to our explanation of delinquent behavior and dropout. It appears to us that Cloward and Ohlin linked anticipated failure to achieve success goals and extrapunitive explanations of such failure to the form of alienation Seeman [203] and Dean [45] describe as normlessness. Seeman defines normlessness as "a high expectancy that socially unapproved behaviors are required to achieve given goals" and notes that the goals in question are general social goals, such as those associated with success [203, p. 788]. This definition, like Dean's, closely parallels Cloward and Ohlin's description of the conditions that lead to alienation and the subjective beliefs of persons who are alienated; it is also consistent with the distinction between the legitimacy and moral validity of norms. Therefore, we interpret Cloward and Ohlin's hypothesis regarding alienation as an assertion that the failure to achieve success goals, when attributed to inaccessibility of conventional opportunities, leads to collective feelings of normlessness or a group-supported belief that nonconforming behavior is required to achieve socially valued goals. The three variables—aspiration-opportunity discrepancy, external attribution of blame, and normlessness—are the social-psychological counterparts of the structural features emphasized by Merton in his work on anomie. In Cloward and Ohlin's formulation, these variables account for the motivational stimulus to delinquency and the attenuation of the regulatory power of conventional norms on behavior. Given this condition, the individual is free to explore alternative, albeit nonconforming, means for realization of his goals. Dropout, we propose, is a retreatist adaptation, a disengagement from social relationships in school, and a return to the less frustrating context of the home and neighborhood. Appropriate to this view is De Grazia's definition of social isolation as "a feeling of separation from the group or of isolation from group standards" [48, p. 5]. Lichter and his co-workers note that "dropouts left school because they were motivated to *run away* from a disagreeable situation; they did not feel impelled to *run toward* a definite and positive goal. . . . Dropping out was not only the easiest course to take but a passive, not an active, resolution of the educational problem" [128, pp. 247-8]. It may be obvious that youth who run away from school to avoid frustration and failure are in some way alienated from the school. This suggests that the dropout experiences isolation from peers and activities in school and from peer-group standards [45].

There is empirical evidence that delinquency is associated with normlessness [6; 29; 125]. In a review of studies relating deviance to alienation, normlessness was the only specific form of alienation consistently related to delinquency [138]. Unfortunately, many of the relevant studies have employed general measures of alienation, rather than a specific measure of normlessness. Earlier in our discussion of context goals, we reported evidence that in each context failure is related to alienation; however, context-specific measures of normlessness have not been used.

The available data support the proposition that dropout is associated with social isolation. According to Cassel and Coleman, dropouts frequently report a feeling of not belonging [23]. Tesseneer and Tesseneer point out that a perception of belonging to the school or to a peer group within the school is an important factor influencing the student's decision to stay in or leave school [234]. Other investigators report that the dropout does not identify with the school [22; 25]. Consistent with our hypothesis that failure to achieve status in the peer culture primarily motivates youth to drop out is the fact that school activities and peers are the basic referents for this form of alienation.

No clear conclusion about the hypothesized relationship between failure, external attribution of blame, and delinquency emerges from the available data. Studies in which delinquent and nondelinquent samples are compared on the basis of Rosenzweig's measure of punitiveness yield inconclusive results [70; 106; 111; 159; 186]. Jessor and his co-workers fail to find any significant relationship between measures of internal-external control and deviance [110]. Examining the relationship between anticipated occupational failure, external attribution of blame, and delinquency, Hirschi concludes that "it does not matter whether the boy blames himself or the social system for potential [occupational] failure; ascription of blame is essentially unrelated to the commission of delinquent acts" [103, p. 184].

Delinquent Learning and Performance Structures

Questions concerning the origin of delinquent subcultures and their differentiation are tangential to our interest in explaining delinquent behavior and dropout. However, implicit in Cloward and Ohlin's discussion of learning and performance structures is the idea that exposure to delinquent patterns of behavior in group contexts is a variable linking aspiration-opportunity disjunction and normlessness to delinquent behavior. Though our concern at this point is with illegitimate opportunities, Cloward and Ohlin correctly view access to legitimate and illegitimate opportunity structures as variable. Following Sutherland [228], they maintain that delinquent behavior, like conforming behavior, presupposes a pattern of social relationships through which motives, attitudes, rationalizations, and techniques can be transmitted and reinforced [33]. Delinquent behavior is learned in interaction with other persons and primarily in social groups in which delinquent patterns of behavior are supported. According to Sutherland's position, differential exposure to pro-delinquent individuals and groups accounts for the learning of delinquent behavior, and such exposure varies from one social context to another [47]. The meaning of differential association is not restricted to contacts with organized criminal operations or to urban areas; the general proposition is that access to illegitimate learning and performance structures is differentially available in various social settings.[15] Access to illegitimate means "can usefully refer to differences in exposure of individuals to the *everyday manifestations* of deviant behavior by other individuals in the environment, or to differences in daily, even fortuitous, opportunities to transgress. This more general view of the idea of access to illegitimate means makes possible an account of deviance which is not necessarily institutionalized in gangs or organized over time" [110, p. 68].

In this sense the presence of delinquent groups in one's social milieu provides opportunities for learning attitudes and rationalizations supportive of delinquent behavior and engaging in delinquent acts with the support of the group. Existent delinquent subcultures provide a social context for the learning and performance of delinquent acts. Delinquent subcultures presumably exist in some form in most communities, although the participants may not exhibit the characteristics of a gang or the degree of specialization suggested by Cloward and Ohlin. Differential access to delinquent opportunity structures is an important variable in the etiology of delinquency, because the person who comes to believe that he cannot succeed through legitimate means "cannot simply choose among an array of illegitimate means, all equally available to him" [33, p. 145]. The person who anticipates failure in legitimate pursuits is motivated to seek illegitimate alternatives. He actively searches for groups that provide opportunities for learning and participating in illegitimate activities, but the accessibility of such groups is variable. If the individual gains access to a delinquent group, then the learning and performance of delinquent acts is likely.

The idea of exposure to criminal or delinquent influences in the home, school, or community implies that there are different reference groups in each of these contexts. In the community, exposure to delinquency occurs primarily through the presence of adult, criminal-role models and organized criminal activity. In this instance the reference group is comprised of older, out-of-school youth and adults. The cultural transmission of criminal values, norms, attitudes, and skills presumably involves the integration of different age-levels of offenders, as described by Cloward and Ohlin [33]. There is empirical evidence that association with adult criminals and access to adult criminal opportunity structures is related to delinquency. Short and Strodtbeck report that members of delinquent gangs perceive greater illegitimate opportunities for financial success than nongang boys [217]. Spergel finds that delinquents more frequently say they know adults who could teach them to be a strong-arm man, a shoplifter, or a racketeer; he concludes that more delinquents than nondelinquents are oriented to persons in the neighborhood, particularly older delinquent youth and adult criminals [225].

Exposure to delinquent influences within the school occurs through peer-group influences and contacts with delinquent youth cultures. The accumulated evidence supporting the relationship between association with delinquent peers and delinquency is impressive [41; 42; 68; 77; 127; 177; 225; 248]. Not only are the findings consistent, but the relationships are generally strong. Further, Toby and Toby indicate that failure in school initiates a search for a more satisfying group membership, which typically results in the acquisition of delinquent friends [238]. They propose that a change in reference groups is the link between failure and delinquency.

Exposure to pro-delinquent influences in the home involves indirect socialization experiences supporting delinquency. In rare instances, parents may play the role of Fagin, but they are not likely to participate in or offer direct encouragement for their children's delinquent activity [110; 139; 184]. Influences in the home relevant to delinquency involve parental attitudes and practices that undermine the law and respect for authority rather than provide direct exposure to or support for criminal behavior.[16] The extent to which a juvenile is committed to or dependent upon his parents is also germane.

The theory of differential association is not one of contagion; it does not suggest that delinquency is simply an effect of association with persons involved in delinquent or criminal behavior. Rather, Sutherland's formulation is concerned with subtle types of reinforcement and social support for delinquency [228]. The dimension of intensity in Sutherland's theory suggests the importance of the meaning an individual attaches to his peer-group associations.

Adolescence is often described as a period in which a juvenile breaks away from parental control and looks to peers for social definitions, values, and appropriate standards of behavior. Nevertheless, youth differ in the extent to which they are committed to peers and parents. It is possible that contact or association with delinquents might have little effect on youth who are neither committed to peers nor dependent upon them for social approval. On the other hand, dependence upon a group of delinquent friends should be more conducive to delinquent behavior since the individual is apt to be more open to their influence.

Opinions on the direct effects of peer commitment are conflicting. Coleman claims that commitment to peers weakens ties with parents and conventional norms [39]. In contrast, Hirschi proposes that attachment to peers is not conducive to delinquency [103]. He says that strong attachment to peers reduces the likelihood of delinquent acts. Hirschi supports his position with empirical evidence, but he only relates attachment to prior delinquency. Other investigators have reported a positive relationship between peer attachment and delinquency. According to Rothstein delinquents emphasize friendship and peer associations to a greater extent than nondelinquents [188]. Erickson and Empey report that commitment to peers is highly correlated with delinquency; in fact, commitment to peers is more highly correlated with delinquent behavior than association with known delinquents [68]. Erickson and Empey's data are quite compelling. Nevertheless, we believe that the effect of association with delinquent peers should be greatest for youth who are committed to their friends for social support. This view does not require that attachment to peers is generally conducive to delinquency. Rather, strong attachment to peers serves to accentuate peer influence, whether it be for deviant or conforming patterns of behavior. This argument would also apply to attachment to or dependency upon parents.

Parental influence may be contingent upon the juvenile's commitment to them; if this is the case, then stronger attachment would produce greater influence. There is a clear supposition in Coleman's analysis that strong commitment to peers is associated with weak commitment to parents [39]. It would be under this specific condition that the delinquent peer group's influence would be maximized.

In any event, the key issue with respect to associational ties and delinquency is one of causal order. Do youth who are delinquent choose other delinquents as friends or do nondelinquent youth who begin to associate with delinquent youth subsequently become delinquent? Is differential association with delinquent peers a cause or an effect of involvement in delinquency? The theory of differential association implies one temporal sequence, whereas Glueck observes that "birds of a feather flock together" and argues for the opposite hypothesis [75]. Both interpretations may be correct; if so, the relative strength of the directional relationships becomes the issue. To our knowledge no one has examined the predictive utility of delinquent associates on *subsequent* rates of delinquent behavior. Hirschi addresses the question of causal order, but the delinquent activity he measures occurs *prior* to his measurement of associational patterns [103]. While his data are relevant to the "flocking" hypothesis, the probability that law-abiding youth with delinquent friends will become delinquent at some future point in time cannot be determined with cross-sectional data.

To this point we have argued that students who experience some aspiration-opportunity disjunction and attribute their difficulties to their own personal deficiencies are likely to drop out if they become isolated from the school. Just as we proposed earlier that the motivation for delinquency—failure and subsequent normlessness—is not adequate to account for its occurrence, we argue that failure and social isolation are not sufficient to account for a capable student's decision to leave school. Therefore, we hypothesize that exposure to dropout is a necessary variable in the causal chain leading to dropout. The argument is essentially the same as the one developed for patterns of differential association and exposure to delinquency. In the home or community a low value may be placed on education. In the community a student may associate with youth who have dropped out of school, and he may have parents or siblings who failed to complete high school. These contacts provide the potential dropout with the opportunity to observe the consequences, both positive and negative, of leaving school and to assess whether dropping out of school will resolve his problems. Further, they may provide some group support—perhaps even group pressure—for this action. The probability of dropout is maximized when an individual has contacts with peers, parents, or siblings who have dropped out and who encourage dropping out by placing little value on education.

We believe that dropout, like delinquency, is a group-supported phenomenon; members of particular groups are more likely to become isolated from the peer system of the school and drop out. Interestingly, patterns of differential association with dropout peers have not been examined in studies of dropouts, although a few investigators have recognized the influence of family and friends. Cervantes reports that dropouts have more family members and friends who are dropouts than do graduates, and the dropouts' friends are less school-oriented than the graduates' friends [25]. Nelson [158] found that two-thirds of the parents of dropouts had negative or indifferent attitudes toward school, and Hausken [98] observes that the majority of dropouts come from families in which neither parent completed high school.

One other issue deserves mention. We are not suggesting that the joint effects of the etiological variables on delinquent behavior are not related to social class; rather, we question the extent to which failure, alienation, and exposure to delinquency are found only among lower-class youth. If these conditions and states are not unique to them, then our causal chain constitutes a general explanation of delinquency that can account for middle-class and female delinquency as well as lower-class male delinquency. Class may be related to some of the variables in our explanation, but we believe that the significance of class linkage has been exaggerated. At best, the relationship between class and delinquency is weak, and there are researchers who argue that delinquent behavior is *not* a class-related phenomenon [50; 92; 103; 162]. Because our etiological variables are not "class bound," this poses no special problem for our theoretical explanation.

There do not appear to be class differentials in the incidence of delinquent behavior, although it is clear that there are such differences with respect to dropout [15; 25; 62; 234]. The relationship between delinquency and dropout may be more complex than we have suggested. Part of the explanation for the class differential in dropout undoubtedly is the greater rate of failure among lower-class youth [91]. It may also be the case that lower-class youth are less extrapunitive; they may be more likely to attribute failure to luck, chance, or fate [149; 151]. If this is the case, they would be more inclined toward a "low-achiever" or dropout adaptation. Such explanations avoid the issue of blame and do not imply permission for deviance.[17] Another possibility is that lower-class youth are more frequently pushed out of school through suspension or expulsion. Among students capable of completing high school, a rudimentary basis for distinguishing subtypes is to consider whether the student's departure was voluntary or involuntary. Juveniles who leave school voluntarily may require a different explanation than adolescents who are forced out by official action. The obvious inference is that delinquency or adolescent rebellion in the school may result in permanent, though involuntary, departure from school. If it is the school that generates the greatest strain on adolescents, then the motivational stimulus for delinquency should be reduced once youth are out of school and free from its competitive pressures. This inference is at odds with the prevailing view that dropout increases the likelihood of delinquent behavior.

Summary

We have presented a general theoretical explanation of delinquent behavior and dropout in which these outcomes are viewed as alternative adaptations to failure. The adoption of one alternative as opposed to the other depends upon the individual's explanation of failure, type of alienation, and exposure to delinquent or dropout influences. It is not only anticipated failure to improve one's economic status in the community that accounts for delinquent behavior; failure to achieve valued goals can occur in the context of the community, school, or home, and the effects of failure may be cumulative.

The way an individual explains failure largely determines his course of action; selection of a delinquent or dropout adaptation hinges on the individual's internal or external attribution of blame. Dropout and delinquency involve not only different explanations for failure but also different forms of alienation. External attribution of blame and normlessness account for the absence of conventional restraints and freedom to explore delinquent alternatives. However, motivation and freedom to explore deviant alternatives do not fully account for the adoption of delinquent means. The individual must also have access to an environment in which he may learn the necessary social definitions and skills as well as receive appropriate social and psychological reinforcement. Similarly, dropout is a consequence of internal attribution of blame, social isolation, and exposure to dropout influences.

We hypothesize that the school is the most important context—delinquency and dropout are primarily adaptations to school-related problems. Resentment toward the school and its norms may find expression in delinquent behavior or in retreat from a frustrating situation. This view challenges the idea that delinquency and dropout are generated primarily in the home.

Our theoretical formulation represents a relatively complex explanation of delinquent behavior and dropout, but it has a special appeal because it is testable. Extending the work of others, we have specified relevant goals, types of blockage, and particular forms of alienation that lead youth to explore delinquent means. The relationships between these variables and exposure to delinquents and dropouts are delineated as well as the temporal sequences involved. Although one may find ambiguities in our statement, the theory can be tested empirically; if the theory is verified, there would be a number of implications for delinquency prevention.

Notes

1. Similarities and differences in the theoretical formulations of Merton, Sutherland, and Cloward and Ohlin are considered at greater length in our earlier report [61].

2. Following Cloward and Ohlin [33], we reject Miller's [151] and De-Lamater's [49] view that delinquency is behavior that conforms to the general culture into which one is initially socialized; this approach would ultimately require separate explanations for lower- and middle-class delinquency and appears to be inconsistent with the available empirical evidence on the pervasiveness of conventional values and norms. We take the position that delinquent behavior is learned by youth who were initially socialized into conventional society and who have internalized conventional values, goals, and norms. An excellent review of the logic and empirical evidence for our position is presented by Jessor and his co-workers [110].

3. The problem of measurement is considered in Chapter 4.

4. It is not clear whether conduct illegal only for children, such as truancy and incorrigibility, is to be included.

5. Some researchers only consider students who leave school voluntarily as dropouts, whereas others include all persons who fail to graduate for any reason other than death or severe physical disability.

6. We suggested that students with limited academic ability generally leave school early—often before entering senior high school. Presumably, among youth who drop out of school later, there are few who lack the requisite ability to complete high school.

7. While this hypothesis is analogous to Merton's explanation of deviance, it involves a different level of explanation. Merton's perspective is sociological, whereas Cloward and Ohlin's formulation is social-psychological.

8. In another paper on these Chicago youth, Rivera and Short report that both gang status and race were related to expectations for upward social mobility—gang members and Negroes anticipated less mobility [179]. They also note that relatively few youth in the Chicago study, which included lower-class gang boys, anticipated occupational failure: "it is clear that high mobility expectations are widespread among adolescents, although there are variations related to social origins, race, and gang membership. At this early age no group can be characterized as giving serious thought to the possibility of actual failure" [179, p. 78].

9. This was calculated by collapsing the cells in Table 60 [103, p. 172]. Hirschi employs the comparison based upon one or more delinquent acts. We have not included in our recalculations those few individuals whose expectations exceeded their aspirations as they do not logically fit into either of the two comparison groups implied in Hirschi's conclusion. We have not calculated the statistical significance of these differences as Hirschi did not report such tests in support of his conclusion.

10. This was calculated from Table 68 [103, p. 183]. Again, we did not include respondents whose expectations exceeded their aspirations in the disjunction group. Hirschi observes that in his sample, educational expectations are nearly as high as aspirations, even among Negroes. A maximum of 19 percent

of the white boys could be classified as anticipating any degree of educational failure, and only 5 percent of the boys who aspire to attend college do not expect to obtain any college education. Hirschi also reports a low proportion of students having occupational aspirations that exceed their expectations; he concludes that frustrated educational or occupational aspirations cannot be an important antecedent of delinquency [103, p. 182].

11. As is the case in the community and school, the home may facilitate or impede the adolescent's feelings of acceptance and personal worth. Youth from broken and disorganized homes are less likely to find affection and acceptance, particularly during their teen years. Rosenberg found that children from broken homes tend to have lower self esteem than those from intact homes [185]. We do not postulate a direct relationship between broken homes and delinquency; rather, we suggest that the structure of the home is related to the adolescent's perception of his acceptance. This factor may account for the relationship observed between broken or disorganized homes and delinquency [104; 184; 237].

12. While there obviously is a relationship between academic failure and anticipated failure to achieve long-range educational and occupational goals, these types of failure are not functional equivalents.

13. In contrast, Cloward and Ohlin's formulation implies that delinquency will continue into adulthood. However, position discontent and failure to achieve economic goals do not disappear with high school graduation or the transition from adolescence to adulthood.

14. Cloward and Ohlin do not mention explanations involving luck or fate [see 149; 151]. Perhaps they accept Rosenzweig's view that for practical purposes such explanations are impunitive and should not lead to feelings of alienation [186].

15. Concerned with the differential accessibility of criminal opportunity structures, Cloward and Ohlin assume the existence of gangs and rackets in some urban settings. Concentrating on stable criminal structures, they focus on a special case [110].

16. There is some relationship between recorded criminal activity on the part of parents and delinquency [18; 76; 140]. There is also a low degree of association between recorded delinquency on the part of one child and delinquency among siblings [100; 229]. We assume that direct socialization for delinquency is more likely to occur outside the home than within the context of the family.

17. Rotter's I-E measure [189] considers fate and luck as sources of external control while Rosenzweig considers them impunitive explanations of failure. Such explanations of failure may be related to feelings of powerlessness, but presumably would not lead to feelings of normlessness. If one believes he has no control over life because it is governed by fate or luck, he would have little reason to expect to be any more successful in criminal endeavors than conventional ones.

3 The Research Setting and Design

The goals of science are prediction and control, and they are best achieved through the development and testing of systematic theory [21; 171; 253]. The major purpose of this investigation is to evaluate the adequacy of our theoretical scheme. This objective requires discussion of appropriate sampling procedures, research design, and analytic techniques. Obviously, the question of sampling involves the selection of schools and students within schools, but given our interest in evaluation of a theory, we must consider the theoretical relevance of the sample itself [21; 71; 171].[1]

The ideal sample for this study would include cases that exhibit the appropriate variables and combinations of variable values required to test the theory, *and* the cases having these values would be represented proportionately. Such a sample would fulfill two conditions. First, it would permit a test of each substantive hypothesis. Second, it would enable us to determine whether the propositions established for the sample may be generalized to the population of existing cases. The first condition may be satisfied with a purposive sample, though such samples do not necessarily afford proportionate representation. To meet the second condition investigators have traditionally employed probability sampling techniques; however, probability samples often do not provide adequate representation of variable values.[2] The latter type of representativeness is important because samples that vary in representativeness will produce different values of the probabilities at issue.[3] Nevertheless, if a choice must be made between (1) the representation of cases having the requisite values of the variables and combinations thereof specified by the theory and (2) proportionate representation of cases having these properties, Camilleri opts for purposive sampling rather than probability sampling to insure variable representation [21].

We do not propose that probability samples are necessarily inappropriate. Nor is the choice between sampling and enumeration of some finite population the issue. Rather, the essential point is that in devoting attention to the selection of a probability sample representative of an existing population, investigators have given only cursory attention, usually in the form of a pious hope, to whether the sample contains the requisite combinations of variable values to evaluate their theory.

If our objective were to estimate precisely the delinquency and dropout rates in a specific community, a probability sample would be essential, but this is not our primary purpose. Consequently, the problem of sampling becomes one of choosing finite units from which inferences can be made about the postulated

39

relationships between the conceptual variables in the theory. Unfortunately, there is no procedure available to select a probability sample from the infinite hypothetical universe specified by a theory.

There is a solution to this dilemma. In a cogent discussion of theory, probability, and induction, Camilleri argues that while sampling may increase efficiency:

The scope of the induction provided by the sampling is, however, limited to the finite set of elements upon which the sampling procedure was employed. There is no procedure for *selecting* a probability sample from the infinite hypothetical universe specified by the coordinating definitions. To extend the scope of the sampling induction to the hypothetical universe requires us to *postulate* explicitly a specific connection between the existent elements and the hypothetical universe. [21, p. 172]

We are required to postulate a relationship between existing elements and the hypothetical universe of such elements; this is the case whether one uses purposive or probability sampling.

Further, it is not always feasible or practical to select a probability sample. In this particular investigation, selection of a probability sample would require resolution of a number of difficult problems. Among these are problems of (1) identifying the local, regional, or national school population to be representative of all existing students, the infinite hypothetical universe to which our theory is relevant; (2) enumerating and sampling the population after it has been identified; (3) obtaining approval from the various administrative units, both with respect to the inclusion of particular students and the nature of the information to be obtained from these subjects; and (4) increasing cost associated with extensive geographical dispersion of students.[4] Considerations of this kind often force investigators to neglect one type of representation—variable or population—for the other. Such was the case in this study.

Following the advice of Camilleri [21; see 71; 78] on this crucial issue, we have selected cases to obtain the required combinations of variable values—that is, we have employed a purposive sampling technique.[5] We based our decision on the conviction that variable representation is more important than proportionate representation of the population because generalization beyond one's sample is difficult, even on the basis of a probability sample. The consequence of this decision is a limited scope of inference with the sample being, in essence, the target population. Generalization of the relationships observed in this study to other populations cannot be made with a known degree of accuracy. Although statistical tests of significance are inappropriate for a purposive sample, there are logical grounds for making inferences beyond the target population:

For instance, if some correlations are found to hold for a heterogeneous sample ... there will be a high degree of confirmation to the generalization hypothesis, even though this confirmation cannot be measured in the way statistical generalization hypotheses are measured (by means of confidence levels and significance levels). Consequently, purposive samples can also be used, provided they are heterogeneous enough, preferably even representative. [71, p. 59]

Camilleri also notes that purposive samples facilitate the replication of studies by keeping the sample size within manageable limits and by clearly specifying the conditions, apart from selection biases, that would make the studies comparable [21]. It is our intention to describe the characteristics of the study population and to identify the conditions upon which inferences to other populations or samples may be made.

It is more important to validate a theory on a limited population than it is to be able to generalize to a larger universe with a known degree of accuracy; representation of variables is more important than proportionate representation of a population through probability sampling. It is our view that the latter has been overemphasized. Consequently, investigators have been preoccupied with demonstrating that their findings may be generalized to a larger finite population. Less attention has been devoted to the question whether the data offer substantive support for the theory under scrutiny. To reiterate, evaluation of a proposition's effectiveness in accounting for the variability in the dependent variable is more important than generalization to a larger population on statistical grounds.

The Research Setting

In this research a type of cluster sample was used in which the basic sampling unit was a school, rather than a person. In one sense we did not sample—we enumerated one grade within the schools we selected. We sampled only in our choice of particular schools. Our selection of schools was not a probability sample of all schools, but a purposive selection of 8 schools located in 2 metropolitan areas. The area in southern California comprised three contiguous communities and surrounding sections of the county. The other study area, located in northern California, consisted of a single community. In southern California a single, unified school district serves the area at the junior and senior high school levels. This unified district operates 7 junior high schools (grades 7 through 9) and 5 senior high schools (grades 10 through 12). The community in northern California is served by a single four-year high school (grades 9 through 12). This school is also part of a large, unified school district, but only the one school in this administrative unit was included in the study.

Both areas are suburban in character—in neither case is the central city or core of the metropolitan area included. In both study areas, the growth patterns are similar to those of many metropolitan areas in which the outlying sections have experienced more rapid growth than the central city. In the area in southern California, two satellite cities contain the majority of the school district's total population. In 1940 the populations of these municipalities were approximately 10,000 and 5,000 and increased to approximately 35,000 and 46,000, respectively, by 1965. In other parts of this area, the population more than doubled between 1940 and 1965.

There are socio-economic and ethnic differences within the southern California area. Illustrative of these differences are the demographic characteristics of the three largest communities: percentage Negro, 0.1, 3.5, 4.0; percentage with Spanish surname, 6.8, 12.7, 27.0; median years of school completed, 12.2, 10.9, 9.9; median family income, $6,969, $5,574, $5,333; percentage of deteriorating and dilapidated housing, 4.5, 12.8, 20.0; and percentage of males in white-collar occupations, 45.6, 33.5, 28.2. As might be expected, there is considerable variation within each community, which is partially masked by these figures.

The community in northern California also experienced rapid growth. From a population of 2,000 in 1940, it grew to approximately 25,000 by 1965. About 70 percent of the residences are less than 10 years old—a reflection of rapid growth in a previously undeveloped area. Although of modest value, the homes in this community are generally in sound condition. Only 3 percent of the dwellings have deteriorated to a point that they need more repairs than would be provided by normal maintenance; these homes are located primarily in the oldest section of the community. On the other hand, 18 percent of the housing units are overcrowded. The median value of the owner-occupied units is $13,000, a figure $5,400 below the median in the county. The income of the residents— $6,300 per family—is also lower than the county median of $8,100. More than 40 percent of the population are Negroes. Almost two-thirds of the employed persons in the community work in blue-collar occupations; in contrast, in the county only 40 percent of the workers have blue-collar jobs. Comprising 5 percent of the total county population, the target community has more dependent persons than the county in which it is located. Thirty-five percent of the residents of the county are under 18 years of age, but in this community, 50 percent of the population are children under 18 years of age. The community also has 27 percent of the cases of Aid to Needy Children; 11 percent of the admissions to the tax-supported community hospital for general care; 25 percent of the births; and 11 percent of the public health nursing visits. There is, of course, considerable variation within the area itself. Although not located in the core of a city, this community has the same general problems as the typical slum, and these vary only in degree of intensity. (For a discussion of the characteristics of slums see Clinard [32].)

The Study Population

Within each school we enumerated the students in the ninth grade. This sampling design was used for several reasons. First, it permitted selection of a variety of school settings and guaranteed inclusion of students with a wide range of social, economic, and racial or ethnic characteristics. A classification of milieu, similar to that developed by Reiss and Rhodes [175], was constructed on the basis of the distribution of occupational, educational, and racial-ethnic characteristics of the population in each school's attendance area. Although such comparisons are not reported in this volume, the selection of specific types of milieu would permit comparison of lower- and middle-class subjects in school contexts where each was the dominant class and where each was a numerical minority. Similarly, schools were selected to include Anglos, Negroes, and Mexican-Americans in school contexts where each was dominant and in schools where each was a minority. This would permit assessment of the school milieu while controlling for class and ethnicity. Second, enumeration of a grade level within each school allows a relatively complete sociometric mapping of the groups within each school context. Comparable data are available for each person in the network; this would not be the case if a sampling technique was employed. These data are crucially important in this research. Information on each subject's associations in school allows direct assessment of peer influence. Third, cluster sampling has practical advantages, particularly reduction in the cost and effort expended in interviewing, administering questionnaires, searching records, and obtaining official clearance for research from school administrators.

An important factor involved in selection of the sample was a consideration of age. There is evidence that students experience failure in school and at home quite early [103; 238]. Ideally, we would begin with preschool subjects and follow them through high school graduation. However, each additional year in a longitudinal study accelerates expenses and increases sample attrition. Yet, to establish temporal sequences, measures of the independent variables must be obtained prior to the time any substantial portion of the student population drops out of school. Various investigations show that the first major period of dropout occurs between the ninth and tenth grade [51; 241; 243; 244]. Initiation of the study while the respondents were in junior high school thus allowed measurement of the effect of movement from one type of school context to another.

Because delinquency is treated as a behavioral variable rather than as a personal attribute, the problem of establishing temporal sequences is somewhat different for delinquent behavior. It is reasonable to assume that the majority of juveniles are involved, more or less, in delinquent behavior, and in many instances their initial experience occurs relatively early in life. In our definition of delinquency we do not merely distinguish between those who have or have not engaged in this type of behavior; rather, our interest centers on differences in the frequency and seriousness of delinquent behavior. Knowing that we could not obtain measures of the independent variables prior to all of the subjects' initial involvement in delinquent behavior, we hoped to demonstrate the effect of these variables on subsequent rates of delinquent behavior and changes in the frequency and seriousness of delinquent acts through time. In considering the important variable *age* with respect to sample selection, we emphasized the age range in which maximum rather than initial involvement in delinquent behavior takes place. We concluded that the study should begin prior to and extend beyond the period of maximum involvement in delinquency. Unfortunately, there is little information available regarding the relationship between age and rates of self-reported delinquent behavior. For example, Short and Nye discuss a number of correlates of reported delinquent behavior, but age is not one of these [216]. In a number of subsequent studies of self-reported delinquency investigators controlled age by confining their respondents to one or two grades (see Chapter 4). To the extent that official delinquency statistics accurately reflect this relationship, we expected the rates of delinquent behavior to be highest for persons between the ages of 15 and 17 [165]. It appeared that if data were gathered initially during the ninth grade and at regular intervals until the usual date of high school graduation, this would provide observations prior to the time the vast majority of dropouts left school, as well as during the years of maximum involvement of juveniles in delinquent behavior.

On the basis of these considerations, 7 junior high schools and 1 four-year high school were selected as the sampling units, and all students who entered these schools as ninth graders in September 1963 comprised the target study population. The potential number of respondents was 2,721. The attendance areas for the 7 junior high schools were congruent with 5 senior high schools; this greatly facilitated the maintenance of contact with the study cohort. Except for dropouts and transfers, the cohort progressed through the ninth, tenth, eleventh, and twelfth grades in these schools and remained essentially intact throughout the entire study period.[6]

The sex, ethnic, and social class distributions of the respondents by school in the junior and senior high schools are presented in Table 3-1. The schools vary in size. In the junior high schools the enrollment range is 173 to 455, whereas among the senior high schools, including the 1 four-year school, the range is 284 to 441. With the exception of Junior High School G and Senior High School A the percentages of males and females are nearly equal. Mexican-Americans comprise sizable percentages of 3 junior and 3 senior high schools. The Negro respondents are concentrated in High School E, the single four-year school included in this study. By design, the schools show considerable variation in the social class of the students. For example, in High School C one-fifth of the students are in Class 2 and two-fifths are in Class 3. In contrast, one-third of the students in High School E are in Class 5.

Table 3-1

Sex, Ethnicity, and Social Class Distributions in Study Schools (Percentages)

Junior High School	N^a	Sex		Ethnicity				Class				
		Male	Female	Anglo	Negro	Mexican-American	Other	1	2	3	4	5
A	(302)	50	50	81	–	11	8	0	5	31	46	18
B	(455)	49	51	93	–	6	1	7	23	37	24	9
C	(212)	49	51	61	1	32	6	2	1	19	44	34
D	(376)	51	49	88	1	7	4	1	8	38	41	12
E	(414)	52	48	73	1	22	4	–	4	30	48	18
F	(342)	49	51	86	–	9	5	1	9	23	53	14
G	(173)	56	44	53	–	43	4	2	–	24	42	32
Senior High School												
A	(284)	46	54	73	1	21	5	–	3	29	50	18
B	(381)	52	48	87	–	10	3	0	8	38	42	12
C	(481)	51	49	94	–	4	2	8	21	41	21	9
D	(366)	52	48	75	–	21	4	1	6	25	50	18
E	(343)	50	50	30	57	3	10	3	4	22	39	32
F	(419)	48	52	72	0	21	7	1	4	28	44	23

aWith the exception of High School E, the four-year high school, these data reflect enrollment in September 1964 when the cohort entered the tenth grade. Dropouts and out-of-district transfers are not included. For High School E, like the junior high schools, these figures reflect enrollment at the beginning of the study; addition of the Ns for the seven junior high schools and High School E total 2,617.

The Research Design

The research design specified that initial observations would be obtained when the study population entered the ninth grade, and additional observations would be made annually until the usual date for graduation from high school for the cohort. Data were to be gathered in the period from September 1963 to September 1967. Questionnaires were to be administered at four points: early ninth grade, mid-tenth grade, mid-eleventh grade, and twelfth grade, prior to graduation.

As noted in Chapter 1, use of a longitudinal design permits determination of the temporal order of events and, therefore, an assessment of postulated cause-effect relationships. However, this type of design introduces problems not encountered in cross-sectional studies. A major concern in longitudinal studies involves the conceptualization of time. A single academic class, ninth graders, was selected for investigation to control or to hold relatively constant the effects of age or maturation—a problem that intrudes in comparing groups at different age levels at any particular point in time. Limitation of the study population to a single class with a rather narrow age range reduces the possible interpretations of time. Maturation effects are limited to differences observed from year to year, but cannot account for differences between subjects at any given point in time.

As the population was selected prior to the onset of dropout or extensive involvement in delinquency, a second salient issue in this type of design involves the likelihood of obtaining the required observations through time. In a pretest estimates of delinquency and dropout rates were calculated for two schools in a nearby school district [60]. These rates provided a basis for estimating the required sample size and gave some assurance that with a sample of 2,000 or more the necessary values of the dependent variables would occur with sufficient frequency to complete the type of analysis planned. While the pretest involved a retrospective follow-up, it also provided a basis for estimating attrition rates, another factor to be considered in determining that the size of the cohort was adequate.

Data-Gathering Procedures

In this investigation data were obtained from official records and through the use of survey research techniques. Throughout the study school records were examined regularly.[7] In the first year, data were gathered from a variety of sources to obtain extensive benchmark measurements. Questionnaires were administered to each of the subjects in the study population, teachers' evaluations were obtained, and the mother or mother surrogate of each respondent was interviewed. The records of law enforcement agencies were also examined. In each additional year of the study, each subject—both students and dropouts—completed a questionnaire or was interviewed. In addition to the annual data-gathering procedures, each respondent who left school was interviewed as soon as it was determined he or she had dropped out. Each time a student left school, a dropout interview was attempted. At the conclusion of the study the records of law enforcement agencies were again examined, and an effort was made to obtain comparable data for mobile subjects.

The Annual Student Questionnaire. In each annual data-gathering phase, most of the subjects in the cohort completed standardized questionnaires. In the first year of the study—the academic year 1963-1964—information was obtained from each of the respondents through the administration of questionnaires in a group setting in the several junior high schools and in the single high school. Thereafter, for subjects who were in school, the questionnaires were again administered in a group setting in the several high schools. Similar procedures were followed each year. Most of the groups consisted of 20 to 30 students, though in the last year larger groups were utilized in some instances because of scheduling problems. Each group of subjects was given oral instructions, and questions were clarified for individuals as they arose. Each questionnaire was checked for completeness as soon as a student finished it. The students generally spent 40 to 60 minutes completing the questionnaires, although in each year some students found the questionnaire to be a useful device to avoid up to 90 minutes of their routine school activities. The students were not coerced to answer every question, but probes were used to obtain meaningful responses in instances where there were no answers or only vague answers to key questions.

For subjects who dropped out of school, a trained interviewer attempted to contact them individually. An alternate form of the student questionnaire was designed to be completed by these subjects with the interviewer's guidance. In the dropout schedule, inquiries about current school experiences were deleted; items pertaining to employment, marriage, and other out-of-school experiences were substituted.

We attempted to make personal contact with each respondent in the original cohort during each of the annual data-gathering phases, including those who dropped out as well as those who transferred to another school. Most of the dropouts and transfer students were in the San Diego, Los Angeles, or San Francisco Standard Metropolitan Areas and were accessible to our interviewers. In cases of respondents having moved beyond one of these areas, faculty members in nearby colleges or universities were contacted to arrange for competent interviewers to administer the questionnaires. The efforts made by these interviewers to contact the subjects were extensive and at times remarkable.[8] This mechanism for follow-up of the students who had transferred as well as the mobile dropouts proved to be effective during the course of this study.

Administration of the first annual student questionnaire was initiated in the district in southern California in October 1963, and continued until December 1963. During December, efforts were made to contact students who were absent on the days the research team visited their school. Forty students were also absent on subsequent visits to their schools and were finally excluded from the study population. A total of 2,309 questionnaires were completed—there were only 4 student refusals.

In the first week of May 1964, questionnaires were administered in the one school in northern California.[9] During the second week of May, efforts were made to contact absentees. We were unable to contact 18 students who were subsequently excluded from the study population. A total of 349 questionnaires were completed—there was only 1 student refusal in this school.

Any student who indicated at the outset that he or she did not wish to complete a questionnaire was given a pass from the classroom to the school library. Such a student was told that participation in the study was voluntary and that the investigators preferred that students not participate if they had any objection to providing the kind of information requested in the questionnaire. It was also explained that these students would be dropped from the study population but this fact would not be known to the school. In no way would failure to participate prejudice a student's position in the school, since the school administrators, while cooperating with the researchers in the conduct of the study, were not party to the administration of it. Two of the 5 students defined as refusals voiced objection after having partially completed their questionnaires; each of these 2 questionnaires was destroyed when only the student involved was present.[10]

The Parent Interview. During the first year of the study, the mother or mother surrogate of each respondent was interviewed in the respondent's home. In the event that an interview with the mother was not feasible, the father or guardian was interviewed. For this purpose a standardized schedule was used. Two equivalent forms of the parent interview schedule were required for English- and Spanish-speaking parents. After the English form of the schedule was developed and pretested, persons fluent in both English and Spanish were employed to develop a comparable Spanish form that did not differ substantively in translation. A number of pretests, involving a limited number of respondents on each occasion, were made. Finally, both forms were pretested with parents of 100 ninth-grade students who were not a part of the study population. Mexican-Americans, Caucasians, and Negroes were interviewed in this pretest.

Adult interviewers from the community, many of whom had previous interviewing experience, participated in a training program during the latter part of December 1963, and in January 1964. A total of 26 interviewers completed the twenty-hour training program. Early in May 1964, a second group of prospective interviewers participated in a comparable program; this provided 21 persons to conduct interviews with the parents of the respondents in the single four-year high school included in the study.

When the interviews with the parents of the ninth-grade students were initiated, each of the completed schedules was checked for completeness, particularly from the standpoint of coding requirements. With the growing familiarity of the interviewers with the schedule, this procedure was replaced by spot checks of the completed schedules.

The interviewers and parents were matched on the basis of sex and ethnicity insofar as possible. Of the 49 field interviewers, 6 were males and 43 were females. There were 23 Caucasian, 18 Negro, 1 Oriental, and 7 bilingual Mexican-American interviewers. During the course of parental interviewing, a time-cost schedule was maintained for each interviewer, as was a count of the interviewer's number of refusals. Such information was essential to control expenses and to limit attrition and enabled us to release the less efficient interviewers.

The refusal rate in interviewing parents was extremely low; only 41 (1.5 percent) of the 2,658 attempted interviews resulted in a refusal. The success in completing interviews is attributed to a combination of several factors—the adequacy of the interviewers' training, the screening of inefficient interviewers, and the interest of community leaders.[11] Another factor involved in maintaining a low refusal rate was the assignment of initial refusals to interviewers who had demonstrated outstanding ability in routine assignments. Such additional attempts to complete the interviews proved to be quite effective; the more adept interviewers found it possible to establish good rapport in cases where others had not succeeded in gaining access to the respondent's home. At the conclusion of each interview with a parent or guardian, permission to reinterview the respondent's child annually for the next three years was requested. In the event this permission was not granted, the subject was excluded from the study cohort. Thus, 2,617 parents (of the 2,658 students who completed the first annual questionnaire) completed interviews *and* granted permission to include their children in the subsequent stages of the study.

The Dropout Interview. Each dropout was interviewed after it was determined that he or she had left school. Personal interviews were conducted following a standardized schedule; the primary focus was on the factors associated with the subject's decision to leave school. The instrument was pretested with 40 dropouts from high schools in an adjacent school district. Once a month, a member of the project staff examined the register in each of the schools to obtain the names of subjects who had transferred to another school, who had dropped out, or who had been expelled, excluded, or exempted from school by administrative order.[12] With the exception of the students who had transferred, these subjects were immediately assigned to an interviewer who attempted to complete the dropout interview. A separate file of the names of the out-of-school students was maintained.

The names of students who presumably transferred to another school were also maintained separately. Until a request for a transcript was received from a student's new school, it was not known whether the subject was attending school or had dropped out. If after 30 days no request for a subject's transcript was received, we assumed the respondent was a dropout, and the procedure followed with dropouts was initiated. In some instances, the interviewer discovered these persons were actually enrolled in school. In such cases, the interviewer's efforts to contact the subject provided the information necessary to keep accurate records.

When a request for a transcript was received for a subject, a form letter, a return post card, and a "flagging" sticker were sent to the new school to (1) verify that the student had entered the school, (2) obtain the subject's new home address for our records, and (3) flag the student's record to insure that we would be notified should he or she drop out or transfer again. At times, a school received a request for a transcript but was later notified that the subject had registered but not entered the school. An interviewer then attempted to contact these persons in order to complete the dropout interview. Our experience indicates that when students leave school, it is often difficult to determine whether they are planning to enroll in another school or drop out.

Teachers' Evaluations. Because teachers are presumably in close contact with students, it has often been suggested that they are in an ideal position to identify youth who are likely to become delinquent or drop out of high school [121]. During the first year of the study, we obtained teachers' evaluations of the ninth-grade students with respect to their (1) academic or classroom performance, (2) social adjustment, (3) hostility toward teachers, (4) reading ability, (5) likelihood of dropout, and (6) probability of getting into trouble with law enforcement agencies.

In each of the schools, every faculty member, including classroom teachers, coaches, counselors, and administrators, was given a set of instructions and questions, as well as a deck of mark-sense cards. The name of each ninth grader was printed on a separate IBM card. A member of the research team explained the procedure to the teachers at one of their regular faculty meetings. Teachers were instructed to evaluate each student they knew well enough to rate; the remaining cards were to be discarded. It was left to the teacher to determine whether he or she had sufficient knowledge of a student to provide an evaluation. Because of differences in teaching assignments, there was variation in the number of students each teacher rated; the number of ratings received by each subject also varied and ranged from 0 to 15. The students in the study population were rated by an average of 6.5 teachers, though in 13 cases no evaluations were made. On the basis of the modal rating, each subject was assigned one of the probability levels specified in the response categories (see Appendix B). There was no mode for 362 students.

Official Records. In addition to the use of survey research techniques, we examined school records to obtain I.Q. scores, achievement test scores, grades, and information on absenteeism and disciplinary action for each respondent. The records of the local police and sheriffs, juvenile divisions of the county probation departments, and juvenile courts were also checked to determine which individuals in the cohort had official contact with law enforcement agencies. Information was recorded on the nature of the offense, the date of the offense, and the disposition of the case by the police. The probation department records included information on the filing of petitions and court action for cases referred to the probation department by the local police or sheriff.

In view of the mobility of the population, it was also necessary to have records examined in a variety of other locations. To obtain comparable information about respondents who left the two primary study areas, letters were sent to the police and probation departments in every location in which a subject had, according to our records, resided during the course of the study.[13] Each school a subject entered was also contacted to obtain school records.

Response to these requests was excellent; 92 percent of the record checks were completed satisfactorily. The level of completion achieved in this phase of our research not only provides a highly adequate record of each subject's officially recorded delinquent acts, but also indicates the feasibility of departing from the usual cross-sectional design and the willingness of school officials and law enforcement personnel to cooperate with investigators. The available data provide a satisfactory base upon which to analyze school records and permit an accurate estimate of the cohort's involvement in officially known delinquent activity.

Cohort Attrition

A fundamental problem in longitudinal studies involves the loss of subjects over the course of the investigation. Obviously, attrition may affect a study's findings. The seriousness of this problem is related to the rate of attrition and selectivity in the loss of cases and constitutes a crucial problem in descriptive studies in which attrition is correlated with the variables being measured. In explanatory studies, selective mortality is generally not a critical problem.

In this study subjects were lost through refusals and changes in residence. Although prospective subjects were excluded during the first data-gathering phase because of a subject's or a parent's refusal to cooperate, refusals encountered during subsequent data-gathering periods were not eliminated from the cohort. After the first year of the study, 19 subjects—10 males and 9 females—refused to participate. These were distributed evenly: 6 in the second year, 7 in the third year, and 6 in the fourth year. Eleven of these subjects eventually graduated, whereas 8 either dropped out prior to or subsequent to refusing to provide information. Clearly, a sizable proportion of the refusals (42 percent) were dropouts.

To minimize case attrition due to residential mobility, rather elaborate tracking techniques were developed. This was essential because 23 percent of the students left the schools in the two study areas. The procedures used to locate these subjects included the usual checks through post office forwarding addresses, public utility addresses, and requests for school transcripts. Using a card similar to those employed by the schools to obtain names of persons to contact in case of emergency, each year we asked subjects to provide the names and addresses of persons who would always know their whereabouts. In most instances, one or more of these techniques proved to be satisfactory in locating mobile subjects. Because most mobile subjects entered a school in their new community, efforts to follow them were greatly facilitated. In many instances, however, we had to rely on the ingenuity of our interviewers in obtaining leads on subjects temporarily lost. At the conclusion of the study, there were only 8 subjects whose whereabouts were completely unknown. There is no evidence of selectivity by sex, ethnicity, or initial involvement in delinquency on the part of these subjects; however, all 8 were from the lower half of the class distribution, all were dropouts, and all but 1 came from a school milieu that provided limited opportunity. When the project was terminated, there were 235 subjects, including the 19 refusals, for whom we had incomplete data for the last data-gathering phase, even though we had addresses for them and knew whether or not they had graduated. Limitations of time did not permit further efforts to secure complete information from these subjects. Persons for whom information was missing appeared to be similar to the study cohort with respect to ethnicity and class. However, they were predominantly male (62 percent) and reported significantly higher initial involvement in delinquent activities than the cohort. An attrition rate of 9 percent appears low, given the length of time the subjects were followed. Further, the effect of incomplete data for 235 subjects was not as serious as would have been the case in a study of shorter duration because data gathering during the first three years were available for most of these subjects. Consequently, trends for major variables could be established.

General Form of the Analysis

In the preceding chapter we presented theoretical linkages that imply the existence of causal relationships. To establish a causal relationship investigators must demonstrate (1) that a statistical association between an independent variable *A* and a dependent variable *B* exists, (2) that *A* is causally prior to *B*, and (3) that the relationship between *A* and *B* is not spurious [104; 107].[14] The first of these requirements is undoubtedly the easiest to fulfill. In a longitudinal study the problem of temporal sequence is partially overcome by the design. Yet we face the difficult task of instituting appropriate controls to test for spuriousness. We attempt to deal with the problem of spuriousness through the design of the study and at specific points in the analysis. However, our major concern is demonstration of the association between variables in the correct temporal sequence; we measure the association between initial values of our predictor variables and subsequent dropout or delinquent behavior.

Temporal Order

To clarify the temporal sequence of independent and dependent variables the years in the study were divided into 5 analytic periods. Each of these periods begins or ends with the administration of an annual questionnaire. The chronology of events during the study and the delineation of analytic time periods are indicated in Figure 3-1. Period I does not have a specific beginning point but ends with the administration of the first annual questionnaire.[15] In

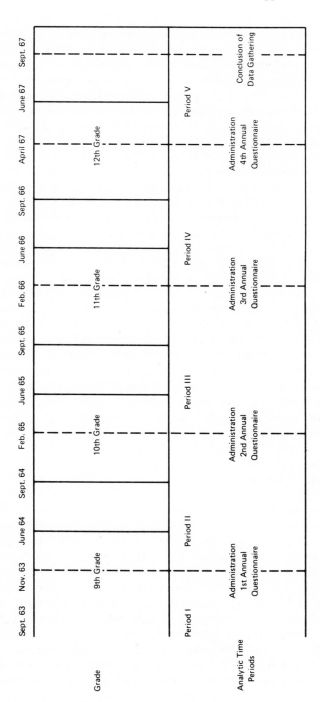

Figure 3-1. Analytic Time Periods

this study we do not attempt to account for events that occurred during Period
I. Rather, measures of the experiences and events during this period serve either
as predictors of future delinquency and dropout or as controls in the analysis.
Measures of self-reported delinquent behavior and police contacts were obtained
for Period I, but these serve primarily as a base against which increases or
decreases in delinquency are measured. Delinquent acts cannot be explained by
data gathered after the fact. Period I, in which the first annual questionnaire was
administered, was the most important data-gathering phase of the study because
initial values for the predictor variables were obtained in this period and base
rates for the dependent or criterion variables were established.

Period II begins immediately after the first annual questionnaire was administered; it ends with completion of the second annual questionnaire in February
1965. Measures of the dependent variables in this time period may be considered
consequences of the predictor variables of Period I; further, new measures of the
independent variables obtained in subsequent periods constitute revised predictors for dropout and delinquent behavior in the following time periods. This
permits a lagged analysis with the predictor measures always being temporally
antecedent to the dependent variables, delinquency and dropout. Period V
covers the time after the expected date of graduation to the following fall, when
most of the subjects would have reached the age of 18. Inclusion of Period V
(April to September, 1967) permits accurate classification of a number of
subjects who neither dropped out nor graduated. Of the nongraduates, some did
not return to school in September 1967, whereas others did and were
progressing toward graduation when the study terminated. The study period
covers the majority of each subject's adolescent years (14 to 18) and includes
most of the period during which the subjects were likely to come into contact
with the police and courts as juveniles.

The Dependent Variables

In this investigation, information about official police contact and self reports of
delinquent behavior were obtained. In subsequent analyses, these data are
extensively compared. However, in tests of our theoretical propositions attention is focused on self-reported delinquent behavior. Two types of measures
were established for the dependent variable, delinquent behavior. The first was a
raw frequency score—a simple enumeration of delinquent acts admitted to on a
"self-reported delinquency" questionnaire. Frequency scores were calculated for
Period I, the time prior to our initial contact with the study population, and for
Periods II through IV, the duration of the study. In the delinquency analysis,
Period II to IV is treated as a single time period. Our primary interest lies in the
scores for Period II to IV because it is their variability that is to be explained by
the independent variables. In a causal argument, only those delinquent acts

occurring after the initial measures on the independent variables can be viewed as effects of these variables.

The frequency scores adequately reflect the extent of juveniles' involvement in delinquent activity during the course of the study, but they ignore the relative increase or decrease in the subjects' delinquency. For example, 2 subjects with 0 and 20 offenses in Period I may both commit 10 offenses during the course of the study. Because only the magnitude of their delinquency during the study is considered in the frequency scores, both subjects would be considered equally delinquent when, in fact, they are not. To overcome this problem we developed measures of change that reflect both prior and subsequent levels of delinquent activity.

There is some controversy about the appropriate technique for measuring change [94; 101; 133; 134; 145; 146]. Essentially, this involves the relative advantages and disadvantages of raw gain scores in comparison with residual gain scores. We employ residual gain scores as our second measure of delinquency because they ordinarily are more reliable than raw gain scores [69; 146]. Further, raw gain scores tend to be negatively correlated with initial scores whereas residual gain scores are, by definition, not correlated with initial scores.[16] Conceptually, the latter feature is of particular importance. While a raw gain score is simply a subject's second score minus his first, the residual gain score is the difference between the observed second score and a predicted second score based upon the regression of first scores on second scores in the general population. Thus, a residual gain score statistically controls the effect of a subject's prior involvement in delinquency. This control is important for two reasons. First, there is reason to believe that delinquency may cause further delinquency; in the absence of influence from other causal variables, prior involvement in delinquency may be a sufficient cause of further delinquency. If this presumption is correct, then a certain portion of a subject's delinquent behavior during the study may be attributed to his prior delinquency. In this case it would be important to control for the "effect" of prior delinquency, which can be accomplished with a residual gain score. In a sense it represents an adjustment of the subject's raw frequency score for the study period and reduces his score by the amount that is statistically predicted or "explained" by his prior involvement in delinquency.

Even if one questions the idea that prior delinquency causes subsequent delinquency, there is another reason for holding prior delinquency constant in the analysis. This guarantees that the relationships between the independent variables and subsequent delinquent behavior are causal. Specifically, it insures the temporal sequence required for a causal argument. If raw gain scores were used, relationships could be found simply because the independent variables were associated with prior levels of delinquency [135]. However, the dependent-independent relationship would involve an incorrect temporal sequence—delinquency would be the causal variable. The control for prior delinquency is also a control for the desired temporal sequence.

On the basis of these considerations, residual gain scores are employed as the primary measure of delinquent behavior in the analysis. Given a subject's prior level of delinquent activity and the pre-post delinquency relationship in the population, his residual gain score may be either positive or negative and indicates whether the extent of his delinquent behavior during the study was higher or lower than predicted. The sign of the residual gain score indicates the direction of change; a negative sign indicates a relative decrease, whereas a positive sign denotes a relative increase. The magnitude of the residual gain score indicates the amount (positive or negative) of delinquency directly attributable to the operation of other variables—it is this difference between the predicted and the observed score that requires explanation.[17] The strongest causal argument can be made with the measure of residual gain. Raw frequency scores are also presented for comparative purposes and because residual gain scores do not unequivocally reflect the extent of involvement in delinquent acts. Persons with low residual gain scores may be either frequent or infrequent offenders. A single measure of delinquency does not reflect the actual magnitude and the relative change in delinquent activity.

Several measures of dropout were developed (see Chapter 4). In the correlational analyses, a dichotomy of dropouts and nondropouts among intellectually capable subjects is employed. On the other hand, a measure of current enrollment is employed in the longitudinal analyses. The latter is a simple dichotomy that indicates for each analytic period whether the subject was in school or dropped out at some time during the period. In the analysis of successive time periods, subjects who left school in an earlier time period are eliminated because the postulated temporal order is reversed for them—measures of the independent variables include possible effects of dropout. This measure is not cumulative, but reflects dropout in each specified time period. The analysis involves the calculation of in- to out-of-school transition rates or the probability of dropout during the period for respondents *in* school at the beginning of the period [44].[18]

Origin and Gain Predictors

In most instances, four separate measures of each independent variable were obtained; with the exception of Period V, a measure was secured at the end of each analytic time period. Two types of predictors were derived from these measures. The first is an origin predictor that reflects the subject's score on that measure at the beginning of the study. For example, the initial measure of a student's exposure to dropout constitutes an origin predictor for dropout during Period II and any subsequent period.

While the level of exposure at the beginning of the study is a predictor for subsequent dropout or delinquency, it only represents a single measure in time.

It does not reflect the dynamic nature of the independent variable. A person with moderate initial levels of exposure may be in the process of moving toward higher or lower levels of exposure; the direction of this movement may be the critical factor in relation to his delinquent activity. The amount and direction of change through time constitutes a second type of predictor. We refer to measures of this type as gain predictors. Together, the origin and gain predictors relate the initial level on an independent variable and its trend through time to subsequent delinquency and dropout.

In all cases the orgin predictors were based on raw scores that were converted into standard scores or normal deviate units. Residual gain scores were used as gain predictors. Four gain predictors were calculated for each independent variable: the gain from Period I to II, from Period I to III, from Period I to IV, and the average of these three scores. Only the first, second, and fourth scores were used in the analysis; the average score was used as the measure of gain for the entire study period because it is more sensitive to relatively short-run changes occurring within each specific time period than the gain calculated only from Period I and Period IV scores. The average gain also was used as the gain predictor for the delinquency analysis because the second measure of self-reported delinquency was cumulative for Period II to IV. Status as a dropout was determined independently for each study period; hence, each of the gain predictors was used in the dropout analysis as appropriate.

Summary

In this study the basic sampling unit was a school rather than a person. Eight schools located in 2 metropolitan areas were purposively selected to provide adequate representation of the appropriate variables and combinations of variable values required to test our theory. Within each of these schools, we enumerated the students in the ninth grade. The study population included students with a wide range of social, economic, and racial or ethnic characteristics. The potential number of respondents in these schools was 2,721. Intensive efforts to contact 58 of these students during the first year of the study were unsuccessful because of their repeated absence from school. These potential respondents were excluded from the study population, as were 5 students who refused to participate. In addition, 41 students were excluded from the study population because their mothers either refused to be interviewed or to grant permission to include their children in subsequent stages of the study; this reduced the study population to 2,617 respondents.

The research design specified that initial observations were to be obtained when the study population entered the ninth grade, and additional observations were to be made annually until the usual date of graduation from high school for the cohort. Data were to be gathered in the period from September 1963 to

September 1967. This time span was divided into 5 separate data-gathering periods covering each of the 4 years of school and the period after the expected date of graduation to the following fall. Use of a longitudinal design presents a number of special data-gathering problems, but it permits assessment of postulated cause-effect relationships. The initial observations were calculated to precede dropout and extensive involvement in delinquent behavior in order to permit accurate determination of the temporal order of events.

In this investigation data were gathered from official records and through the use of survey research techniques. In the first year of the study, data were gathered from a variety of sources to obtain benchmark measurements. In addition to the administration of questionnaires to each of the students in the cohort, the mother or mother surrogate of each respondent was interviewed. Teachers' ratings were also obtained. In each subsequent year of the study, each subject (both students and dropouts) completed a questionnaire or was interviewed. Further, each respondent who dropped out was interviewed after he or she left school. Throughout the study the records of the schools were examined to obtain grades and achievement test scores, to maintain an accurate record of each respondent's current address, and to detect dropouts. A variety of techniques were successfully used to minimize cohort attrition; at the termination of the study the whereabouts of only 8 subjects were completely unknown. Time limitations resulted in incomplete data for an additional 235 subjects, although we knew whether they graduated or dropped out prior to graduation.

Official and self-reported delinquency data were collected in this investigation permitting a number of comparative analyses. However, tests of our theoretical propositions were conducted on the basis of self-reported delinquent behavior. Two measures of the dependent variable, delinquent behavior, were developed. One was a raw frequency score or an enumeration of delinquent acts committed during the study period. Residual gain scores were computed to control for the effect of subjects' involvement in delinquency prior to the initiation of the study. For the other dependent variable, dropout, different measures were used in the correlational and longitudinal analyses. In the latter, a simple dichotomy was employed to indicate for each analytic period whether a respondent was in school or dropped out at some time during this period.

Two types of predictor variables were derived from the repeated measures of each independent variable. For a given independent variable the initial measure is treated as an origin predictor. The origin predictors are based on raw scores that were converted into standard scores. Gain predictors were also developed to assess the amount and direction of change through time for a given independent variable. Four gain predictors (residual gain scores) were calculated for each independent variable. Together, the origin and gain predictors relate both the initial level and the trend with respect to an independent variable to subsequent delinquency and dropout.

Notes

1. In devoting primary attention to the theoretical relevance of the sample—or the population from which the sample is selected—we depart from the usual point of emphasis in empirical investigations conducted by sociologists. On the advice of statisticians, sociologists have eschewed purposive samples. Probability samples have been employed almost routinely, though at times it is impossible to obtain such samples as occur, for example, in research focused on drug users or homosexuals, in which case convenience samples are necessarily employed. According to Camilleri convenience samples are unsatisfactory as representative of the existing population and "unless these samples are huge they will usually not contain enough of the right combinations of variable values to make an adequate test of the theory" [21, p. 173]. Recognizing that sampling introduces a source of error not present if a population is enumerated, researchers have used statistical tests of significance to determine the risk entailed in drawing inferences from a probability sample. Although there is disagreement regarding the propriety of this use of significance tests, it is clear that statistical significance has been confused with theoretical or substantive importance. Sociological journals have been enlivened in recent years by debates on the uses and misuses of tests of significance; critics have raised serious questions about the use of these tests in sociological research [21; 53; 78; 112; 122; 144; 207; 221]. Gold argues that tests of significance cannot be used as a basis for generalization to a population, but he contends that a decision about *substantive* importance can be made using a random process model: "When lack of statistical significance by any test is found in a universe or a given set of data (keep in mind, not a sample), we can say that in the empirical world the association produced by nature is no greater than that produced by a chance (e.g., random pairing) process. And it would seem a fair rule of thumb that, given our present state of knowledge about associations among sociological variables, we cannot with any confidence attribute substantive importance to associations of such magnitude" [78, p. 44]. At any point in this research that we use tests of significance, we do so not to measure sampling error but random processes.

2. The first condition makes a probability sample impractical if a number of variables or certain combinations of these variables are relatively rare in existing populations, because an extremely large sample is required to obtain a sufficient number of the infrequent types. If the necessary information were available—often it is not—stratification would permit selection of a sample of manageable size. One of the reasons why social scientists know considerably less about the behavior of upper-class persons than lower-class individuals is their reliance on probability sampling. We know, for example, very little about delinquent behavior among upper-class juveniles; the limited number of upper-class respondents included in most probability samples requires their grouping with middle-class subjects.

3. Because there is no way to determine this type of representativeness for any particular sample, Camilleri asserts: "We are obliged therefore to postulate a statistical relationship between the existing cases and the hypothetical pool. By virtue of this postulate a complete inspection of the existing cases would be interpreted as a probability sample of the hypothetical population. A probability sample of the existing cases would also be appropriate." [21, pp. 172-3]

4. The federal government requires that in funded research the rights of human subjects must be protected. At a minimum researchers must obtain the consent of parents prior to gathering data from students.

5. During the years the authors were in graduate school "the state of the art" was such that the importance of probability sampling was not questioned. It was, therefore, only after extensive discussion with our colleague, S. Frank Camilleri, that we selected a purposive sample.

6. The 7 junior high schools and 5 of the 6 senior high schools constituted 1 entire school district; consequently, a sizable proportion of the transfers in and out of these schools were in the study population.

7. School personnel gave invaluable help in the conduct of this research. To facilitate communication between the school's staff and the researchers, we attached a bright red one-inch square sticker to the file folder of each student who was part of the study cohort. As a result of the excellent cooperation of school personnel, it was possible for us to confine our examination of school records to the summer months, with the exception of the monthly checks of the school registers. This not only fit our academic schedule, but also minimized our intrusion into the normal operation of a school. It may be that the most important effect was not measurable. Students in the study population only saw us once a year when questionnaires were administered, and various negative definitions of the researchers—as agents of the school and so on—were avoided because our examination of school records was unobtrusive.

8. For example, one interviewer in the Phillipines traveled 250 miles by almost every means of transportation known to man only to find that the subject had recently returned to the mainland United States. This mechanism for follow-up of transfers and mobile dropouts proved to be costly but effective.

9. These questionnaires were administered late in the school year because initially we had planned to include schools operated by two districts in southern California. Difficulties in one district led us to change our plans with the eventual selection of the school in northern California [249].

10. In addition to the 5 student refusals, 41 respondents who completed the first annual questionnaire were excluded from the study population as a result of the parent interviews.

11. Before the interviewers entered the field their names were sent to local Chiefs of Police, the various Chambers of Commerce, the Better Business Bureau, the Federal Bureau of Investigation, and the principals and school administrators in the local area. This precaution was taken so that potential

respondents could readily determine, if they desired, whether the interviewer was associated with the project.

12. Good provides the following definitions of these terms. Exclusion is "(1) an order refusing a pupil the right to participate in the work of the school for a limited period of time; (2) an order granting a pupil permission to remain out of school for a limited period." Exemption refers to "those conditions under which youths are freed from the requirements of the state's compulsory school-attendance laws (equivalent schooling, physical inability, mental inability, lawful employment, etc. are examples of the more common exemptions; poverty and distance from school used to be generally accepted exemptions, but they are being rapidly dropped from the statutes)." Expulsion is "the act of forcing a pupil to withdraw from school; applies particularly to cases of extreme misbehavior or incorrigibility where the youth is ejected under pressure of school authority." Finally, suspension is "the temporary, forced withdrawal of a pupil from school, resorted to for various disciplinary and other reasons by school officials" [85].

13. The respondents were first contacted in the ninth grade, and previous addresses were not obtained. Consequently, it is possible that subjects who had not always lived in the study areas could have had police contacts elsewhere prior to the initiation of this study. Presumably there would be few cases of this type.

14. Hyman proposes an additional criterion, the identification of one or more intervening variables linking the independent and dependent variables. We agree with Hirschi and Selvin that this is desirable substantively and psychologically, but it is not essential.

15. In some instances questions were phrased in such a way that the beginning of the seventh grade serves as the initial point in this period.

16. Bereiter notes that when the first score is partialled out of the second score, the resulting residual gain score is not correlated with the *observed* initial score, but it is positively correlated with the *true* initial score [10].

17. If the correlation between prior delinquency and delinquency during the study were zero, the residual gain score would equal the raw frequency score for the study period. In this case, none of the later delinquency could be attributed to prior delinquency. The upper limit of the residual gain score is the raw frequency score for delinquency during the study. The two measures would also be equal if a subject's prior delinquency score was zero. Toward the other extreme, if the correlation were 1.0 (assuming equal variances) the residual gain score would equal the raw gain score. In practice, then, a residual gain score lies in the range between the raw gain score and the second raw frequency score. The constant in the regression equation was omitted in the derivation of these scores, because all comparisons were between subgroups of the population and would not be affected by the value of the constant. If comparisons between populations with different parameters were undertaken, these constants would have to be considered.

18. Those already out of school when a given predictor variable was measured were excluded from the relevant analyses because the temporal sequence for such subjects would be incorrect.

4 Measurement of Delinquency and Dropout

Having discussed conceptual difficulties in Chapter 2, we turn now to the problem of measurement, or the linkage of appropriate operational definitions with the usage of the concepts *delinquency* and *dropout* specified in our theory. Resolution of the problems of measurement is of crucial importance in studies such as this, which propose to test a theoretical scheme, because the value of the test is directly related to the adequacy of the measurements employed.

Delinquent Behavior

As conceptualized in this study, delinquency refers, first of all, to a class of behavior. Acceptance of a behavioral conception of delinquency requires consideration of the appropriate dimensions of behavior that should be reflected in the operational measures of delinquency. Scrutiny of our theory suggests that it is necessary to measure three dimensions. The fundamental dimension is the frequency of delinquent behavior. The basic measure of delinquency must provide an estimate of the number of delinquent acts committed by a respondent during particular time periods. Two additional facets must be considered—the relative seriousness of particular acts and the specific nature of each act. The need for such measures is indicated by Cohen: "On the basis of interviews, questionnaires and tests we must differentiate these samples into delinquents and nondelinquents of various degrees and kinds. In this manner alone can we achieve a valid conception of the distribution, by degree and kind, of delinquency within sectors and strata of the population" [34, pp. 170-1]. Researchers have traditionally been interested in the seriousness dimension because it reflects the degree or magnitude of delinquency [147; 206]. Measurement of this dimension necessitates consideration of the response to behavior, rather than intrinsic characteristics of delinquent acts. Cloward and Ohlin propose that the anticipated response to an act has important implications for a potential violator: "To the offender, the anticipated official response is a highly significant element of the total situation, one that gives different meanings as well as different risks to various delinquent acts" [33, p. 6]. A measure of seriousness should, therefore, reflect the likelihood that social control agents will respond officially—minor offenses are more likely to be ignored than serious violations.[1] The third behavioral dimension, involving the nature of delinquent offenses, is relevant for the postulated relationship between social contexts and particular patterns of delinquent behavior.

63

Self-Reported Delinquent Behavior

The official figures that purport to measure the volume of juvenile delinquency are challenging and complex. Although they may be appropriate in the investigation of the labeling process, the records of law enforcement agencies are of limited utility for an analysis of delinquent behavior. Official statistics provide only an imperfect index of the total volume of delinquency. It is obvious that not all delinquent acts are officially recorded, and the recorded acts are not a random sample of the acts which occur [82; 116; 155; 164; 183; 200; 205; 216; 247]. Further, empirical investigations demonstrate that there are variations in the exposure, detection, and apprehension of juveniles on the basis of their socio-economic status, ethnic background, demeanor, age, sex, and even physical size [153; 166; 210; 216; 232; 233].

The biases inherent in offical statistics led to the exploration of alternative ways to measure delinquent behavior [155; 161; 172; 200; 215; 254]. A number of measurement techniques have been developed, and prominent among these is the use of self reports as an alternative to analysis of official records.[2] The self-report technique involves a direct questioning of youth about their delinquent activities. This approach avoids the biases in official records produced by variations in the exposure, detection, and apprehension of juveniles by law enforcement agencies.

Although the self-report approach raises certain methodological issues, particularly in the areas of reliability and validity, it appears to be more appropriate for this research than exclusive reliance on official records or the use of other techniques, such as direct observation.[3] Consequently, a self-report instrument was developed to provide a direct measure of delinquent behavior. This instrument, a modification of the Nye-Short delinquency checklist, consists of 12 of Nye and Short's original 21 items [161]. Whereas the question about sexual behavior was eliminated at the request of representatives of the school district, other items were eliminated because they did not involve delinquent acts; that is, they were not defined as felonies or misdemeanors in the penal code. The general format of the questions was similar to that used by Nye and Short (see Appendix B). The items pertained to auto theft, petty theft (worth less than $2), thefts of medium value ($2 to $50), gang fights, grand theft (over $50), robbery, purchasing liquor, destroying property, truancy, and running away from home. Two additional items from the Nye-Short checklist—driving a car without a license and defying parental authority—were included in the questionnaire but were not included in the measure of self-reported delinquency (hereafter cited as SRD).

The SRD items were included in the questionnaires administered to the study population during the first and fourth data-collection waves. Like the question format, the instructions were similar to those provided by Nye and Short [161]. The instructions in the first wave indicated that the time period covered by the self-report questions included the 3 years of junior high school (grades 7 through 9), whereas the time period covered in the instructions in the fourth period included the 3 senior high school years (grades 10 through 12). With the exception of an additional item concerning drug use, the instrument used in the fourth period was identical to the one employed initially.

In retrospect, it is regrettable that self reports of delinquent activities were not obtained during the second and third data-collection periods. The decision not to use the SRD instrument annually was a practical one. Initiation of this study produced community pressure on the participating schools to avoid sensitive areas of inquiry [249]. The available data limit the analysis of self-reported delinquent behavior to two time periods, because changes in the independent variables observed in Periods II and III cannot be related directly to self-reported delinquency in those periods.

The essential dimensions of delinquent behavior are, however, measured by the SRD items. The basic analytic procedure involves calculation of the frequency of self-reported offenses by a serious and nonserious classification and by type of offense. To score the frequency of delinquent acts we transformed the response categories of the SRD items into frequencies, as follows: "No" or "None" equals 0; "Once or Twice" equals 1; "Several times" or "Three times" equals 3; and "Very often" equals 4. This scoring procedure provides a conservative estimate of the actual frequency of reported delinquent acts.

We explored various approaches to the classification of offenses with respect to seriousness and found that the different measures produced somewhat divergent orderings.[4] We resolved this problem by adopting and extrapolating the distinction between felonies and misdemeanors in the California Penal Code [19]. According to the circumstances, participation in a gang fight could lead to charges of assault or disorderly conduct, which are, respectively, a felony and a misdemeanor. Legally, medium theft and petty theft constitute misdemeanors, although the California Penal Code (§ 487) states that whenever the accumulation of thefts over any twelve-month period exceeds $50 (in some instances $200), the offense constitutes a felony. Thus, responses that indicate multiple offenses involving between $2 and $50 each could constitute a felony. This logic could be applied to thefts of less than $2, but the frequency required to accumulate a total value in excess of $50 renders this a less likely possibility. Both gang fight and medium theft were treated as felonies, because these offenses are likely to be viewed as serious by policemen and court officials and may constitute felonies. Similarly, drug use was defined as a felony. The distinction between serious and minor offenses in the law has a counterpart in the operation of social control agencies; a decision to file a petition with the juvenile court in response to a juvenile's behavior, rather than handling the case informally, reflects the definition of certain acts as serious infractions.[5] Those self-reported offenses that are felonies or under reasonable circumstances could be felonies—robbery, grand theft, auto theft, drug use, gang fights, and thefts of medium value—are categorized as serious offenses. Acts that constitute misdemeanors—petty theft, run away, vandalism, liquor law violations, and truancy —are categorized as nonserious or minor offenses.

For each of the 10 acts in the SRD measure, the frequency and the mean number of self-reported delinquent acts are presented in Table 4-1 according to grade level and sex. The scoring procedure employed to convert the responses on the SRD instrument into frequencies provides a conservative estimate of the subjects' involvement in delinquent behavior. It is also noteworthy that while only 10 acts are included in the SRD measure, a number of other acts would have met our definition of delinquent behavior. Nevertheless, the study population reported a considerable volume of delinquent behavior. For the 3 years of junior high school, the 2,617 subjects reported an estimated 10,073 delinquent acts, whereas their responses in senior high school reflect involvement in 13,141 offenses. Thus, over the six-year period the study population reported a total of 23,214 delinquent acts or an average of 9.63 infractions for each subject. Males reported an average of 4.81 delinquent acts in junior high and 7.43 infractions during their years in senior high school, or 12.24 offenses each for the six-year period. In comparison, female subjects reported an average of 6.90 infractions over the period of six years.

Although the differences in the frequency of delinquent acts are not as great as might be expected on the basis of official statistics in which the ratio of males to females is 4 or 5 to 1, comparison of the males and females reveals expected differences (Table 4-1). Females consistently report fewer offenses than males, and the differences are greatest for serious offenses. Among the females the frequencies are particularly low for gang fights, auto theft, and robbery; these offenses are usually committed by males.

Comparison of the frequencies reported in the junior and senior high school years shows the expected trend. The median age of the cohort is 13 in junior high school (eighth grade) and 16 in senior high school (eleventh grade); it is not surprising that the total volume of delinquent behavior increases substantially as the cohort moves from junior to senior high school. The volume of delinquency increases with the shift in school milieu, but the change is not uniform. Petty thefts and vandalism decrease, while liquor violations, truancy, gang fights, and auto thefts increase.

It is difficult to compare these estimates of the frequency of delinquent behavior with the findings of other investigators employing self reports because some form of scale analysis has usually been used to differentiate most and least delinquent categories; analysis of the frequency or seriousness of self-reported delinquency is relatively rare. The volume of delinquent behavior reported by the subjects appears to be reasonable in comparison with the findings of Porterfield [172], Erickson and Empey [67], and Kupfer [119]. Porterfield's

Table 4-1
Frequency of Specific Self-Reported Delinquent Acts, by Sex and Grade Level

| | A. Junior High School | | | | |
| | Males | | Females | | |
Nonserious Offenses	Frequency	Mean	Frequency	Mean	Total Mean
Petty Theft (< $2)	1478	1.110	921	0.724	0.921
Liquor	1340	1.004	1035	0.812	0.910
Vandalism	804	0.601	300	0.235	0.422
Truancy	634	0.474	426	0.334	0.406
Run Away	313	0.234	269	0.210	0.222
Serious Offenses					
Gang Fights	712	0.532	174	0.136	0.338
Medium Theft ($2 to $50)	489	0.366	241	0.189	0.279
Auto Theft	324	0.242	91	0.071	0.158
Grand Theft	217	0.162	145	0.113	0.138
Robbery	140	0.104	20	0.015	0.061
Total	6451	4.810	3622	2.840	3.850

| | B. Senior High School | | | | |
| | Males | | Females | | |
Nonserious Offenses	Frequency	Mean	Frequency	Mean	Total Mean
Petty Theft (< $2)	1170	0.983	569	0.514	0.757
Liquor	2447	2.059	1775	1.526	1.795
Vandalism	699	0.587	136	0.114	0.352
Truancy	1589	1.334	1202	1.019	1.117
Run Away	332	0.279	270	0.228	0.253
Serious Offenses					
Gang Fights	770	0.659	186	0.161	0.412
Medium Theft ($2 to $50)	474	0.398	164	0.138	0.268
Auto Theft	384	0.322	164	0.138	0.230
Grand Theft	206	0.176	109	0.094	0.135
Robbery	109	0.091	17	0.014	0.053
Drugs	262	0.221	107	0.090	0.156
Total	8442	7.430	4699	4.060	5.780

200 male subjects reported an average of 17.6 offenses for their precollege years on a 55-item checklist, whereas the 137 females admitted an average of 4.7 offenses prior to entering college. Comparison with the data reported by Erickson and Empey is also difficult because they examine four subsamples, including persistent offenders on probation and incarcerated offenders. Further, they do not specify the time period covered by their research. However, one of their subsamples, 50 randomly selected 15- to 17-year-old high school boys who had never been to court, is comparable to part of our study population; these subjects report—presumably for their lifetime—an average of 45.5 offenses for the 10 acts in our SRD measure. In response to the same set of 10 SRD items, Kupfer's subjects report an average of 4.41 offenses for a two-year period covering the ninth and tenth grades. In addition to such comparisons, the volume and distribution of offenses through time and the observed sex differences indicate that the SRD has face validity. Because it is such a critical issue in self-report studies, a direct assessment of the validity of the SRD is essential.

Validity. Critics question whether adolescents address themselves seriously to self-report inquiries and suggest that concealment or deliberate falsification may occur [79; 82; 92; 141]. Respondents may invent offenses, forget violations, confess accidental offenses, or report trivial acts as delinquent behavior. There are a number of ways in which the truthfulness of self reports might be investigated, but in this research attention centers on falsification by exaggeration and concealment. When adolescents respond to self-report items, to what extent do they exaggerate their involvement in delinquency and to what extent do they conceal their depredations? Fortunately, there is a growing body of research directed to these questions.

The most direct attempt to establish the validity of self reports involves comparison of responses to specific self-report items with an external criterion, such as official police or court records. Several investigators report high response validity on the basis of comparison of self reports of arrest or police contact with official police records [27; 67; 93; 174; 175; 247]. Comparing self reports with offenses known to the police, Voss indicates that 4 of 52 known offenders denied one act that appeared on their record, but 95 percent (79 of 83) of the recorded offenses were admitted [247]. Erickson and Empey state: "None of those who had been to court failed to say so in the interview, nor did anyone fail to describe the offense(s) for which he was charged" [67, p. 459]. Nevertheless, the question has been raised whether the validity of self reports can be established by reference to police or court records, as those who use self reports do so in an effort to avoid biases in the official records [141].

Hardt and Bodine note that invalid responses may also be detected through the inclusion of "lie" scales and social desirability scales in a questionnaire [92]. A related procedure involves inclusion of items that do not pertain specifically to delinquency, but involve negative self reports; for example, "I was questioned at the police station," "I was suspended from school," "How many days in this school year (since September) were you: late for school? absent from school?" Summarizing the use of these comparisons, Hardt and Bodine comment: "The technique has been employed in a number of recent studies, and is beginning to provide evidence of the relatively high validity of self-reports" [92, p. 19].

Another validation technique utilizes comparison of "known groups" or groups believed to differ with respect to delinquency involvement. Nye and Short conclude that their delinquency scale scores, based on self reports, discriminate between boys institutionalized as delinquents and high school boys with 86 percent accuracy [161]. Similar results are reported by Voss [247]. Using two measures, Reiss and Rhodes could differentiate moderately well between boys with and without court records [174]. Dentler and Monroe report a "known group" validation; boys assigned the roles of bully and fighter through sociometric choices had high scores on a Theft Scale [50].[6] Dentler and Monroe conclude: "The preliminary evidence supports the validity of a [self-report] Theft Scale. Following Guttman's distinction between internal and external validity, we have found that the scale predicts a series of outside variables and that these predictions are themselves coherent" [50, p. 741]. Measures of self-reported delinquency have been used successfully to differentiate groups assumed to differ with respect to involvement in delinquency; to this extent they appear to be valid.[7]

Reliability. Questions about the reliability of self-report measures have not received the attention devoted to validity. Clark and Tifft [31] report a type of self-report validation, which DeFleur [46] suggests is essentially an investigation of the reliability of self reports. While their techniques may have produced more valid responses, they clearly offer useful information about the reliability of self reports. Clark and Tifft compare a series of successive measures of the frequency of delinquent acts: (1) initial responses to self-report items on a questionnaire, (2) responses in a post-questionnaire interview in which subjects were asked to reconsider their initial questionnaire responses, and (3) responses made during a post-interview polygraph examination. Comparison of the initial and final responses reveals that 81.5 percent were identical, but underreporting was three times as common as overreporting. In the response category, "None," 92 percent of the original answers were unchanged. Shifts in responses were to a considerable extent in the admitted frequency of acts. However, analysis of the error rate indicates that questionnaire accuracy and extent of involvement in delinquent acts are not related. Clark and Tifft conclude:

The main finding of this study is that self-reporting of delinquency is rather accurate when a wide range of behaviors is considered simultaneously, but that there is differential validity on specific questionnaire items. . . . Self-report techniques are well suited for etiological research, and it is time for some causal propositions to be operationalized and tested using these techniques. [31, p. 523]

Readministration of self-report items has not been common, but researchers who have obtained test-retest data report adequate levels of reliability. According to Hardt and Bodine [92], Clark obtained test-retest coefficients of reliability of about .80. Dentler and Monroe state that after a two-week interval responses to a five-item Theft Scale were identical in at least 92 percent of the cases [50]. And only 2 percent of the respondents shifted more than one step within the set of multiple response categories. They assert: "The self-report responses were thus internally consistent and stable" [50, p. 735]. The available evidence concerning reliability and validity indicates that continued use of self reports to measure delinquent behavior is warranted.

Procedure. The attempts to validate SRD measures discussed to this point are important post facto evaluations. We made similar validity checks, but a discussion of the procedures used to obtain the data is in order because we deliberately attempted to maximize the truthfulness of responses. The causes of invalid responses, particularly underreporting, presumably involve such factors as the respondent's desire to protect himself from exposure and possible sanction or to meet the expectations of researchers. Consequently, a research situation as free as possible from personal threat was created. First, confidentiality of responses was guaranteed. No respondent's name ever appeared on a questionnaire, and no school personnel were present during the administration of the questionnaires. The longitudinal nature of the research precluded complete anonymity; however, it was explained to the respondents that names would be retained only until all the data were collected and that the lists associating identification numbers and names would be destroyed at that time. Thereafter, responses would be anonymous.[8] Not only was this procedure described fully to each group of respondents, but related questions were also answered in detail. Second, the degree of threat posed by the items was minimized by providing instructions and response categories implying that some, but not all, would have engaged in particular forms of behavior. Several inquiries pertaining to nondelinquent behavior, for example, defying parental authority, were purposely included, and we expected high frequencies of positive response to these items. Finally, the SRD measure was embedded in a long questionnaire; the primary focus of the research concerned educational and occupational career opportunities and aspirations. In our opinion, the general orientation of the questionnaire was not threatening, and good rapport was established with the students; the low refusal rate and the limited number of incomplete questionnaires provide indirect evidence that this was the case. It may be noted that one of the advantages of a longitudinal study is that subjects who are initially hesitant to provide honest responses may freely do so in subsequent contacts because they know parents, school personnel, and law enforcement officials were not informed of their previous responses.

Another potential source of error in self-report data is an unintended distortion in recall; that is, the respondent attempts to be honest, but simply cannot recall accurately the information requested. Response error in retrospective questions is affected by the ambiguity or remoteness of the time period specified in the questions, the type of information solicited, and the respondent's current attitudes and situation [107]. With respect to the items concerning delinquent behavior, respondents may wish to forget their experiences. If this is the case, then the length of time intervening between the event and an investigator's inquiry is of considerable importance. To minimize such problems, the time periods involved in the self reports were specified as 3 years, a relatively short time. Another advantage is that the ages covered by the 2 three-year reporting periods are 11 to 17; the self reports are therefore comparable with official juvenile records because the latter rarely include youth below 10 or over 18 years of age.[9]

To reduce the possibility of response set, the ordering of responses to the SRD items was occasionally reversed. This accomplishes two ends. First, it demands greater attention on the part of the respondents to each item, which hopefully increases the validity of the responses. Second, it provides a basis for identification of uncooperative or unreliable respondents who consistently check the first or last response category. On this basis, the information provided by 3 (0.1 percent) students in Period I and 45 (1.7 percent) respondents in Period II to IV was considered unreliable. These subjects were excluded from further analyses involving reported delinquent behavior.

Validity Checks of Self-Reported Delinquency

One type of validity check used in this study involves comparison of self-report data with police and court records, whereas another utilizes internal comparisons by grade level, sex, social class, and ethnicity, as well as teachers' nominations of "potential" delinquents. A search of official records, including a Central Index maintained by each of the 2 county probation departments, local city police files, and the records of county sheriffs, was conducted at the beginning and end of the study to determine which subjects had police contacts or juvenile court records. Mail contact with local officials produced comparable information for 92 percent of the mobile respondents who moved from the areas in which the study was conducted.

Recorded and Reported Offenses. As the SRD measure is restricted in scope, comparison of official records with self reports is limited to the acts included in the SRD measure. The percentages of respondents for whom an official record of a delinquent act (similar to one of the acts in the SRD) was located, but who failed to report that type of delinquent act are shown in Table 4-2.

Offense-specific comparisons of self-report and official data have rarely been

Table 4-2

Subjects Known to the Police for Specific Delinquent Acts Who Fail to Report Those Offenses (Percentages)

Offense[a]	Junior High School (Period I)		Senior High School (Period II to IV)	
	N	Percentage Not Reporting	N	Percentage Not Reporting
Robbery	1	100	0	0
Grand Theft[b]	3	67	14	43
Auto Theft	11	18	35	26
Drugs			8	25
Petty Theft[b]	113	16	141	16
Liquor	1	0	75	4
Run Away	40	20	83	16
Vandalism	75	32	31	39
Truancy	7	14	19	11
Total	251	22	406	17

[a]Multiple types of offenses by a given subject are taken into account, but multiple offenses of a given type for a single subject are not. A subject having one or more police contacts for a specific type of offense who reported *any* frequency was considered to have reported accurately for that type of offense.

[b]A report of medium theft met the reporting requirement for an official record of grand theft. Those known to police for petty thefts who reported any *more serious* levels of theft were also considered to be accurate in their reports.

presented. They are difficult comparisons to make, because the offense recorded in police records may not coincide with the respondent's report for reasons that have nothing to do with the actual behavior involved. The respondent's report may be accurate, but may not coincide with the official records. This could occur when the respondent reports a theft involving more than $50 in value, but is charged with petty theft. In another instance, the subject may report a robbery, but the official charge is grand theft. The lack of correspondence between offenses listed in official records and subjects' reports of their behavior requires little documentation, but it poses a serious problem for investigators who wish to compare self reports with official records.[10] To offset this, a report of a theft is considered to be accurate if the respondent indicated a level of theft equal to or greater than that for which he was charged. However, this represents only a partial solution, and similar standards cannot readily be developed for the other types of behavior covered in the SRD measure.

The overall level of error in Table 4-2 is not great—22 percent for Period I and 17 percent for Period II to IV. However, the error level for the serious offenses is quite high. Clearly, the serious offenses are more frequently underreported than are the minor violations. These results are remarkably similar to the findings of

Clark and Tifft [31] and Gold [80] who reported error levels of 15 and 17 percent, respectively. However, the offense-specific accuracy levels differ in one important respect from those reported by Clark and Tifft. They observe the greatest error in the admission of nonserious offenses, while we find the greatest error in the reporting of serious offenses. Clark and Tifft specifically note that in view of their procedures the low frequencies of admitted serious offenses may have produced a spurious relationship between accuracy and seriousness. The argument that underreporting is due to a perceived threat, whether of sanctions or the presentation of a socially undesirable image, would lead one to expect a positive relationship between underreporting and seriousness.

There is considerable consistency in the level of error in the 2 administrations of the SRD instrument, even though in many instances different subjects reported inaccurately.[11] The slightly lower rates of error for the senior high school years (Period II to IV) may be the result of better rapport with the subjects after repeated contacts with them. It is also possible that as junior high school students the subjects were not as aware of fine legal distinctions.

In general, the offense-specific comparison of self-reported delinquency with official records suggests that the SRD measure is valid. Although it must be recognized that variation in error level among specific offenses is considerable, and substantial error in serious offenses is evident, the offense-specific comparison constitutes a rather rigorous validity check. Perhaps it is too rigorous—to some extent the errors uncovered are a consequence of the vagaries that affect the recording of delinquent acts.

A less rigorous check can be made by examining the percentage of subjects who fail to report any delinquent act of the same or greater degree of seriousness than their officially recorded offense(s), as shown in Table 4-3. Again, the analysis is limited to SRD offenses. A considerably higher level of accuracy is reflected in this analysis; for the 2 periods combined, the error rate is 5 percent.

Table 4-3
Subjects with Police Contact Who Fail to Report Any Delinquent Acts of the Same Degree of Seriousness, By Time Period

	Period I		Period II to IV	
Police Contacts	N^a	Percentage Not Reporting	N^a	Percentage Not Reporting
Nonserious	202	6	285	2
Serious	15	20	52	19
Total	217	7	337	4

aJuveniles who admitted both levels (serious and nonserious) of delinquent behavior are included in both categories; hence, the total in Period I does not reflect 217 separate persons nor does the total in Period II to IV refer to 337 different subjects. The smaller N in this table, in comparison with Table 4-2, is a result of collapsing categories.

Voss reports a 5 percent error in a comparable analysis [247]. The trends in Table 4-3 are similar to those noted in Table 4-2. There is a higher level of accuracy with respect to nonserious offenses, and accuracy is slightly higher in Period II to IV. Nearly all of the persons with police contacts admit one or more offenses of the same level of seriousness.

An implicit assumption in the foregoing analyses is that juveniles apprehended by the police for delinquent acts did in fact commit those acts (see note 24). No legal determination of fact has been made in these cases, and some of the observed errors may be due to unreliability in the official data. If this is the case, then adjudication would provide a more reliable indicator of delinquent behavior than police .contacts, because the court presumably makes some determination that the alleged offender committed the delinquent act. In simple terms, court data are less comprehensive but contain fewer errors.

A comparison of the official charges filed against juveniles adjudicated during Period I, the junior high school years, and their self-reported behavior late in the ninth grade reveals that 95 percent (52 of 55) of the adjudicated delinquents reported an act of the same or greater seriousness than the offense listed in the official complaint. Of the remaining 3, one had a serious charge but reported only minor offenses, while the other 2 reported no delinquent acts at all. A similar analysis of those adjudicated during Period II to IV indicates that the accuracy of their self reports is 100 percent.

These comparisons provide some information pertinent to the problem of underreporting, but they do not allow a precise estimate of the magnitude of concealment, nor are they relevant to the problem of overreporting. Although there is some question about the accuracy of reporting serious offenses, these comparisons do not suggest that extensive concealment occurs on SRD measures. We conclude that responses to the SRD are valid indicators of the nature and extent of involvement in delinquent activities.

Internal Comparisons. The average number of serious and nonserious offenses reported in junior and senior high school by sex, social class, ethnicity, and teachers' nominations is presented in Table 4-4.[12] Inclusion of the distinction between junior and senior high school approximates a comparison of different age levels; reports covering the 3 years of junior high school (Period I) are contrasted with those for the 3 years of senior high school (Period II to IV). At the midpoints of these grade levels, the eighth and eleventh grades, the modal ages of the cohort are 13 and 16 years, respectively. Examination of Table 4-4 reveals an increase in the frequency of serious and nonserious offenses for the ethnic and class groupings as the population moves from junior to senior high school. A similar pattern is observed for four of the five categories of teachers' nominations; the one exception is the group nominated as most likely to "get into trouble with the law." The latter subjects report more delinquent offenses during junior high school than in senior high school. Although age is measured in terms of grade level, the general trend is consistent with the relationship between age and officially recorded delinquent acts that has been known for some time.

Sex. The offense-specific means of males and females are shown in Table 4-1. The data in Table 4-4 are presented according to the distinction between serious and nonserious offenses, but the same general conclusions hold about the involvement of males and females in delinquency. All of the differences by level of seriousness and time period or grade level are statistically significant and substantial. The sex difference with respect to the mean number of serious offenses is particularly great. In both periods, females report approximately one-third as many serious offenses as males. The data reflect the sex differential observed in official statistics, but the 3 to 1 ratio of males to females is considerably lower than the sex ratio of 5 or 6 to 1 typically reported on the basis of official records. If the self reports are accurate, these data suggest a substantial sex bias in the detection of juvenile offenders.

Ethnicity. A comparison of the means for Anglos, Mexicans, Negroes, and Orientals generally fails to yield significant differences, although some substantial differences appear in the serious category in each time period. The Anglo-Mexican difference in Period I is significant at the .01 level; however, no other paired comparisons produce significant *t* values. Further, the one significant difference disappears in Period II to IV. In fact, the mean for Anglos is slightly higher than the mean for Mexicans. Comparison of the 2 time periods reveals a stable rate of serious offenses among Mexicans and Orientals, whereas Anglos and those classified as "Other" show substantial increases. With time, there is a moderate increase among Negroes in the occurrence of serious offenses. Apparently Mexican and Negro youth commit serious delinquent acts at an earlier age than Anglos, but with the exception of the Orientals there is little support for the notion that there are ethnic differences in the rate of delinquent behavior. Examination of self-reported and official data gathered in Hawaii supports the idea that Oriental youth have low rates of delinquency [247]. In this investigation, Oriental subjects consistently report fewer delinquent acts than other respondents. Although official delinquency statistics indicate that there are ethnic differentials, we fail to find such differences with the SRD measure. This implies either distortion in our delinquency measure or an ethnic bias in official data or both. However, our findings are generally consistent with other studies.[13]

Social Class. Hollingshead's Two-Factor Index, based on the occupational level and educational attainment of the principal wage earner in the respondent's home, serves as the measure of class in this investigation [156, pp. 24-6].[14] With one important exception, no statistically significant differences are found in either time period. The single exception is the average number of serious

Table 4-4
Mean Number of Serious and Nonserious Self-Reported Offenses, by Grade Level, Sex, Ethnicity, Social Class, and Teachers' Nominations

Period	Self-Reported Behavior	Sex			Ethnicity[a]					
		Male	Female	t Value	A	M	N	Or	Other	F Ratio
I[b]	Nonserious (Ns)	3.41	2.31	9.35**	2.88	3.01	2.70	2.57	2.67	.56(NS)
	Serious (S)	1.41	.53	10.50**	.91	1.23	1.21	1.08	.93	2.26(NS)
	Total (T)	4.81	2.84	11.03**	3.78	4.25	3.91	3.64	3.60	.82(NS)
II to IV[c]	Nonserious (Ns)	5.25	3.33	14.11**	4.53	4.32	4.04	3.85	4.38	1.20(NS)
	Serious (S)	1.85	.64	12.94**	1.33	1.29	1.49	1.05	1.77	.74(NS)
	Total (T)	7.10	3.97	15.70**	5.86	5.61	5.52	4.90	6.15	.67(NS)
N		1338	1279		1943	360	193	61	60	

$p > .05$ = Not Significant (NS)

*$p < .05$

**$p < .01$

[a]A = Anglo; M = Mexican-American; N = Negro; Or = Oriental.

[b]Period I (S)   A:M $p < .05$
               All others NS

[c]Periods II to IV All NS

Period	Self-Reported Behavior	Social Class						Teachers' Nominations					
		1	2	3	4	5	F	1	2	3	4	5	F
I	Nonserious (Ns)	2.83	2.79	2.76	2.88	3.07	.85(NS)	8.64	5.97	4.58	3.11	1.83	123.41**
	Serious (S)	.52	.86	.84	1.03	1.19	2.78*	6.23	3.69	2.01	.98	.38	117.31**
	Total (T)	3.34	3.65	3.59	3.91	4.26	1.76(NS)	14.86	9.57	6.59	4.09	2.21	155.08**
II to IV	Nonserious (Ns)	4.00	4.53	4.43	4.51	4.32	.44(NS)	7.45	8.10	6.22	4.80	3.20	76.45**
	Serious (S)	1.05	1.36	1.30	1.36	1.39	.27(NS)	4.05	3.85	2.15	1.34	.82	43.41**
	Total (T)	5.05	5.89	5.73	5.87	5.71	.35(NS)	11.50	11.96	8.37	6.14	4.10	81.89**
N		58	220	768	1082	489		22	68	355	591	1206	

t values:

I
Ns   All NS
S   1 vs. 3, 4, 5 p < .01
     3 vs. 5 p < .01
     All others NS
T   3 vs. 5 p < .05; All others NS
II to IV
Ns   All NS
S   All NS
T   All NS

t values:

I
Ns   All Sig. p < .05
S   All Sig. p < .01 except 1 vs. 2 p < .05
T   All Sig. p < .01 except 1 vs. 2 p < .05
II to IV
Ns   All Sig. p < .05 except 1 vs. 2, 3-NS
S   All Sig. p < .01 except 2 vs. 3 p < .05
     1 vs. 2-NS
T   All Sig. p < .01 except 1 vs. 2-NS
     1 vs. 3-NS

offenses in Period I. These means are substantially different; the means for Classes 4 and 5, the two lowest categories, are twice as large as the mean for Class 1, the highest level. Further, comparisons of categories reveal significant differences between Class 1 and Classes 3, 4, and 5, as well as between Classes 3 and 5.

In Period I the means are rather consistently ordered from low to high as one moves down the class scale. Although most of the differences in means in Period I are not statistically significant, the rank ordering of the means for nonserious, serious, and total offenses produces a trend similar to the one observed in official records. The self reports obtained in Period I offer partial support for Gold's argument that lower-class youth commit more delinquent acts as well as more serious violations [80]. However, the data collected in Period II to IV do not reveal the same trend. None of the F values approach statistical significance, and none of the comparisons of adjacent categories produce significant values. Neither does a rank ordering of the means show a trend similar to the one observed in Period I. Consequently, there is no support for the presumption of a class differential in delinquency in the self reports of delinquent behavior during senior high school.

Before we examine the implications of our findings, a review of the self-report studies on the class distribution of delinquency is essential. One of the most controversial findings in the study of delinquency was reported by Nye, Short, and Olson: "There is no significant difference in delinquent behavior of boys and girls in different socio-economic strata" [162, p. 388]. The work of Nye and Short was extensively replicated with contradictory results. Some of these studies challenge the presumed inverse relation between social class and delinquency [1; 30; 50; 103]. However, class differences are reported by a number of investigators [68; 80; 175; 222; 250].

There are a number of points relevant to these contradictory results. Short and Nye conducted their research in high schools in rural areas and small towns; their subjects were not drawn from metropolitan areas nor were non-Caucasians included. Akers retested the null hypothesis of the Nye-Short investigation in a large northeastern Ohio community, but his subjects were junior high school students. Similarly, Dentler and Monroe studied seventh and eighth grade students in 3 small Kansas communities. Part of the explanation of the negative findings lies in the use of delinquency scales to differentiate most and least delinquent groups, because those respondents who admit some delinquent acts are contrasted with those who admit little (usually one or two positive responses) or no involvement in delinquency. Rejecting use of omnibus scales, Dentler and Monroe nevertheless employed a delinquency scale based on theft items. Slocum and Stone used a five-item scale; those who admit no delinquent acts other than drinking alcoholic beverages are defined as conformists, while those who admit the 5 acts comprise their "delinquent-type" respondents. For subjects similar to those of Nye and Short, they found that the children of white-collar workers are more likely to be conformists than are the children of blue-collar workers, but essentially Slocum and Stone's results are similar to the findings of Nye and Short. In contrast, Gold constructs two delinquency indices in which the frequency and seriousness of delinquent acts are considered. For white males from a metropolitan area, he finds a weak inverse relation between class, as measured by paternal occupation, and delinquent behavior. Clark and Wenninger report differences among status areas, but they do not find significant differences in self-reported delinquency by social class. Their findings suggest that differences between small towns and metropolitan areas partially explain why some researchers do not find differences in delinquent behavior by class. Hirschi concludes that there is "no important relation between social class as traditionally measured and delinquency" [103, p. 75]. Unfortunately, in his analysis approximately three-fourths of the respondents, including all Negro students, are eliminated. It should be noted that Reiss and Rhodes use a composite measure of official and self-reported delinquency; their results are not strictly comparable with the findings of other analyses of self-reported delinquency. Voss found more self-reported delinquency in the middle class, but this may be explicable in terms of the unique ethnic composition of his sample—specifically, the concentration of Japanese respondents in the lower class. Erickson and Empey report a significant correlation between low class position and involvement in delinquency as measured by 3 scales. Their subjects are white males between 15 and 17 years of age, but their sample consists of 4 randomly selected subsamples, including 50 high school boys, 30 boys who had been to court once, 80 probationers, and 40 incarcerated offenders. In contrast with other researchers, they did not analyze a random sample from the general population; rather, their sample reflects different stages with respect to the judicial process.

Using self reports we find a relationship between class and delinquency while the respondents are in junior high school, but not during senior high school. This difference may partially explain the contradictory findings produced by cross-sectional analyses of self-reported delinquency. Our results suggest that the age composition of the population studied is of crucial importance. The difference between the two periods is not attributable to a loss of dropouts; in this study dropouts also completed the SRD items for Period II to IV. It would appear, therefore, that age is an important variable specifying the relationship between class and delinquent behavior. Further, the findings suggest that lower-class youth become involved in delinquency at an earlier age than middle-class adolescents. This apparently is also the case for minority-group youth, and their concentration in the lower class lends credence to this interpretation.

Teachers' Nominations. The final comparison in Table 4-4 involves teachers' nominations or their evaluation of the probability that a subject would come to the attention of law enforcement agents.[15] The 5 categories shown in Table 4-4 reflect teachers' consensus. The students in category 1 are the ones the teachers believe are most likely to come to the attention of law enforcement agencies. Interestingly, they have the highest mean number of ratings; they apparently are the most widely known youth in school.[16]

The differences among the 5 categories of teachers' nominations in the mean frequency of delinquent behavior are tremendous. Not only do the means of the several categories differ significantly (F Ratio), but with one exception the mean of each category is significantly different from the mean of every other category (t test). Only the comparison between levels 1 ("very sure") and 2 ("fairly sure") in Period II to IV failed to show a significant difference. There is a high degree of association between teachers' evaluations of a subject's probability of police contact and the student's involvement in delinquent behavior, as measured by the SRD.[17] The teachers' nominations of "potential" delinquents and nondelinquents provide impressive internal evidence for the validity of the SRD.

Official Delinquent Behavior

The second type of measure of delinquent behavior employed in this study is based on official police contact reports. To estimate rates of delinquent behavior, it is desirable to have both self-reported and official data because these sources are complementary. Together they provide a more complete picture of the frequency and nature of delinquent behavior. In addition, the availability of both types of data permits exploration of the relationship between these divergent sources.

Few would argue that any type of official records of delinquent acts constitutes a representative sample of such behavior in the juvenile population. Recognition of processing biases has led some sociologists to adopt an egalitarian position; that is, *all* differences in official records merely reflect bias and hence may be "explained away" by invoking the concept of bias. A more moderate position is adopted by others who suggest that *some*—presumably not all—differences may be attributed to processing bias. It is evident that the records of the police and courts comprise an incomplete coverage of their respective universes. The fact that institutional records cover their universe more accurately than the others might lead one to conclude that institutional statistics offer the best index of the incidence of delinquency. Germane is a simple point: the use of any index is based on the assumption that there is a consistent relation with time between the total incidence of delinquency and the recorded volume [8]. Perlman believes that such an assumption is permissible with respect to annual comparisons in national data, but not for local data or for inter-areal comparisons [164]. Sellin indicates the relative merit of the various types of official statistics: "The value of a crime rate for index purposes decreases as the distance from the crime itself in terms of procedure increases" [205, p. 346; see 116]. As indicators of delinquency rates, police investigation reports are more trustworthy than statistics on arrests, judicial records, or institutional figures. Case attrition in the judicial process is extensive; many offenses known to the police are handled informally and do not result in court appearance [165].

Whatever biases are operative in the processing of offenders vary in effect at different stages from informal or formal handling by the police to court appearance to adjudication to institutionalization [232; 233]. We have defined delinquency in behavioral terms, but the official records reflect the influence of what are, insofar as delinquency is concerned, nonbehavioral factors such as age, sex, ethnicity, and social class. Consequently, the major limitation of official records as a measure of the extent of delinquent behavior is the confounding of delinquent behavior with such nonbehavioral characteristics of juveniles. Of the various official statistics available, offenses known to the police furnish the most comprehensive and hence the least biased official record of delinquent acts [116]. These reports constitute the record of the initial contact between suspected offenders and law enforcement agents. Although these data reflect differential police activity, they do not show subsequent decisions regarding arrest, the filing of petitions, or court action. The latter information is, however, available in probation department records (see Chapter 3).

The official measure incorporates the same dimensions of behavior reflected in the SRD measure—the frequency and seriousness of delinquent acts and the type of offense. Not all police contacts involve delinquent acts, as defined in this research, and only offenses involving a violation of the California Penal Code are included in the official measure of delinquent behavior. In addition, all traffic violations are excluded. The criterion of seriousness is again the distinction between felonies and misdemeanors.

The frequency and percentage of specific types of offenses are presented in Table 4-5, and the mean number of serious and nonserious offenses are shown in Table 4-6. Through May 1, 1967, the termination date for Period IV, the 2,617 subjects had 1,486 contacts with the police.[18] Of this number, 523 offenses were recorded prior to our first contact with the respondents or in Period I. The number of offenses recorded during the subsequent study periods were: Period II, 415; Period III, 305; and Period IV, 243.[19] Suprisingly, approximately one-third of the police contacts for delinquent behavior occurred prior to the initiation of this study. This is noteworthy because the modal age at the time the first questionnaires were administered was 14 years. Clearly, the subjects were involved in a substantial amount of delinquent activity at relatively early ages, and many of them were known to the police.

Sex. The data in Tables 4-5 and 4-6 indicate that there are sizable sex differentials in the frequency of contact with the police and in the specific offenses recorded. Serious offenses apparently are concentrated among the

Table 4-5
Frequency and Percentage of Officially Recorded Offenses, by Sex

Offense	Males		Females		Totals	
	N	Percentage	N	Percentage	N	Percentage
Robbery	3	0.26	1	0.30	4	0.26
Burglary	147	12.63	8	2.47	155	10.45
Theft	260	22.35	78	24.14	338	22.80
Auto Theft	50	4.29	2	0.61	52	3.50
Disorderly Conduct	81	6.96	9	2.78	90	6.07
Vagrancy	149	12.81	28	8.66	177	11.94
Liquor	70	6.01	16	4.95	86	5.80
Incorrigible	251	21.58	140	43.34	391	26.38
Truancy	18	1.54	16	4.95	34	2.29
Assault	48	4.12	6	1.85	54	3.64
Sex	32	2.75	12	3.71	44	2.96
Drugs	7	0.60	1	0.30	8	0.53
Forgery	3	0.26	2	0.61	5	0.33
Weapons	29	2.49	0	—	29	1.95
Gambling	1	0.08	0	—	1	0.06
Escapee	1	0.08	1	0.30	2	0.13
Violent Property Destruction	3	0.26	0	—	3	0.20
Fraud	3	0.26	0	—	3	0.20
Obscene Literature	1	0.08	0	—	1	0.06
Other	6	0.51	3	0.92	9	0.60
Total	1163		323		1486	

males; burglary, auto theft, and assault constitute a larger percentage of the offenses for males than females. There is one exception—sex offenses; these account for a slightly larger percentage of the girls' offenses than of the boys. In this population a charge of robbery is relatively rare. Although the number of males and females apprehended for truancy are similar, "skipping school" constitutes a greater percentage of the offenses recorded against females. Two-thirds of the females' offenses are recorded as incorrigibility or theft, whereas these offenses include only 44 percent of the charges against males. The males' offense pattern indicates substantial involvement in a variety of offenses.

On the basis of frequency of police contact, the sex ratio is approximately 4 to 1, but for serious offenses the sex ratio is much greater—8 to 1. The apprehension rate for females is relatively low, particularly for serious offenses. Previous research on the basis of official data revealed similar offense patterns and sex ratios.

Table 4-6
Mean Number of Nonserious and Serious Police Contacts, by Sex, Ethnicity, and Social Class

	Sex			Ethnicity						Class					
	Male	Female	t test	Total	Anglo	Mexican	Negro	Oriental	F-ratio	1	2	3	4	5	F-ratio
N	1338	1279		2617	1943	360	193	61		58	220	768	1082	489	
Nonserious	.651	.228	**	.440	.435	.553	.477	.409	NS	.171	.341	.366	.499	.589	**
Serious	.218	.025	**	.120	.106	.168	.368	.049	**	.021	.100	.084	.122	.255	**
Total	.869	.253	**	.560	.541	.721	.845	.458	*	.192	.441	.450	.621	.844	**

$* = p < .05$
$** = p < .01$
NS = Not Significant

Ethnicity and Social Class. The average number of police contacts for the various ethnic and class categories are also similar to those previously reported in official statistics. The highest rate of police contact is found in the lower class and among Negroes and Mexican-Americans, whereas Orientals have low rates of police contact and Anglos are intermediate. The class and ethnic differentials are particularly great for serious offenses. The mean number of police contacts for serious offenses among Negroes is more than three times as great as the mean for Anglos; similarly, the average number of police contacts for serious offenses of those in the lowest social class (Class 5) is twelve times as great as the mean of respondents in Class 1. With one exception, the rank order of the classes by serious, nonserious, and total offense means is consistent. Exceptional is the average number of serious offenses in Classes 2 and 3; otherwise, there is a perfect inverse relation between social class and police contact rates. With the exception of the average number of police contacts for misdemeanors among Mexicans, the ethnic categories are ordered as follows: Negro, Mexican, Anglo, and Oriental.

Comparison of Measures of
Delinquent Behavior

Most studies employing a self-reported measure of delinquent behavior have guaranteed anonymity to subjects. Unless some procedure is devised to link questionnaires with respondents, this approach precludes a direct comparison of self-report with official measures of delinquent behavior. (For an example of unobtusive linkage see Voss [247].) The procedures used in this research--the questionnaires were coded by identification numbers—permit this kind of comparison. It is possible to estimate the (1) amount of "hidden" delinquency in the population, (2) probability of police contact on the basis of the frequency of delinquent behavior reported, and (3) conditional probabilities of police contact in terms of the sex, ethnic ancestry, and social class of the offender, as well as the seriousness of the delinquent act involved.

The accuracy of these estimates is dependent upon the precision of the official and self-report measures. Bias in the official records and recording errors on the part of law enforcement agents are beyond our control. The official records were searched carefully, and our data accurately reflect police contacts, although any biases or errors in these records are not eliminated. On the basis of our scoring procedure and validity checks, as well as Clark and Tifft's study [31], we believe that inaccuracies in the self-report measure likely to influence these estimates are in the direction of underreporting of delinquent behavior on the SRD instrument. The amount of such error is assumed to be small, but its effect is to make our estimate of the amount of hidden delinquency a conservative one and our estimate of the probability of police contact somewhat high. Further, our comparisons are necessarily restricted to those specific offenses—10 in all—included in the SRD measure.[20] The ratio of police contacts to self-reported behavior varies considerably by type of offense, and these estimates cannot be construed as general estimates for the total range of possible offense categories.

The number of police contacts per 100 self-reported offenses by the sex, ethnic ancestry, and class of the offender, and the seriousness of the offense is presented in Table 4-7. The overall police contact rate is 4.816; in other words, there are approximately 5 police contacts for each 100 self-reported offenses. In similar analyses Erickson and Empey reported 10 police contacts per 100 self-reported offenses [67], while Gold reported 3 per 100 [80; 82]. Police contact occurs for only a small proportion of the delinquent acts admitted by the study population. Of the self-reported offenses, 95 percent are not recorded—they remain hidden from the scrutiny of law enforcement agents. Comparing the serious and nonserious offenses, we find a higher contact rate for nonserious offenses, which is contrary to the common assumption that the more serious offenses are more likely to result in official action. This may be due either to the greater effort serious offenders make to avoid detection or to errors in measurement, such as systematic underreporting of minor violations in comparison to serious acts. Although we failed to find this type of systematic error (in fact we found the opposite to be true), this remains a plausible explanation because our validity checks did not permit a precise estimate of the amount of underreporting.[21] It is also reasonable to assume that the accuracy of recall is related to the seriousness of the act. If this is the case, then nonserious offenses are more readily forgotten. These possibilities force us to view this particular finding with caution, although we question the tenability of the assumption that serious offenses more frequently result in police contact.

The volume of delinquent behavior uncovered by the official and self-reported measures varies greatly, but the rates of delinquency through time, as reflected by these measures, are reasonably consistent. Thirty-eight percent of the police contacts for SRD offenses and 43 percent of the self-reported offenses occurred prior to the initial questionnaire administration in the ninth grade. This suggests that the rates of delinquency and police contact increase, but not dramatically, from the junior to the senior high school years. Also, these data imply that there is a fairly consistent relation between the incidence of delinquency and the recorded volume.

There is a substantial sex differential in the police contact rates, particularly for serious offenses where the males' contact rate is four times as great as the females' rate. Police contact reports include only 1 percent of the serious offenses admitted by females. This is not simply a reflection of differential involvement in delinquency on the part of males and females; rather, the official records are biased in favor of girls. Comparison of the sex ratios derived from self-report and official data for auto theft offers a specific example. The

Table 4-7

Number of Serious and Nonserious Police Contacts per 100 Self-Reported Offenses, by Sex, Ethnicity, and Social Class

Police Contacts[a]	Total Population	Sex		Ethnicity				Class				
		Males	Females	Anglo	Mexican	Negro	Oriental	1	2	3	4	5
Nonserious	4.948	5.841	3.502	4.750	6.057	6.142	5.106	1.771	3.784	4.269	5.493	6.576
Serious	4.398	5.486	1.166	3.705	6.071	12.851	2.300	1.337	3.468	3.084	4.142	8.953
Total	4.816	5.751	3.101	4.512	6.060	8.069	4.789	1.692	3.710	4.120	5.337	7.382

[a]Limited to SRD offenses. (For all police contacts see Table 4-5.)

male-female ratio according to the SRD is slightly more than 2 to 1, but the same ratio for police contacts is 26 to 1. Although females perceive themselves as partners in the theft of automobiles, apparently police officers apprehend only their male companions. For the full range of delinquent acts handled by the police, it might be argued that differences in sex ratios are due to the relatively greater involvement of females in offenses that have a low probability of detection, such as sex offenses [170]. However, in this analysis, sex offenses are excluded because this offense category was not included in the SRD measure.[22] Consequently, this explanation is of dubious merit for the specific offenses we compared. Females either grossly overreport offenses, particularly serious ones on the SRD, or there is a serious sex bias in official police contact reports. The latter alternative is more likely.

Anglos have the lowest overall police contact rate, followed by Orientals, Mexicans, and Negroes. The rate for Negroes is almost twice that of Anglos. Negroes have 8 police contacts for every 100 self-reported offenses, whereas Anglos have fewer than 5. Ethnic and racial differences are particularly great in the serious offenses, and these essentially account for the overall differences among ethnic categories. For serious offenses the police contact rate for Negroes is three times higher than the rate for Anglos, twice as great as that for Mexicans and five times greater than the rate for Orientals. The risk of formal police contact for a serious offense varies considerably according to a juvenile's ethnic ancestry. Among Negroes, the police contact rate for serious offenses is significantly higher than it is for nonserious offenses. This suggests, but does not demonstrate, that officers ignore many petty offenses on the part of Negro adolescents.

The risk of police contact also appears to be related to the social class of the offender. With one exception, there is a consistently higher police contact rate as one moves from Class 1 (high) to Class 5 (low). The risk of a police contact in Class 5 is more than four times higher than in Class 1. As was the case with both sex and race, the class differences are accentuated in the category of serious offenses—the risk of police contact for those in Class 5 is six times higher than for juveniles in Class 1. The respondents in Class 5 provide the second exception to the generalization that police contact rates are higher for nonserious than serious offenses. Both Negroes and respondents in Class 5 have higher police contact rates for serious than nonserious offenses, and these relationships are independent of one another; that is, the relationship between class and police contact rates and the higher rates for serious offenses persist when ethnicity is controlled.

The greatest differences between adjacent categories are consistently found between Classes 1 and 2 and Classes 4 and 5. On the one hand, offenders from Class 1 appear to be particularly successful in avoiding police contact, while those in Class 5 are quite unsuccessful in avoiding such contacts. The differences between the intermediate class categories—2 and 3, 3 and 4—are relatively small.

The police contact rates vary by sex, ethnicity, and social class; males, members of minority groups, particularly Negroes, and lower-class offenders encounter a relatively greater risk of police contact for each delinquent act they commit. It appears that sex, ethnicity, and class affect the probability of detection, as indicated by the filing of an official investigation report. Previous investigators have demonstrated that these variables influence subsequent steps in the legal processing of suspected offenders [84; 232; 233].

These findings raise serious questions concerning the adequacy of official data as a measure of delinquent behavior. Yet, theoretical explanations of delinquency involve the variables of class, ethnicity, and sex. This suggests that exclusive reliance upon official data in tests of theoretical propositions could be misleading. "Because much delinquent behavior is not followed by official processing, studies which use some type of official contact as the criterion of delinquency may reveal spurious differences between delinquents and nondelinquents" [251, p. 4]. We view the analysis of delinquent behavior by means of self reports as a viable alternative to exclusive reliance on cases known to the police or courts. Our position is that self reports are best conceived as complementary to official data rather than as a potential replacement. The apparent biases in police contacts suggest that official data are of limited utility in research designed to test theoretical propositions. Yet, limitations in the official data do not preclude their utilization in studies in which persons serve as the unit of analysis. Official data would be useful in analyses of factors involved in police officers' decisions to take formal or informal action or in an examination of the effect of official labeling on the individual's subsequent perceptions, beliefs, and behavior [113].

Delinquent Persons

To construct a measure of delinquent persons poses special conceptual difficulties because it entails both an individual's involvement in delinquent behavior and the action of social control agents in response to that behavior. Although sociologists who adopt the interactionist perspective have little to say about the actor's initial involvement in delinquent acts, we accept the interactionists' view of delinquency as a process. The formal application of the label *delinquent* to a person is the final phase of a process beginning with the individual's initial delinquent act [73; 190]. Legally, one becomes a delinquent, that is, a delinquent person, upon adjudication, but juveniles who commit delinquent acts begin the process leading to adjudication, and they may be classified according to their proximity to legal definition as a delinquent. This approach permits us to consider persons as more or less delinquent; their position is dependent upon their location in the process terminating with the acquisition of the legal status of a delinquent. Each step in this process implies movement toward formal designation as a delinquent; the final stage includes youth formally adjudicated as delinquents by a juvenile court. In this sense we divide the process into three general phases: involvement in delinquent behavior, apprehension by law enforcement agents, and the formal application of the label *delinquent* through court action. Within the first two phases further differentiation may be made with respect to the seriousness of the behavior and the type of offense.[23] The stages then become: (1) involvement in nonserious delinquent behavior, (2) involvement in serious delinquent behavior, (3) police contact for a nonserious delinquent offense, (4) police contact for a serious delinquent act, and (5) adjudication by the court. With the inclusion of the residual category, no self-reported or official record of delinquency, each subject is located in one of these stages. Self-report, police contact, and court data were available, and the previously described measure of seriousness for self-reported behavior and police contacts was utilized. Because the measure of delinquent persons is conceptualized as a status measure, a subject's experience in the delinquency process is treated as cumulative from one time period to the next. Therefore, a subject's status in any time period is always equal to or greater than his status in the preceding time period.

It is not essential to argue that the 6 stages have additive, cumulative, or unidimensional properties, although it is reasonable to assume that they might satisfy the requirements of a Guttman scale in which the underlying dimension would be the delinquency process. There is also some question regarding the ordering of stages 2 and 3, for it is problematic whether a police contact for a nonserious offense constitutes an advanced stage over involvement, albeit undetected, in serious delinquent behavior. A decision on this issue requires specification of the priority of seriousness and detection by the police. Assuming that adolescents known to the police, regardless of the seriousness of the act, are closer to adjudication than juveniles with whom the police have not had contact, we assign greater weight to apprehension.

However, scaling provides evidence about the correct ordering of the stages. The distribution of subjects according to the stages in the delinquency process is presented in Table 4-8. The Coefficients of Reproducibility and Minimum Marginal Reproducibility indicate that the scale meets the requirements for Guttman scales for males and females. The resulting order of the stages supports the assumption that a police contact for a nonserious delinquent act constitutes a more advanced stage in the delinquency process than hidden serious delinquent behavior. However, juveniles known to the police for either serious or nonserious offenses generally admit serious delinquent behavior on the SRD measure. Adolescents known to the police comprise 26.2 percent of the study population, and 80 percent of these respondents admit serious delinquent behavior. Conversely, 73.8 percent of the population have never had any recorded contact with the police, and 48.5 percent of them admit serious delinquent acts. This suggests that the dichotomy based on official records typically used in delin-

Table 4-8
Final Distribution on the Delinquency Status Scale

Stage	Scale Score	Total Population			Males			Females		
		N	Percentage	Cumulative Percentage	N	Percentage	Cumulative Percentage	N	Percentage	Cumulative Percentage
No Self Report or Official Record of Delinquency	0	115	4.4	4.4	38	2.8	2.8	77	6.0	6.0
One or More Nonserious Self-Reported Acts	1	878	33.6	38.0	310	23.2	26.0	568	44.5	50.5
One or More Serious Self-Reported Acts	2	938	35.8	73.8	499	37.3	63.3	439	34.3	84.8
One or More Police Contacts—Misdemeanors	3	403	15.4	89.2	267	20.0	83.3	136	10.6	95.4
One or More Police Contacts—Felonies	4	126	4.8	94.0	108	8.1	91.4	18	1.4	96.8
Court Adjudication	5	157	6.0	100.0	116	8.6	100.0	41	3.2	100.0

Coefficient of Reproducibility:
Males = .98859 (Period I); .99391 (Period IV)
Females = .97683 (Period I); .97130 (Period IV)
Scale Scores: Male Mean = 2.33; Female Mean = 1.67; $t = 14.84$ $p < .01$

Minimum Marginal Reproducibility:
Males = .88531 (I); .85891 (IV)
Females = .83587 (I); .82063 (IV)

quency research has some general validity. Yet, it would be misleading as a measure of individual involvement either in serious or nonserious delinquent behavior. If an investigator used official contact to distinguish between delinquents and nondelinquents, 80 percent of the subjects he identified as delinquents would have some involvement in serious delinquent acts, but he would not have a representative sample of juveniles involved in delinquent behavior.[24] Specifically, 42 percent of the adolescents admitting serious delinquent behavior and 27 percent of the youth reporting nonserious delinquent behavior would be identified as delinquents. If the usual procedure were also followed in the selection of a control group, juveniles in the general population would be assumed to be nondelinquent in the absence of police contact; however, the self-report data demonstrate that many of the potential controls are highly involved in delinquent activities. Our measure of delinquency status represents an essential refinement of the typical persons measures derived from official data, because it reflects the seriousness of the subject's delinquent behavior and the official response, if any, to that behavior.

The Delinquency Status Scale scores in Table 4-8 indicate that of the subjects in the study population, 95 percent report some participation in delinquent behavior, 62 percent admit serious delinquent acts, 26 percent are known to the police, and 6 percent are adjudicated delinquents. The distribution of males and females reveals expected differences. Approximately 50 percent of the females and 26 percent of the males have little or no involvement in delinquency (status scores 0 and 1). Relatively few females are known to the police for felonies or are adjudicated, whereas the proportion of males in status categories 4 and 5 is more than four times that of females.

The Delinquency Status Scale does not include a quantitative dimension; consequently, it does not reflect the frequency of involvement in delinquent behavior. A person admitting one serious delinquent act is categorized in the same stage as a juvenile admitting many serious delinquent acts. Conceivably, youth adjudicated delinquent could have committed fewer serious delinquent acts than juveniles known to the police for serious delinquent offenses or even those who have escaped police contact but admit serious delinquent acts. This raises an important question regarding the measure of delinquent persons: Is placement in one of the stages of the delinquency process associated with a greater frequency of delinquent acts? Examination of the mean number of SRD and officially recorded offenses by delinquency status shows a striking association between delinquency status and the reported frequency of delinquent acts (see Table 4-9). The differences in the means for the total range of self-reported behavior are sizable; subjects in Status Category V report more than four times the number of offenses admitted by respondents in Status Category I. The mean frequency of total, serious, and nonserious self-reported offenses decreases regularly with decreasing delinquency status; the only exception is the average number of serious offenses reported by juveniles in Status Categories II and III.

Table 4-9
Mean Number of Self-Reported Offenses and Police Contacts, by Final Delinquency Status Scale Scores

	Delinquency Status[b]					
Delinquent Behavior[a]	Adj. V	S PC IV	Ns PC III	S SR II	Ns SR I	Total Population
N	157	126	403	938	878	2617
Total Self-Report	18.87	15.60	13.23	11.85	4.35	8.55
Ns Self-Report	13.23	10.59	9.87	8.48	4.35	6.38
Ser. Self-Report	5.83	5.05	3.36	3.38	–	2.01
Ns Police Contacts	3.07	1.13	1.49	–	–	0.454
Ser. Police Contacts	1.20	1.26	–	–	–	0.189

[a]Nondeliquent N = 115

[b]Adj. = Adjudicated
S PC = Serious Police Contact
Ns PC = Nonserious Police Contact
S SR = Serious Self Reported
Ns SR = Nonserious Self Reported

Total SR	$F = 204.9445 2p < .01$ All $t:p < .05$
Ns SR	$F = 174.76601 p < .01$ All $t:p < .01$; except 3 x 4
Ser. SR	$F = 114.37851 p < .01$ All $t:p < .01$; except 4 x 5; 2 x 3
Ns PC	$F = 480.4727 p < .01$ All $t:p < .01$
Ser. PC	$t:$ NS

Juveniles known to the police are more frequent offenders with respect to both serious and minor violations. Similarly, subjects formally adjudicated are involved more frequently in both serious and nonserious offenses than are those known to the police, but not adjudicated.[25] Examining the total number of police contacts, we observe that juveniles adjudicated by the court (Category V) had a mean of 4.27 contacts in comparison with 2.39 for the respondents known to the police for serious offenses and 1.49 for youth known only for nonserious violations (Category III). When the type of police contact is controlled, the trends are not entirely consistent. The adjudicated delinquents (Category V) have two to three times more police contacts for nonserious offenses than subjects known to the police who are not adjudicated (Categories III and IV); in contrast, respondents who have serious police contacts (Category IV) have *fewer* nonserious contacts than do youth in Status Category III whose only contact with the police is for nonserious violations. Further, the adjudicated delinquents (Category V) have approximately the same number of serious police contacts as persons in Status Category IV.

The analysis of the relationship between the measure of delinquency status and the frequency of self-reported delinquent behavior reveals that youth with the highest delinquency status, adjudication by the court, are the most serious and frequent violators and that there is decreasing involvement in delinquent behavior associated with a decreasing status score. The frequency of police contact is also associated with delinquency status.[26] Reflecting the seriousness of an individual's delinquent activity and the official response to that behavior, delinquency status is also correlated with the frequency of delinquent acts. To the extent that these are the salient dimensions of the delinquency process, the Delinquency Status Scale is an adequate measure of delinquent persons.

High School Dropouts

While dropout, like delinquency, may be conceptualized in either behavioral or persons units, analysis of the data reveals little variability among dropouts in the frequency with which they terminate school enrollment. The vast majority of the dropouts left school only once, and none dropped out more than twice. Because there is so little variation in the frequency of leaving school, the only unit of analysis utilized in this research is a "persons" unit.

Although frequently used to characterize persons who have temporarily or permanently left school, the term *dropout* has been used in reference to at least three separate distinctions: (1) persons who "quit" school at some point prior to high school graduation as opposed to those whose attendance is continuous to graduation, (2) persons out of school at a specific point in time as opposed to those attending school at that time, and (3) juveniles in an age cohort who have or have not graduated. These distinctions are logically independent, because a person who leaves school may return and may subsequently graduate. Thus, in terms of the first distinction, at a specific point in time, a juvenile may or may not be considered a dropout, depending on whether the time of classification is prior to, during, or after his period of absence. By definition, all dropouts were in school prior to dropping out; some returned to school at a later date. Similarly, those who spend some time out of school and who are either in or out of school at a given point may in the course of time be either graduates or nongraduates. Therefore, while each of these distinctions is important, no one of them is sufficient.

The apparent confusion is at least in part a consequence of the use of cross-sectional designs. Studies of dropouts are characteristically static in nature, and it is the time perspective that renders the distinctions independent of one another. If all dropouts were to leave school at the same time, never to return, these distinctions would disappear. The longitudinal nature of this research forced us to consider each of these distinctions; in addition to using a descriptive definition of dropout, we classified the respondents in terms of Attendance Status and Graduate Status.

Descriptive Definition

We adopted the following description as our working definition of dropout:

A dropout is a pupil who leaves a school, for any reason except death, before graduation or completion of a program of studies and without transferring to another school. . . . Such an individual is considered a dropout whether his dropping out occurs during or between regular school terms, whether his dropping out occurs before or after he has passed the compulsory school attendance age, and, where applicable, whether or not he has completed a minimum required amount of school work. [173, p. 13]

Although more explicit than most, this definition fails to specify any minimum length of time a person has to remain out of school to be classified as a dropout. There was considerable movement in and out of school over the course of the study period; for various lengths of time students were ill, temporarily suspended, excluded, expelled, truant, or absent from school for undetermined causes. However, the concept dropout implies either a personal decision to leave school, presumably permanently, or an official decision by educational authorities to exclude a student from school. In either case, the result should be a more extended absence than is implied by truancy, suspension, or minor illness. Consequently, we specified a minimum period of absence as a further criterion for classification as a dropout.[27] Juveniles were considered dropouts only if they remained out of school for 30 or more consecutive days during any regular school term.[28] The point of dropping out was defined as the first day of this minimum period of absence. This criterion not only excludes those temporarily out of school who fully intend to return but also distinguishes such students from those who intend to drop out as well as those officially prohibited from attending school in the district.[29] On the basis of these criteria, 558 persons—21 percent of the study population—were classified as dropouts. Identical percentages of males and females were dropouts.

Attendance Status. Attendance Status was measured independently to indicate for each time period whether the subject was attending school or was a dropout *for that period.* (See Chapter 3, especially Figure 3-1, for definition of the time periods.) Some dropouts returned to school and were classified as in attendance in subsequent study periods. Attendance Status reflects this distinction for each time period, and it provides an essential time dimension for this longitudinal study of dropouts.

The Attendance Status of the cohort for each time period is presented in Table 4-10. During Period II, 129 students left school, but 14 of them returned to school before the end of the period. At the beginning of Period III, 2,502 of the original cohort were in school, 115 were out of school, and 1 subject was lost. At the beginning of Period V, 2,142 subjects were in school, 469 were out of school, and 8 were lost. During the next 2 months, immediately prior to graduation, 123 respondents left school, and 48 subjects returned to school. The data in Table 4-10 reflect extensive movement in and out of school on the part of subjects classified, at one time or another, as dropouts. During the 4 years of

Table 4-10
Attendance Status, by Sex and Time Period

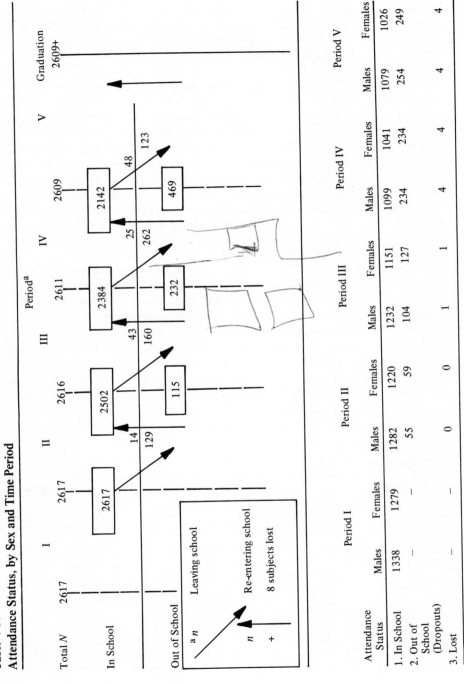

Attendance Status	Period I		Period II		Period III		Period IV		Period V	
	Males	Females	Males	Females	Males	Females	Males	Females	Males	Females
1. In School	1338	1279	1282	1220	1232	1151	1099	1041	1079	1026
2. Out of School (Dropouts)	—	—	55	59	104	127	234	234	254	249
3. Lost	—	—	0	0	1	1	4	4	4	4

the study, the 558 dropouts left school 674 times. Of the 130 reentries, 89 percent subsequently dropped out again. In each period the proportions of males and females leaving school were nearly identical, but 63 percent of the dropouts who returned to school were males.

Graduate Status. Graduate Status reflects the educational outcome for each subject and distinguishes between graduates and nongraduates at the termination of the study. Determination of Graduate Status is complicated by the fact that one may receive a diploma or certificate of completion through a regular day high school, night school, continuation school, military educational program, or by successfully passing a high school equivalency examination (hereafter cited as GED). Dropouts need not return to school, nor are they required to transfer formally to any specific school program to become high school graduates. The distinction between graduates and nongraduates has a temporary quality. Many studies in which graduates and dropouts are compared fail to consider anything but the conventional route to graduation and define those who do not graduate from a regular day high school as dropouts. The accuracy of our measure of Graduate Status is limited by the termination of the study three months after the usual graduation date; however, for the time period between dropout and the end of the study, we took into account all paths to Graduate Status. Any person receiving a high school diploma or certificate of completion through the GED is defined as a graduate. Because there is some interest in the proportion of dropouts who graduate, in the measure of Graduate Status we differentiate between dropout graduates and graduates who were never dropouts. Also distinguished are two kinds of nongraduates—those in attendance and those out of school at the termination of the study. The Graduate Status of the respondents is presented in Table 4-11. As of September 1967, 79 percent of the

Table 4-11
Graduate Status, by Sex

Graduate Status	Sex				Total Population	
	Male		Female			
	N	Percentage	N	Percentage	N	Percentage
Graduate						
Nondropouts	1016	75.9	994	77.7	2010	76.8
Dropouts	31	2.3	23	1.8	54	2.1
Non-Graduates						
Attending	32	2.4	9	0.7	41	1.6
Dropouts	255	19.1	249	19.5	504	19.2
Lost	4	0.3	4	0.3	8	0.3
Total	1338	100.0	1279	100.0	2617	100.0

cohort had graduated, whereas 19 percent had dropped out and remained out of school at the end of the study. Approximately 2 percent were still enrolled in school. The percentage of dropouts is slightly lower than the figures reported for the state of California and school districts near the areas where this study was conducted.[30] While dropout graduates constitute only 2 percent of the total study population, they comprise approximately 10 percent of all dropouts. The proportions of males and females who graduated are almost identical, though a slightly higher proportion of male than female dropouts graduated.

Types of Dropouts

After reviewing the relevant empirical studies, we identified three types of dropouts—involuntary, educationally handicapped, and capable. Only intellectually capable students who left school as a result of external circumstances over which they had no control were classified as involuntary dropouts. Dropouts are usually defined as students who leave school prior to graduation for any reason except death. There were 2 deaths in the study population; for convenience these cases are included in the category of involuntary dropouts. Respondents classified as capable dropouts either had a cumulative grade point average (hereafter cited as GPA) of 2.00 (C average) at the time of dropout *or* achievement and I.Q. test scores above the 30th percentile according to national norms. Students with test scores between the 20th and 30th percentiles were also considered capable if their GPA was at least 1.00 (D average). The dropouts with GPAs below 1.00 and test scores between the 20th and 30th percentiles were classified as educationally handicapped, as were those whose test scores were below the 20th percentile. The mean I.Q. scores of the capable dropouts were at the 51st percentile, whereas the mean for educationally handicapped dropouts fell at the 23rd percentile according to national norms.

The distribution of types of dropouts is presented in Table 4-12. Sixty-six percent of the dropouts are classified as capable, 2 percent as involuntary

Table 4-12
Types of Dropouts, by Sex

Type	Males		Females		Total	
	Number	Percentage	Number	Percentage	Number	Percentage
Educationally Handicapped	97	33.9	83	30.5	180	32.0
Involuntary	4	1.4	8	2.9	12	2.0
Intellectually Capable	185	64.7	181	66.5	366	66.0
Total	286	100.0	272	100.0	558	100.0

dropouts, and 32 percent as educationally handicapped. These figures are comparable to the percentages reported by other investigators [51; 124; 142]. In this cohort health-related problems are not a significant factor in the etiology of high school dropout. A slightly higher proportion of the male dropouts are classified as educationally handicapped, whereas more female dropouts are categorized as either involuntary or capable dropouts. We do not attach substantive significance to these minimal differences.

Early in the study we discovered a potentially important distinction—some capable dropouts leave school voluntarily as a result of a personal decision, while others are forced to leave school by official action [62]. Interviews with respondents in the latter category indicate that a majority of them neither wanted to leave school nor previously contemplated dropping out. Our hypothesis concerning delinquency and dropout as alternative responses to problems encountered in the context of the school was based on the assumption that dropout constitutes a voluntary decision on the part of the adolescent; this supposition clearly would not apply to students forced out of school by administrative authority, often because of their rebellious behavior. Consequently, we attempted to differentiate between "pushouts" and voluntary dropouts among those classified as capable dropouts. Only in instances when an official rule was invoked by a school administrator to suspend or expel a student was he or she considered a pushout. A subject who left school to take a job or to marry was defined as a voluntary dropout, whereas a student who was forced to leave school was classified as a pushout. A student who did not return to school following a brief suspension was also classified as a pushout. It was clear who made the decision for all but 21 cases. These are not included in comparisons of pushouts and voluntary dropouts.

The numbers and percentages of capable dropouts who were pushouts or voluntary dropouts are shown in Table 4-13. Almost three-fourths are voluntary dropouts, whereas pushouts comprise one-fifth of the capable dropouts. A larger percentage of males than females are classified as pushouts, although the difference is small. The predominant reason for suspension or expulsion of females was a rule prohibiting attendance by married or pregnant students; on

Table 4-13
Types of Intellectually Capable Dropouts, by Sex

Types	Males		Females		Total	
	Number	Percentage	Number	Percentage	Number	Percentage
Pushout	42	22.7	37	20.4	79	21.0
Voluntary	126	68.1	140	77.4	266	74.0
Indeterminate	17	9.2	4	2.2	21	5.0
Total	185	100.0	181	100.0	366	100.0

the other hand, official action against males typically involved suspension, exclusion, or expulsion for troublesome behavior in school. The officially recorded reasons for leaving school are shown in Table 4-14.

Reviewing previous studies of dropouts, we attempted to explain the contradictory findings regarding the intellectual ability of dropouts by hypothesizing that educationally handicapped dropouts leave school relatively early in comparison with capable dropouts [62; 252]. The proportion of each type of dropout leaving school during each time period in the study is presented in Table 4-15. In this table, Period V refers to the four-month interval between the last administration of questionnaires in April 1967, and the beginning of school the following fall. During Period II, 22 percent of the educationally handicapped and 16 percent of the capable dropouts left school. The proportion of educationally handicapped students leaving school during the latter part of the ninth grade and early in the tenth grade is somewhat greater than the comparable proportion of capable dropouts. However, the cumulative proportions of educationally handicapped and capable dropouts for each succeeding time period are nearly identical. Except for Period II, the data do not support the hypothesis that those with limited ability leave school early.[31]

The proportions in Table 4-15 show that dropout frequently occurs in Period IV. Forty-two percent of all dropouts left school between the latter half of their junior year and near the end of their senior year. Almost one-half of the voluntary dropouts, a subtype of capable dropouts, left during this period. The majority of the dropouts left at one of two points—the end of summer vacation—that is, they failed to return to school in the fall—and the end of Christmas vacation. The latter point is of special significance, because it is shortly after students return from the Christmas holidays that graduation lists are prepared, and marginal students learn whether they are likely to graduate. Surprisingly, 17 percent of all dropouts left school after April 1 in their senior year. In many cases these students finished the school year, but did not graduate; failing to return to school the following September, they were classified as dropouts.

Final Dropout Status

Our major theoretical interest centers on the 365 intellectually capable dropouts, and in the analyses in subsequent chapters we restrict our attention to these capable dropouts.[32] As we noted in Chapter 2, intellectually capable dropouts cannot be identified on the basis of I.Q. scores, grades, or other information available in school records; indeed, they have adequate reading ability and at least average intelligence levels. It is to this type of dropout that our theoretical explanation is directed, and inclusion of involuntary and educationally handicapped dropouts in tests of theoretical propositions would

Table 4-14
Official Reasons for Leaving School, by Sex and Ethnicity (Percentages)

Reasons	Males					Females				
	Anglo	Mexican-American	Negro	Other	Total	Anglo	Mexican-American	Negro	Other	Total
Marriage	7.0	2.9	1.8	–	5.536	50.5	35.2	27.3	33.3	44.981
Pregnancy	–	–	–	–	–	5.4	1.8	22.7	22.2	6.691
Non-Academic Goals	19.4	37.7	19.0	15.4	23.529	8.2	16.7	4.5	11.1	9.665
Trouble with or Dislike of School Officials	4.3	2.9	–	–	3.460	–	–	–	–	–
General Dislike of School	9.7	11.6	4.8	7.7	9.688	11.4	7.4	–	–	9.293
Academic Difficulties	18.3	10.1	9.5	7.7	15.224	4.3	7.4	–	11.1	4.832
Temporary Suspension or Expulsion	24.2	13.0	47.6	38.0	23.875	9.8	11.1	18.2	11.1	10.780
Illness	1.1	1.4	4.8	–	1.384	4.3	1.8	4.5	11.1	4.089
Institutionalization or Trouble with the Law	–	4.4	–	7.7	1.384	1.1	–	–	–	0.743
Adult School or Over Age	9.7	11.6	–	–	8.996	1.1	5.6	13.6	–	2.973
Family Problems	1.6	–	4.8	7.7	1.730	1.6	7.4	4.5	–	2.973
Trouble with Peers	1.6	–	–	–	1.038	0.5	–	–	–	0.371
No Response	1.1	1.4	–	–	1.038	–	–	–	–	–
Other	2.1	2.9	4.8	15.4	3.114	1.6	5.6	4.5	–	2.602
N	186	69	21	13	289	184	54	22	9	269

Table 4-15

Proportion of Dropouts Leaving in Each Time Period, by Type of Dropout

Type of Dropout[a]		Period				Total N
		II	III	IV	V	
Educationally	p[b]	.22	.20	.39	.19	180
Handicapped	cp[c]	–	.42	.81	1.00	
Involuntary	p	.58	.08	.34	0	12
	cp	–	.66	1.00	1.00	
Intellectually	p	.16	.24	.44	.16	366
Capable	cp	–	.40	.84	1.00	
Pushouts	p	.24	.24	.32	.20	79
	cp	–	.48	.80	1.00	
Voluntary	p	.14	.25	.48	.13	266
	cp	–	.39	.87	1.00	
Indeterminate	p	.10	.14	.48	.28	21
	cp	–	.24	.72	1.00	
Total	p	.19	.22	.42	.17	558
	cp	–	.41	.83	1.00	

[a]Only the *last* drop is considered for those dropping out of school more than once.

[b]p = proportion

[c]cp = cumulative proportion

confound the analysis. We combined the capable dropouts from the several time periods because the number in any single time period was limited. The advantages of this classification are obvious—there is a larger number of dropouts involved, and the marginal imbalance between dropouts and nondropouts is reduced. To avoid the cumbersome terminology of "dropouts and nondropouts among those who are intellectually capable" we call this classification Final Dropout Status. It should be noted that Graduate Status is not considered in this dichotomy. When capable students dropped out, they were classified as dropouts, regardless of subsequent Graduate Status; similarly, if they were intellectually capable, nongraduates were included in the category of nondropouts.

Summary

In this study a behavioral conception of delinquency was adopted, and a self-report instrument was used to measure delinquent behavior. The SRD measure provides a conservative estimate of the number of delinquent acts committed by each subject. The 2,617 respondents admitted 23,214 delinquent acts—an average of 9.63 infractions per subject—during their junior and senior high school years. The estimates obtained on the basis of the SRD have face validity, and evidence concerning reliability and validity in earlier studies supports the continued use of self reports. In this research several external validity checks were made by comparing police and court records with self reports of delinquent behavior. In Periods I and II to IV, the levels of error are 22 and 17 percent, respectively, for specific offenses; similar comparisons according to the seriousness of recorded and reported offenses reveal less error—7 percent in Period 1 (junior high school) and 4 percent in Period II to IV (senior high school). For the 2 periods combined, the level of error is 5 percent. As expected, the amount of error in the direction of underreporting was substantially greater for serious than nonserious offenses. However, 97 percent of the adjudicated delinquents reported a delinquent act at least as serious as the offense that led to the filing of a petition with the juvenile court. In a further effort to validate the SRD, internal comparisons involving groups assumed to be different with respect to rates of delinquency were made. The expected differences by age and sex were observed, but only partial support was found for presumed ethnic and social class differentials. The latter may exist only in official records as a result of variations in the exposure, detection, and apprehension of juveniles from different ethnic groups and class levels. We do not consider these discrepancies a serious challenge to the validity of the SRD. The teachers' nominations of "potential" delinquents and nondelinquents provided the strongest internal evidence for the validity of the self-report measure. There was a high degree of association between the teachers' evaluations and the students' reported delinquent behavior, and the SRD discriminated among the several categories of teachers' nominations.

Official police contact reports provide a second type of measure of delinquent behavior. Approximately one-third of the 1,486 police contacts occurred before we administered questionnaires to the respondents in the ninth grade. Analysis of the official data shows the expected differentials by sex, ethnicity, and social class. The study population appears to be quite similar to juvenile populations investigated by other researchers.

The self-report and official data permit estimation of the amount of hidden delinquency, the probability of police contact according to the frequency of delinquent behavior, and conditional probabilities of police contact in terms of the sex, ethnic ancestry, and social class of the offender as well as the seriousness of the delinquent act. Comparison of these divergent sources of data reveals that there are approximately 5 police contacts for every 100 self-reported offenses— there is a substantial amount of hidden delinquency in this population. Police contact rates vary by sex, ethnicity, and class; males, members of minority groups, and lower-class juveniles have a relatively greater risk of police contact for each delinquent act they commit. Although official data are potentially useful in studies of police decision-making and the effect of official labeling, the obvious biases in official records limit their utility in tests of etiological propositions. Exclusive reliance on official records is unwarranted, but we view self reports and official data as complementary—the advantages of one partially overcome the limitations of the other.

An effort was made to define delinquent persons by locating each respondent at some stage in the process of becoming an adjudicated delinquent. Specifying stages in this process, we derived a unidimensional scale; the Delinquency Status Scale reflects the seriousness of self-reported delinquent behavior and the official response, if any, to that behavior. Over the course of the study more than 95 percent of the subjects were involved in some delinquent activity, 26 percent experienced official police contact, and 6 percent were adjudicated delinquent by the courts. Position on the measure of delinquency status was related to the frequency of delinquent behavior. Adjudicated delinquents were the most frequent offenders, and there was a decreasing frequency of delinquent acts associated with a decreasing delinquency status score.

In addition to a descriptive definition of dropout, two separate indicators, Attendance Status and Graduate Status, were developed. A dropout was defined as a person who left school for a reason other than death for a period of at least 30 consecutive days. During the course of the study 558 persons (21 percent of the study population) were classified as dropouts; these respondents left school 674 times. Attendance Status refers to the subject's presence in or absence from school during each time period in the study. Graduate Status reflects the final educational outcome at the conclusion of the investigation; 79 percent of the cohort graduated, whereas 19 percent were nongraduates at the end of the study. Approximately 2 percent of the population, who comprise 10 percent of the dropouts, were dropout graduates; that is, they graduated even though at one point they had dropped out of school.

Finally, three types of dropouts—involuntary, educationally handicapped, and capable—were identified. Only 2 percent of the dropouts left school involuntarily; 32 percent were classified as educationally handicapped, and 66 percent were capable of completing high school. Within the category of capable dropouts approximately one-fifth were forced to leave school; the remainder left voluntarily. Only limited support was found for the hypothesis that students with minimal intellectual ability leave school earlier than juveniles with adequate ability. In subsequent analyses, attention is restricted to the capable dropouts, and in the classification labeled Final Dropout Status, capable dropouts and nondropouts are distinguished.

Notes

1. The concept *delinquency* has included noncriminal behavior, but in a "persons" unit of analysis such cases would have to be excluded to be consistent with our definition of delinquent acts.

2. In addition, some investigators have attempted to observe delinquent

activity [236; 258; 261]. Other researchers have relied on reports from detached workers or special observers who made contact with juvenile gangs [152; 209; 217; 218]. However, observation requires an extensive time commitment, is expensive, and introduces difficult problems of standardization.

3. Hardt and Bodine provide a useful discussion of the advantages and disadvantages of this approach, as well as a summary of the findings produced by some 30 studies in which self reports of delinquency were obtained [92].

4. It was not possible to use either Sellin and Wolfgang's measure [206] or Robin's arrest rate index [180]. The self-report data do not indicate the value of property lost or destroyed or the number of victims involved, and this information is needed for Sellin and Wolfgang's classification. Robin's index is not appropriate for 5 of the 10 SRD items because it does not differentiate between various types of theft and excludes truancy. Comparisons of McEachern and Bauzer's index [143], based on the proportion of cases in which petitions are filed for specific offenses, Erickson's police contact-juvenile court action rates [66], the felony-misdemeanor classification, and a Guttman scale analysis of the data collected in the present investigation are presented in Elliott and Voss [61]. At best, the self-report items form a quasi-scale (CR = .85), and the relatively small difference between the Coefficient of Reproducibility and the Minimum Marginal Reproducibility value suggests that the order of offenses may simply be a function of the frequency distribution.

5. One of the potential difficulties involved in the use of procedures such as Guttman scaling with self-report data is that the scale position of an act is, in part, a function of its frequency in the sample under investigation. Yet, the probability of official response to an act is not determined by its volume in the population. On the other hand, for any particular actor the probability of apprehension and official processing is related to the frequency of his or her violations [67].

6. Dentler and Monroe caution against the use of omnibus scales in "known group" comparisons because differences in patterns of behavior are confounded in such scales [50].

7. The findings of self-report studies are controversial to the extent that they challenge generally accepted ideas. This is particularly true of the finding reported by Nye, Short, and Olson regarding the lack of relation between delinquent behavior and social class [162]. Gold challenges this conclusion, but his questions concern the completeness and accuracy with which class is measured and the nature of the acts defined as delinquent in checklists, rather than the validity of self reports [81]. On the other hand, findings in agreement with the bivariate relationships observed in official data have provoked little comment. For example, Dentler and Monroe report higher Theft Scale scores for males than females, older boys than younger boys, and truants than nontruants [50]. Noncontroversial findings concerning age and sex differences have also been described [1, 92; 93; 102; 216; 222].

8. The effect of anonymity on the veracity of answers has not been studied extensively, but it may not be necessary to guarantee anonymity to obtain the cooperation of respondents [92; 118].

9. In California the jurisdiction of the juvenile court includes youth over 18 years of age, only if the court previously had established jurisdiction.

10. To make self-report items match legal categories more closely might pose a threat for respondents. Gold suggests use of interviews in conjunction with responses to delinquency checklists [82].

11. The official records and self-report data were also compared in terms of the frequency of delinquent behavior reported by subjects who gave accurate and inaccurate responses in the offense-specific analysis. For Period I subjects who provided accurate responses reported an average of 7.70 offenses, whereas the inaccurate respondents admitted a mean of 2.69 delinquent acts. For Period II to IV the comparable means are 9.48 and 5.05 for accurate and inaccurate subjects, respectively. Hence, the accuracy of reporting specific offenses is related to the frequency of delinquent behavior admitted on the SRD.

12. Information on ethnic ancestry was obtained during interviews with each respondent's mother or mother surrogate. The ethnic categories were ordered— Anglo, Other, Oriental, Mexican, and Negro—and cases of ethnic mixture were coded in the lower status category. Respondents whose ethnic ancestry was Anglo and Other or Oriental and Other were classified as Other; combinations of Mexican and Oriental, as well as Mexican and Other, were coded as Mexican; and Mexican-Negro, Negro-Oriental, and Negro-Other combinations were classified as Negro.

13. Analyzing self reports of delinquent behavior obtained in Washington, Slocum and Stone find small but statistically significant differences between whites and nonwhites [222], but a number of investigators do not [2; 26; 65; 90; 192]. Commenting on his comparison of the rank order of the major ethnic groups in Hawaii according to official delinquency records with their ordering on the basis of self reports, Voss suggests:

One explanation for the minor discrepancies observed consisted of differences in the frequency or seriousness of delinquent activities. The essential point is that in studies using self-reports greater attention has been devoted to differentiating those who, on the basis of the information they provide, are more or less delinquent, whereas the frequency of their violations, as well as the seriousness of their acts, has been given less attention. [251, p. 60]

Because we emphasize the frequency and seriousness of reported delinquent acts, our analysis is not directly comparable with studies in which most and least delinquent respondents are differentiated.

14. The study population is distributed as follows: Class I, 58; II, 220; III, 768; IV, 1082; and V, 489. This distribution is slightly skewed toward the lower end of the range.

15. There was no mode for 362 students. In addition to the 13 students who received no evaluations, these students are not included in the figures shown in Table 4-4.

16. The mean number of ratings for students in each category are: (1) 8.41; (2) 6.60; (3) 7.14; (4) 6.88; (5) 7.54. The average number of ratings for the 362 students about whom teachers do not agree is 6.48.

17. The teachers' evaluations are more highly associated with previous delinquent behavior than activity in the future. The teachers' evaluations, which were gathered in Period I, reflect the students' involvement in delinquency during junior high school more adequately than they predict the students' behavior during the years in senior high school. The Pearsonian product-moment correlations are −.46 and −.35, respectively. The correlation between teachers' ratings and the number of serious offenses in Period II to IV is even lower, −.26.

18. Each contact was coded as a specific offense.

19. An additional 55 offenses were recorded between May 1, 1967, and June 15, 1967 (the termination date for the collection of delinquency data). These acts are *not* included in Tables 4-5 and 4-6.

20. In the case of "run away" and "gang fights" the matching of self-report and official records could not be done precisely. The police categorize "run away" and a number of other offenses as incorrigibility. Similarly, disorderly conduct and assault include various types of offenses involving fighting. Because the police records did not always specify the nature of the offense within these categories, the total number of police contacts for these three categories—incorrigibility, disorderly conduct, and assault—were used to calculate self-report-official offense ratios. Consequently, these ratios are somewhat conservative estimates of the relationship between the two measures of delinquent behavior.

21. The difference may also be a product of our scoring procedure. For any given offense, the response categories did not reflect frequencies above 4; yet, the response category, "Very often," which was scored as a frequency of 4, was checked more frequently for nonserious than serious offenses. As a result, our estimates are less accurate for nonserious offenses than for serious offenses.

22. Official records suggest that sex offenses constitute a greater proportion of the delinquent acts of females than males. If this is the case, exclusion of questions pertaining to sexual behavior in a delinquency checklist limits the utility of self reports for investigation of delinquency among females.

23. The third phase, involving formal court action, could be divided according to the action taken; the filing of a petition without adjudication and application of the delinquency label to the offender could serve as stages. In this research the number of cases, although large, does not permit this distinction. The majority of the subjects in level 4 had a petition filed, though this did not always result in court appearance. Only those cases in which a juvenile was institutionalized or formally placed on probation as a ward of the court were included in the adjudicated category.

24. On the basis of the subjects' own reports the records of the police reflect involvement in delinquent acts—few are falsely accused.

25. The product-moment correlations between frequency of self-reported delinquent behavior and the Delinquency Status Scale scores are: total, .50; nonserious, .47; and serious, .42.

26. The product-moment correlations are .60 for nonserious official contacts and .51 for serious contacts.

27. One could emphasize the reason for absence, but this is difficult to ascertain. Official reasons for absence are often incorrect or misleading, and those accepted as legitimate by the school are frequently used by students to bypass compulsory attendance requirements.

28. Students who transferred to a continuation school program were considered dropouts only if they attended school less than 20 hours per week.

29. A sustained absence of four or more months (except in a few cases of prolonged illness that resulted in assignment of a home teacher) uniformly resulted in the removal of a person's name from the attendance rolls.

30. The rate for the state of California is reportedly 25 percent. (See the reports of the Los Angeles City School District, [136]; San Diego Unified School District, [193]; and Segel and Schwarm, [204].)

31. It is possible that the retardates leave school prior to the ninth grade.

32. There is one exception to this generalization. In Table 7-9, Part A, teachers' predictions of all dropouts are examined.

5 The Relationship between Delinquency and Dropout

On theoretical grounds we have suggested that delinquency and dropout are alternative responses to the experience of failure and frustration generated primarily in the context of the school. Furthermore, the consequences of adopting either of these alternatives should have implications for the other. We expect delinquency to lead to dropout [60]. If delinquency is a response to frustrations encountered in the school, then those frustrated students who remain in school should encounter increasing conflict with school authorities and greater risk of suspension or expulsion. Not all of the students' depredations will occur within the school. However, we assume that adolescents involved in serious and frequent delinquent behavior in the community will rarely be models of propriety in school. Nor does the school operate in a vacuum; students labeled delinquent by the police or courts are likely to be considered trouble-makers by school personnel. Their withdrawal from school often may be involuntary, as adolescents who are disruptive in school or involved in delinquent acts should have a relatively high probability of suspension or expulsion. In addition, we hypothesize that movement out of the school context reduces school-related frustrations and alienation and thereby decreases the motivation for delinquency. If failure in school leads to delinquency, then dropout should result in decreasing involvement in delinquency [60].

This expectation is consistent with our theoretical framework, though other factors complicate the relationship. A juvenile's prior involvement in delinquent groups or the experience of official labeling may provide continuing motivation for delinquency. In this case, the hypothesized relationship would hold only for those dropouts who were neither participants in delinquent groups nor were labeled, either formally or informally, as delinquent persons. Failure in school may be repeated in the dropout's out-of-school experiences; he or she may trade failure in school for failure in the economic context. In essence, the same motivational stimulus is involved, but failure is experienced in a different setting than the one postulated as the most relevant for delinquency.

The school may be an effective agent of social control because it supervises and regulates the activity of adolescents. If there is a similar level of motivation for delinquency among dropouts and juveniles attending school, then the absence of the restraints imposed by the school should result in a higher rate of delinquent behavior among dropouts. The absence of restraints may compensate for a lower motivational stimulus for delinquency among dropouts with the

109

result that in- and out-of-school delinquency rates would be comparable. Writers who adopt a control perspective argue that this one factor should produce higher rates of delinquency among dropouts [25; 95; 99; 195; 220]. Social control theorists avoid the issue of motivation for delinquency, whereas we examine variables that may positively motivate youth towards delinquent behavior, whether restraints are present or absent. While we propose that departure from school should reduce motivation for delinquency, it may not follow that the rate of delinquency will diminish with dropout if any of these extraneous factors are operative. These are complicating factors, but they would not lead us to expect an increasing delinquency rate to be a consequence of dropout if the reduction in restraints is counteracted by less motivation for delinquency. In an effort to unravel the relationship between delinquency and dropout, we employ controls for many of the presumably important factors such as employment, marriage, and official labeling.

Previous Research

Consistently higher rates of official delinquency among high school dropouts in comparison with the general youth population have been reported—dropouts have three to four times more police contacts than graduates [25; 58; 60; 96; 97; 109; 197; 198; 199; 220]. In fact, Schreiber found the delinquency rate for dropouts to be ten times higher than the rate in the total youth population or for high school graduates [199]. Clearly, these studies have established an association between official delinquency rates and dropout. However, the nature of the relationship has not been determined, nor has a causal relationship been demonstrated with self-reported or official measures of delinquency. In all of the studies cited, police or court contacts were employed to measure delinquency. Although there are two noteworthy exceptions, the temporal sequence between delinquency and dropout has not been examined in these studies; rather, the investigators employed ex post facto designs and failed to note the relative frequency of arrest or court appearance before and after the point of dropout. The studies have been static in nature, and juveniles who differ with respect to involvement in delinquent behavior at some point in time have not been compared in terms of subsequent rates of dropout.

Schreiber [199] and Jeffrey and Jeffrey [109] have been careful to note that existence of an association between dropout and delinquency is not sufficient grounds to argue for a specific causal relationship. On the other hand, Simpson and Van Arsdol have made unwarranted causal inferences from a statistical association [220]. Unfortunately, most writers have assumed that dropout causes greater involvement in delinquency; the folk adage, "idle hands are the devil's workshop," has been translated into a simple scientific proposition. For example, Haskell and Yablonsky suggest that "the school dropout is less likely to secure employment and more likely to engage in delinquent behavior than those who remain in school" [95, p. 304].

The only known studies in which rates of delinquency before and after dropout are compared are those of Elliott [60] and Jeffrey and Jeffrey [109]. Elliott reports that delinquents who dropped out had a higher official referral rate while in school than after dropout. He also notes that male dropouts had a lower police contact rate than boys in school. Elliott's study was retrospective and involved a small sample, a cohort of males in 2 high schools in southern California. Because the study was exploratory (a euphemism for unfunded research), a substantial number of subjects who left the immediate area during the study period were excluded from his analysis. Consequently, his conclusions must be considered tentative. The measure of delinquency Elliott employed was based exclusively on official police records, an inadequate measure of delinquent behavior. Nevertheless, Elliott's study casts doubt upon the common assumption that dropping out of school leads to greater involvement in delinquency.

Jeffrey and Jeffrey employed a unique research design insofar as the temporal sequence of dropout and delinquency is concerned [109]. They compared the delinquency rates of dropouts before and after entry into a special program. The investigators' primary purpose was evaluation of a special educational program designed to help dropouts pass the GED, but they included a comparison of the dropouts' official delinquency contacts before and after entering the program. They conclude: "The number of weeks a student (dropout) was in the project did not deter him from delinquent conduct; in fact, the longer a student was in the project the higher the chances of delinquency" [109, p. 8]. Unfortunately, the investigators do not indicate the types of controls they utilized for variable lengths of time in the program. If dropouts who enter a program differ from all dropouts or the general population of youth, Jeffrey and Jeffrey's results cannot be generalized beyond the universe of dropouts who subsequently enter a specialized training program. Such limitations force us to view their conclusion with caution, but it is consistent with Elliott's finding that higher rates of delinquency are associated with school attendance, not dropout. Although the available evidence is limited, it challenges the control theory recently proposed by Hirschi [103]. Among other things, Hirschi emphasizes the importance of involvement in conventional activities. In his terms, dropout is indicative of a weakened bond of the individual to society. However, if delinquency rates are higher among juveniles in school than among dropouts, then the control perspective would have to be revised. Obviously, additional data are needed to establish the nature of the relationship between delinquency and dropout.

Findings

Persons classified as dropouts at the end of this study had a substantially greater number of recorded police contacts than graduates, as may be seen in Table 5-1.

Table 5-1
Mean Number of Police Contacts and Self-Reported Delinquent Acts, by Final Graduate Status and Sex

Graduate Status	Total Police Contacts		Serious Police Contacts		Total Self Reported		Serious Self Reported		Delinquency Status Score	
	Male	Female	Male	Female	Male	Female	Male	Female	Male	Female
Graduate (G)	.53	.16	.13	.02	10.59	6.33	2.71	1.09	3.09	2.50
Nongraduate (NG)	3.06	1.33	1.06	.11	14.62	6.43	5.03	1.29	4.06	3.67
Dropout (DO)	2.00	.66	.52	.06	16.82	8.74	5.22	1.32	4.09	3.24
t values G vs. NG	<.05	<.05	<.05	<.05	NS	NS	NS	NS	<.01	<.01
G vs. DO	<.05	<.05	<.05	<.05	<.05	<.05	<.01	NS	<.01	<.01
NG vs. DO	NS	NS	NS	NS	NS	NS	NS	NS	NS	NS

The dropouts also reported considerably more delinquent behavior than graduates. Among males and females the mean number of police contacts for dropouts is approximately four times higher than the average for graduates. A similar pattern exists with respect to police contacts for serious offenses, although the dropout-graduate ratio for females is somewhat lower, 3:1. Surprisingly, nongraduates enrolled in school at the conclusion of the study had the highest average number of police contacts both for serious offenses and total number of offenses. It is important to note that 21 percent of these nongraduates were dropouts who had returned to school.

The police contact rates for dropouts and graduates appear to be consistent with the findings of previous research. Using juvenile court records, which are less inclusive than police contact reports, Schreiber reported a 10 to 1 dropout-graduate ratio [199]. For comparative purposes the proportion of graduates adjudicated delinquent was .03; the comparable figure for dropouts was .17. Restricting the analysis to adjudicated delinquents, we observe differences between dropouts and graduates substantially lower than the ratio reported by Schreiber.

Involvement in delinquent behavior was also measured by the SRD, and the differences between the graduates and dropouts are statistically significant and substantial. Male dropouts report a mean of 16.82 offenses; in comparison, male graduates report an average of 10.59 delinquent acts. While the means for dropouts are consistently higher than the averages for graduates, in no case does the mean for dropouts exceed the mean for graduates by a factor of 2. The specific offenses included in the police contact measure are not limited to the ones included in the SRD; the relative differences in dropout-graduate ratios suggest that there is, given a constant number of delinquent acts, a higher risk of official action for dropouts than graduates.[1] The means for nongraduates on the self-report measures are consistently higher than for graduates and lower than for dropouts, although the differences are not statistically significant. This represents a different ordering of the graduates, nongraduates, and dropouts than was observed with the police contact measure.

In terms of the Delinquency Status Scale, dropouts are also more delinquent than graduates, although no significant differences are observed between nongraduates and dropouts. Both the official and the self-reported measures of delinquent behavior support the conclusion that dropouts have been involved in more delinquent behavior than graduates, although the differences on the SRD measure are not nearly as dramatic as those based on official police contacts. Dropouts are more likely to have been adjudicated delinquent, and when not adjudicated are typically further along in the process of becoming officially labeled delinquent.

Some significant differences in rates of delinquency are also found among types of dropouts (Table 5-2). Involuntary dropouts consistently have the lowest mean number of offenses and Delinquency Status Scale scores. In fact, the

Table 5-2
Mean Number of Police Contacts, Self-Reported Delinquent Acts, and Delinquency Status Scale Scores, by Type of Dropout and Sex

Type	Total Police Contacts		Serious Police Contacts		Total Self Reported		Serious Self Reported		Delinquency Status Score	
	Male	Female	Male	Female	Male	Female	Male	Female	Male	Female
Educationally Handicapped (EH)	2.22	.83	.61	.11	17.96	8.95	6.37	2.07	4.18	3.45
Involuntary (IV)	.00	.50	.00	.00	10.67	4.86	3.00	.14	3.00	2.62
Intellectually Capable (IC)	1.92	.59	.48	.04	16.46	8.86	4.75	1.07	4.06	3.17
Pushout (PO)	3.48	.73	.79	.08	17.72	8.54	5.72	1.04	4.60	3.30
Voluntary (VOL)	1.40	.53	.37	.02	16.24	8.93	4.51	1.07	3.87	3.11
Indeterminate (IND)	1.94	1.50	.53	.25	13.00	—	3.50	—	4.24	4.00
t values EH vs. IV	<.01	<.05	<.01	<.05	<.01	<.05	NS	NS	<.01	NS
EH vs. IC	NS	NS	NS	NS	NS	NS	NS	NS	NS	NS
EH vs. PO	NS	NS	NS	NS	NS	NS	NS	NS	NS	NS
EH vs. VOL	NS	NS	NS	NS	NS	NS	NS	NS	NS	NS
EH vs. IND	NS	<.05	NS	<.05	<.05	NS	NS	NS	NS	NS
IV vs. IC	<.01	NS	<.01	NS	<.01	<.05	NS	NS	<.01	NS
IV vs. PO	<.01	NS	<.01	NS	<.01	<.05	NS	NS	<.01	NS
IV vs. VOL	<.01	NS	<.01	NS	<.01	<.05	NS	NS	<.01	NS
IV vs. IND	<.01	<.05	<.01	NS	<.01	<.05	NS	NS	<.01	NS
PO vs. VOL	<.01	<.01	<.01	<.05	NS	NS	NS	NS	<.01	NS
PO vs. IND	<.05	<.05	NS	<.05	NS	NS	NS	NS	NS	NS
VOL vs. IND	<.05	<.05	NS	<.05	NS	NS	NS	NS	NS	NS

means for the involuntary dropouts are similar to the means for graduates, as shown in Table 5-1. On the other hand, the means of the educationally handicapped and capable dropouts are high in relation to the averages of the involuntary dropouts and graduates. While the means of the educationally handicapped dropouts are consistently higher than the means of the capable dropouts, the differences are small and are not statistically significant. Among the capable dropouts, pushouts have more frequent police contact than voluntary dropouts, but these subtypes do not differ significantly in their involvement in delinquent behavior as measured by the SRD. In comparison with the voluntary dropouts, the pushouts' delinquency apparently is more visible, not only to the police but also to school authorities; this may explain the school officials' action to exclude them.

There are four alternative, though not mutually exclusive, ways in which delinquency and dropout could be associated. If dropout is treated as the causal variable, then it is possible that dropout increases or decreases the probability of delinquent behavior. On the other hand, if delinquency is considered as the causal variable, then delinquency may increase or decrease the probability of dropout. The effect of dropout on delinquency can be determined by comparing the dropouts' in- and out-of-school delinquency rates; in this way support may be provided for either the first or second hypothesis. In a similar manner, we compare the dropout rates of subjects with high and low rates of delinquency to ascertain the effect of delinquency on dropout; this approach may provide evidence in support of either the third or fourth alternative. The hypotheses within each of the pairs are mutually exclusive. However, the alternatives in the first set are not necessarily inconsistent with the hypotheses in the second set; for example, delinquency could lead to dropout which, in turn, could produce increasing or decreasing rates of delinquency.

The Effect of Dropout on Delinquency

If dropping out of school leads to increased delinquent activity, a comparison of delinquency rates while dropouts are in and out of school should provide evidence in support of such a causal sequence. In- and out-of-school rates of police contact during each study period are presented in Table 5-3. In this table dropouts are categorized according to the period in which they left school. Dropouts in Period II (hereafter cited as DO IIs) left school sometime during the second period, and the number of days in and out of school during this period had to be calculated for each dropout, as did the number of police contacts prior to and subsequent to his or her leaving school. Individually, DO IIs contributed a variable amount of time and number of police contacts to the in-school and out-of-school rates during Period II. Similarly, dropouts in Periods III, IV, and V (hereafter cited as DO IIIs, IVs, and Vs, respectively) have in-school and

Table 5-3
Total Police Contact Rates,[a] by Subjects In and Out of School

	In School					Out of School			
Periods:	I	II	III	IV	V				
Graduates (N = 2142)	.19	.19	.27	.20	.19				
Periods:	I	II	III	IV	V	V			
DO V (N = 65)	.10	.47	.60	.68	1.12	.43			
Periods:		I	II	III	IV	IV	V		
DO IV (N = 195)		.55	.48	.74	.81	.41	.00		
Periods:			I	II	III	III	IV	V	
DO III (N = 106)			.71	.71	1.64	.30	.01	.00	
Periods:				I	II	II	III	IV	V
DO II (N = 109)				1.00	1.70	.94	.32	.10	.00

[a]Mean number of police contacts per 1,000 days. The summer period from June 15 to September 15 is excluded. For this analysis Period I was assumed to have started in September 1959 when the cohort's mean age was 10 years.

out-of-school rates for the period in which they left school. The vertical line in Table 5-3 represents the point of dropout; values on the left side of the table are in-school rates, and those to the right are out-of-school rates. Because the dropouts are categorized according to the period in which they left school, a comparison of the dropouts' rate of police contact within any particular time period requires examination of the diagonal cells. For comparative purposes, police contact rates by study period are also shown in the first row of Table 5-3 for graduates who were in school throughout the study.

Comparison of police contact rates of dropouts and graduates in Period I clearly demonstrates that, with the exception of the DO Vs, the dropouts had substantially higher contact rates prior to the start of the study. In Period I the rate for respondents who were to drop out in the following year, DO IIs, was five times higher than the rate of eventual graduates. Only one category of dropouts, the DO Vs, had a rate lower than the graduates, and this category, which contains 65 subjects, includes 13 dropout reentries and 52 respondents who tenaciously remained in school until the usual date of graduation without completing the requirements. Further, dropouts consistently had higher police contact rates than graduates for *every* period they were in school; the rates for dropouts were never less than twice the rate of graduates in any single time period. The case of the DO IIs is particularly impressive. While in school during Period II, their rate was nine times higher than the police contact rate of graduates. These data are consistent with the findings reported by Elliott [60]; they demonstrate forcefully that dropouts have higher in-school rates of police contact than graduates.

For each category of dropouts the police contact rates increase with time while they are in school. Furthermore, the highest rate for each category is observed in the period in which dropout occurs. The pattern is similar regardless of when the subjects dropped out; that is, the rate of police contact increases steadily and peaks in the last period the subjects are in school. In contrast, among graduates the rate increases somewhat from Period II to Period III but then declines to the earlier level in Periods IV and V. Among the graduates the magnitude of the rate changes with time is slight, particularly in comparison with the changes observed in each dropout category. The dropouts' increasing involvement with the police while they are in school is not accounted for by the general trend observed in the total population. The higher initial or prestudy police contact rates and the accelerating rates through time are also observed for serious police contacts.

The out-of-school rates for dropouts indicate a dramatic reversal of the in-school trend. In the period in which dropout occurs, the rate for out-of-school police contacts is approximately one-half the magnitude of the in-school rate for DO IIs and IVs; the out-of-school rate declines even more sharply among DO IIIs and Vs. For each category of dropouts the rate systematically declines in the period after which dropout occurred, and it continues to decline in subsequent time periods. In the later periods the police contact rates are substantially lower than the comparable rates for graduates. In Periods IV and V, the out-of-school police contact rates for dropouts are close to 0. The figures for Period V must be treated as tentative approximations because this was a short time period. Nevertheless, these data support the conclusion that dropping out of school is associated with decreasing, rather than increasing, out-of-school rates of police contact. Dropouts who have been out of school for a relatively short time have higher rates of police contact than prospective graduates who are still in school. It is not until Period IV that the official delinquency rates of DO IIs and IIIs reach a level lower than the rates of future graduates. From the standpoint of a causal argument, the most important finding is that dropping out of school is associated with a decreasing involvement with the police.

Use of the SRD measure, rather than police contacts, produces similar findings, as shown in Table 5-4. This analysis is limited to a comparison of graduates with DO IIs who did not return to school, because these dropouts were in school during nearly all of their junior high school years, but were out of school for all of their senior high school years.[2] Thus, the first SRD measure covers the period these dropouts were in school, while the second SRD measure coincides with the period they were out of school. On the other hand, graduates were in school continuously throughout the junior and senior high school years. Because the length of the two periods is identical, means are used rather than rates.

Table 5-4

Mean Number of Self-Reported Delinquent Acts and Percentage Change Scores for Dropouts in Period II and Graduates During Junior and Senior High School, by Sex

	Males						Females					
	Junior High		Senior High		Percentage Change		Junior High		Senior High		Percentage Change	
	Means		Means		Percentages		Means		Means		Percentages	
	Total	Serious	Total	Serious	Total	Serious	Total	Serious	Total	Serious	Total	Serious
Dropouts[a]	8.57	3.59	8.13	2.60	−5.1	−27.6	4.40	1.17	4.21	.50	−4.3	−57.3
Graduates	3.88	.99	6.76	1.71	+74.2	+72.7	2.47	.43	3.83	.67	+55.1	+55.8
t test	3.90**	3.71**	.85	1.00			2.74**	2.31*	.61	−.54		

*p < .05
**p < .01

[a]See Note 2 of this chapter for N.

In Table 5-4, males and females are considered separately to control for the established differences in delinquency rates by sex. It is also assumed that the effect of dropping out might be different for males than for females. During the junior high school years, male dropouts report a mean of 8.57 offenses in comparison with 3.88 for graduates; female dropouts and graduates report 4.40 and 2.47 offenses, respectively. Even greater differences are observed for serious offenses during the junior high school years. Male dropouts report more than three times as many serious offenses as graduates, and female dropouts report twice as many serious offenses as graduates. These differences are all significant statistically. These data are consistent with the findings based on police contacts and indicate that while in school, dropouts have substantially greater involvement in delinquent activity than graduates. However, the magnitude of the differences between the in-school means for dropouts and graduates is less than the differences observed in the police contact data; apparently the dropouts have a higher risk of police contact.

A comparison of the means for male dropouts reveals a decline from 8.57 self-reported offenses while in school to 8.13 after dropping out of school. This represents a 5 percent average decrease in raw scores. The comparable rate of change for female dropouts is a decrease of 4 percent. Substantially greater decreases are observed in the means for serious offenses, −28 percent for male and −57 percent for female dropouts. While the decrease in the total number of offenses is slight, it is, nevertheless, clear that the high rates of delinquency among the dropouts cannot be attributed to their dropping out of school. The dropouts reach a high level of involvement in delinquency *prior* to leaving school, but once they are out of school, their total offense rates decline slightly, and their involvement in serious offenses declines substantially. Unfortunately, year by year changes are not reflected in the SRD measure, and the systematic decline observed in police contacts for each year out of school cannot be replicated with these data. Nevertheless, the findings based on the two measures of delinquency are consistent—there is decreasing involvement in delinquency after dropout.

While the dropouts' involvement in delinquent behavior decreased from the junior to the senior high school years, graduates reported an increasing number of delinquent acts. The change from a mean of 3.88 total offenses for males in junior high school to 6.76 delinquent acts in senior high school represents a 74 percent average increase in raw scores. A similar increase is observed for serious offenses. Female graduates also report substantially more delinquent acts in senior than in junior high school; their average increase exceeds 55 percent for the total number of offenses as well as for serious offenses. Given the sizable increases in delinquent behavior among graduates, the declining rates for dropouts assume even greater importance, because they represent a trend counter to the one occurring in the general population.

In terms of raw scores the dropouts' self-reported delinquency declined slightly after they left school. With the exception of serious offenses among females, in the senior high school period the dropouts' mean SRD scores were slightly greater than the means for graduates, although the differences were not significant. In view of the dropouts' significantly more extensive involvement in delinquency while in school, as well as our assumption that involvement in delinquency leads to further delinquency, we would have predicted higher rates of delinquency for the dropouts during the high school years, even if they had not dropped out of school. It may be that more of the dropouts' involvement in delinquent behavior during the senior high school period may be attributed to initially higher rates of delinquency than is the case for graduates. To assess this possibility residual gain scores were calculated. Examination of the mean residual gain scores in Table 5-5 allows a comparison of dropouts and graduates in terms of SRD scores in which the effects of prior delinquency have been partialled out. The residual gain score for dropouts represents the difference between their out-of-school SRD score and an expected score based upon their prior delinquency level. Similarly, the residual gain score for graduates reflects the difference between their high school SRD score and a predicted score based upon their prior delinquency in junior high school.

For the total SRD offenses the mean residual gain score for males is -1.37 for dropouts and $+.06$ for graduates. For females the comparable means are $-.70$ and $+.04$. Dropouts reported fewer offenses than expected while graduates reported slightly more than expected. Both male and female dropouts reported an average of approximately 1 less offense than expected, given their prior SRD scores. The mean gain scores for graduates were positive, but close to 0. Since the average gain for the population is 0 by definition, this finding was expected. Although none of the differences in Table 5-5 are statistically significant at the .05 level, 3 of the 4 differences are substantial, and the direction of the differences is consistent—all dropout means are negative and all graduate means are positive. The failure to find statistically significant differences is due in part to the relatively small number of dropouts involved in the analysis. Nevertheless,

Table 5-5
Mean Self-Reported Delinquency Residual Gain Scores for Dropouts in Period II and Graduates, by Sex

	Males		Females	
	Total	Serious	Total	Serious
Dropouts[a]	-1.37	$-.03$	$-.70$	$-.22$
Graduates	$+ .06$	$+.03$	$+.04$	$+.05$
t test	$- .91$	$-.08$	$-1.29*$	$-.86$

$*p < .10$ (one-tailed test)
[a]See Note 2 of this chapter for N.

our presumption was correct. The slightly higher SRD means for dropouts than graduates in the high school years are explained by the dropouts' initially higher involvement in delinquency. Once they leave school, dropouts commit *fewer* offenses than students in school with similar levels of prior delinquency.

Whether delinquency is measured in terms of police contacts or self reports, similar patterns are revealed: (1) dropouts show a high level of involvement in delinquency while they are in school, and their involvement declines after they leave school; (2) there is limited initial involvement in delinquency on the part of graduates, but it generally increases in the high school years; and finally, (3) the rates of delinquency for subjects out of school are no greater—and possibly slightly lower—than the rates for students in school. Although Elliott reported a class differential [60], an analysis of the effects of class on the involvement of dropouts in delinquency while in and out of school reveals no significant differences. Significant differences by sex are observed in both time periods.

Because these findings are contrary to the widely accepted belief that dropout leads to an increasing risk of delinquent activity, it is necessary to consider the possibility that the relationship is spurious. The findings we have presented on the relationship between delinquency and dropout are consistent with the results of earlier research; in this study the dropouts' involvement in delinquency is substantially greater than the participation of graduates in delinquency. The fact that these data also confirm a higher in-school and a lower out-of-school delinquency rate makes it unlikely that this finding is due to some unique feature of the study population.

With respect to the measure of delinquency based on police contacts, it might be argued that the lower out-of-school rate is simply a consequence of a decrease in visibility which accompanies dropout. We do not deny that dropout may affect the visibility of delinquent acts, but it is unlikely that this could explain the decrease in delinquency among out-of-school youth, in view of the fact that a similar finding was produced when a self-report measure, unaffected by visibility to the police, was employed. Further, the finding that lower-class and minority-group youth have a higher risk of police contact contradicts this possibility, because these youth contribute disproportionately to the dropout categories. If operative, the effect of police bias would be to exaggerate estimates of delinquency among dropouts in comparison with graduates. Another possibility is that if school officials frequently initiate police action, then those in school are more visible. However, school-related offenses such as truancy are not included in this analysis, and in less than one-half of 1 percent of the police departments' investigation reports are school personnel identified as the source of the complaint. This corroborates Elliott's finding that the school is rarely the agency which initiates action resulting in a police contact [60]. It does not appear that differential visibility can account for the decreasing police contact rate among dropouts.

An alternative explanation of this finding involves the deterrent effect of court action on subsequent delinquent behavior. The effect of apprehension by the police, appearance in juvenile court, assignment to a probation officer, or incarceration in a correctional institution may be a reduction in subsequent delinquent behavior, which certainly is the effect intended and desired by police officers and court officials. Having determined that dropouts have significantly higher rates of police contact and adjudication while in school than graduates, we could argue that the dropouts' extensive contacts with the police and courts may result in dropout or pushout and, simultaneously, a decrease in delinquent activity. If police contact or court action has a deterrent effect on subsequent behavior, then this could account for the decline in police contacts and self-reported delinquent behavior among out-of-school respondents.

A definitive answer to this question is difficult to obtain, and our data, while limited concerning this issue, do not support the deterrent hypothesis. Males adjudicated delinquent prior to the initiation of the study report an average of 8.80 SRD offenses during the study in comparison with a mean of 4.81 for the total male population. Among the females who were adjudicated prior to the initiation of this research, the average number of self-reported offenses is 8.50, whereas the total female population reports a mean of 2.84 offenses. In both instances the difference is statistically significant at the .05 level. These are raw scores; the effect of prior delinquency is eliminated in the residual gain scores. The mean residual gain score for males adjudicated in Period I is −.24; this indicates a slightly lower than average high school SRD score, given their initial levels of delinquency. While in the direction postulated by the deterrent hypothesis, this difference is minimal and not statistically significant. With prior delinquency controlled, the delinquency rate of males adjudicated in Period I appears similar to the rate for all males in the cohort. The mean residual gain for females adjudicated in Period I is 1.40, a positive score, which is significantly different from 0 at the .10 level. For females, adjudication is associated with slightly higher than average SRD scores, given their initial levels of delinquency.[3] These data do not support the idea that adjudication is a deterrent for either males or females.

While the problem of spuriousness can never be resolved, the observed relationship between delinquency and dropout cannot be explained by class or sex differences among dropouts and graduates, by differential visibility, or by the deterrent effect of adjudication. Two additional facts support the conclusion that the relationship is not spurious—the police contact and the self-report measures produce consistent findings, and the overall rates are similar to those reported in earlier studies.

The Effect of Delinquency on Dropout

The observation that dropouts have significantly higher police contact and self-reported delinquency rates while in school than graduates appears to be consistent with our expectation that delinquency increases the probability of dropout (see Table 5-1). However, it does not demonstrate that subjects who were highly involved in delinquency at the beginning of the study or in a particular time period have a greater likelihood of dropping out than respondents with limited involvement in delinquency. To ascertain the effect of delinquency on dropout we compare the in-school with the out-of-school transition rates of subjects stratified according to prior involvement in delinquency [44]. Comparison between the strata indicates the relative probability of dropout during a given period for subjects with and without police contact at the beginning of that period; in this analysis the size of each stratum is held constant as are differences in initial marginal frequencies. The in-school transition rates for subjects with no police contacts and juveniles with one or more police contacts at the beginning of each period are presented in Table 5-6. For convenience of reading the rates are stated in percentages.

The transition rates for respondents who experienced police contact are consistently higher than for juveniles with no official record. For each study period the probability of dropout is more than two times greater for those who experienced police contact than for respondents with no police contact. In Period IV, these probabilities differ by a factor of 3. These data offer strong support for the hypothesis that official contact with the police increases the likelihood of dropout.

In- to out-of-school transition rates for respondents with high, moderate, and low levels of self-reported delinquency at the beginning of the study are presented in Table 5-7. These transition rates reflect the probability of dropout over the entire study period. The data confirm that extensive involvement in delinquent behavior, whether or not it leads to official action, increases the probability of dropout. The transition rates of subjects with high initial SRD

Table 5-6
In-School to Out-of-School Transition Rates, by Time Period, Stratified by Police Contact (Percentages)

| Police Contact[a] | Period | | | | | | | |
| | II | | III | | IV | | V | |
	Rate	N	Rate	N	Rate	N	Rate	N
One or More Police Contacts	0.8	308	1.0	418	2.1	464	1.0	464
No Police Contacts	0.3	2307	0.4	2082	0.7	1876	0.4	1652
t value:	4.55**		5.45**		8.75**		5.26**	

**p < .01

aPersons were classified as being in one or the other of these strata at the beginning of each successive time period. Subjects with no police contact at the beginning of Period II could be in either strata at the beginning of Period III. However, respondents who entered the "one or more" strata at any given point remained in it in subsequent time periods.

Table 5-7

In-School to Out-of-School Transition Rates, by Sex, Stratified by Self-Reported Delinquency in Period I (Percentages)

Self-Reported Delinquency I[a]	Males	Females	Total	N
High	3.5	3.3	3.3	775
Moderate	1.6	2.4	2.0	804
Low	1.1	1.4	1.3	1038
t values:				
High vs. Moderate	6.55**	2.57**	6.36**	
High vs. Low	8.57**	6.55**	10.77**	
Moderate vs. Low	2.13*	4.08**	4.22**	

$*p < .05$
$**p < .01$

[a]The membership in each strata was determined at the beginning of the study on the basis of SRD I total scores and could not be readjusted for each period, as was the case with police contacts. For both sexes, those with less than 2 offenses were considered low; those with 2 to 4 offenses, moderate; and those with 5 or more offenses, high. These cutting points were used to trichotomize the SRD I scores for each sex.

scores are more than double the rates of respondents with low scores; more than one-third of the respondents with high initial SRD scores dropped out of school prior to graduation. The direction and magnitude of the differences in Table 5-7 are similar to those in Table 5-6. Together, these data offer impressive support for the hypothesis that delinquency leads to dropout.

The expected relationship between delinquency and dropout is not a simple one: delinquency increases the probability of dropout, which in turn decreases the probability of delinquency. Measures of delinquency based on police contacts and self reports provide evidence in support of this causal sequence. These relationships were postulated in our theoretical scheme and support the basic proposition that the school is the critical social context for the generation of delinquent behavior.

Delinquency and Post-Dropout Experiences

Earlier, we suggested that dropouts' decreasing involvement in delinquency would depend upon several contingencies in their out-of-school experiences, particularly employment and marriage. Dropout should reduce the motivation for delinquency to the extent that the dropout makes a satisfactory adjustment in the adult, working community. Should he encounter difficulty in obtaining a job, establishing new friendships, and making the transition into an adult role, he has simply traded one type of failure for another, and we would not anticipate any dramatic decrease in his motivation for delinquent behavior.

The circumstances of youth after they have dropped out of school vary widely. The unemployed, unmarried, out-of-school teenager probably comes closest to fitting the popular conception of the aimless, drifting high school dropout. On the other hand, males who are steadily employed and married, as well as females who are married, are viewed as having successfully entered conventional adult roles in the community, and we would not expect continued involvement in delinquent behavior. It was, therefore, hypothesized that dropouts who were employed and married should be less delinquent than unmarried and unemployed dropouts.

In Table 5-8 the rate of police contact for out-of-school dropouts by sex, marital status, and employment status is presented. For Periods II, III, and IV, subjects who were out of school were jointly classified with respect to marriage and employment; the rate of police contact during each period was determined for respondents in each category. Subjects who were employed or married for the major part of a given time period were classified as employed or married for that period. Respondents who were married or employed for less than one-half of the period and subjects unmarried or unemployed for the entire period were classified as unmarried and unemployed. Thus, the rates do not accurately reflect relatively short shifts with time from one marriage-employment category to another *within* a given time period, as all offenses in a particular time period are attributed to the single category that characterized the subject for the majority of the time involved. In part, this procedure was adopted as a consequence of the problem involved in collating employment dates with dates

Table 5-8
Police Contact Rates[a] for Out-of-School Dropouts, by Sex, Marital Status, and Employment Status

		Married	Unmarried	Total
Males:	Employed	6.1	14.9	11.8
	Unemployed	0.0	17.5	15.9
	Total	5.1	15.4	13.3
Females:	Employed	4.0	2.4	3.0
	Unemployed	1.8	6.2	3.1
	Total	2.1	4.7	3.0
Total:	Employed	5.2	10.2	8.6
	Unemployed	1.8	11.7	6.0
	Total	2.6	10.9	7.0

[a]The number of police contacts per 100 dropouts in each marriage-employment category. The number of dropouts involved by period are as follows: Period II, 80; III, 136; IV, 484.

of police contacts, as the former were particularly difficult to specify. The rates in Table 5-8 reflect the total experience of dropouts in various marriage-employment categories through time; a given dropout may have contributed to the unmarried-unemployed rate for Period II, the unmarried-employed rate for Period III, and the married-employed rate for Period IV.

While out of school, male dropouts had 25 official police contacts, and female dropouts had 8. Thus, this analysis involves only 33 offenses. An examination of the rates reveals that for males marital status is the variable most highly associated with police contact. The police contact rate for unmarried males is more than three times the rate for married males. The rate for unemployed dropouts is also greater than for employed dropouts, but the difference is limited. As expected, males who were unmarried and unemployed had the highest rate of police contacts, whereas married and unemployed males had the lowest rate. This finding must be viewed with caution, because there were very few cases of this type—most of the married male dropouts were also employed. Nevertheless, it is clear that marriage rather than employment is the critical variable.

In general, the same conclusions apply to female dropouts, but the limited number of police contacts they experienced forces us to view these findings as highly tentative. Again, the highest rate is found in the unemployed-unmarried category. The rate for unmarried females is more than twice the rate for married females, but there is no difference in the rates according to employment status. The lowest rates are found in the married-unemployed and the employed-unmarried categories. The first of these presumably describes the typical housewife; the second depicts the career woman. Either marriage or employment presumably is a deterrent to delinquency, but marriage and employment apparently do *not* work together to deter delinquency for female dropouts. Dropouts who do not marry or obtain employment appear to have the greatest risk of police contact.

Combining the males and females we confirm the importance of marital status—the delinquency rate of unmarried dropouts is four times higher than the rate of married dropouts. The rate of police contact for all employed dropouts is higher than for unemployed dropouts; however, this is due primarily to the large number of married and unemployed females who have very limited involvement with the police.

The results of a similar analysis employing self-reported delinquent behavior are presented in Table 5-9. This analysis is limited to the respondents who dropped out during Period II and were out of school for the entire time span covered on the second SRD measure. Changes in marital or employment status during the three-year period covered by the SRD measure could not be related to changes in self-reported behavior. Also, the small number of cases did not permit a simultaneous analysis by sex, marital status, and employment status. Consequently, only the mean SRD scores (Period II to IV) for dropouts by

Table 5-9

Mean Total Self-Reported Delinquency Scores for Period II to IV for Dropouts Out of School in Period II, by Marital Status and Employment Status

Employment Status	Marital Status		
	Married Entire Time	Unmarried or Married Part of Time	Total[a]
Employed Part Time	1.50	6.25	6.00 (28)
Not Employed	2.85	6.34	3.95 (19)
	2.53 (17)	6.65 (30)	5.17 (47)

[a]Figures in parentheses are Ns.

marital and employment status are presented. Differences by sex will be discussed, but are not shown in Table 5-9.

The relationships in Table 5-9 are similar to the ones observed with the police contact measure. Marriage again appears to be a more important variable than employment; the mean SRD score of those in the unmarried category is more than two and one-half times the score of married dropouts. This difference was found for male and female dropouts.[4] The difference in means of the employed and unemployed dropouts is misleading, as is the case with the data on police contacts. For unemployed males the mean is nearly twice as large as the mean of the employed male dropouts (8.64 and 4.50); this indicates a relationship between delinquency and unemployment for males. However, employed females report a higher mean number of offenses than unemployed females (4.45 and 3.77); again, this is due to the low mean SRD score for married and unemployed females (2.85). Unmarried and unemployed females report a higher average number of offenses than unmarried and employed females (6.20 and 4.91). The small number of cases (5 and 12) demands that we view these findings with caution; however, it appears that unemployment is associated with higher levels of self-reported delinquency for married and unmarried males, as well as for unmarried females. In no case are these differences as large as the ones observed for married and unmarried dropouts. The number of cases is small, but the relationships are similar whether self-report or police contact data are employed, and this consistency lends credence to the general finding.

Summary

Although previous research has demonstrated that high school dropouts have higher rates of official delinquency than high school graduates, the nature of the relationship had not been determined. The dropouts, both male and female, have four times more police contacts than the graduates, and the dropouts also report more delinquent behavior. Nongraduates, who were in school at the end of the study but did not graduate, are even more highly involved in officially recorded delinquency. Involuntary dropouts report about the same number of delinquent acts as graduates. In comparison, the educationally handicapped and capable dropouts report more delinquent behavior than graduates.

Analyzing the effect of dropout on delinquency, we find that dropouts consistently have higher police contact rates than graduates for every period they are in school, and these rates increase with time while they are in school. However, the police contact rate systematically declines in the period after which dropout occurs, and it continues to decline in subsequent time periods. In the later periods the rates are substantially lower than the rates for graduates. Use of the SRD measure produces similar findings. The dropouts reach a high level of involvement in delinquency prior to leaving school, but once they are out of school, their involvement in serious offenses declines substantially, and the total number of offenses reported declines slightly. In comparison, graduates report an increasing number of delinquent acts, as well as serious offenses, with time. Whether delinquency is measured in terms of police contacts or self reports, similar patterns are revealed. The rates of delinquency for those out of school are no greater—and possibly slightly lower—than the rates for students in school. The effects of class on the involvement of dropouts in delinquency while in and out of school are negligible. The relationship between delinquency and dropout cannot be explained by class or sex differences among dropouts and graduates, by differential visibility, or by the deterrent effect of adjudication.

The expected relationship between delinquency and dropout is observed—delinquency increases the probability of dropout, which in turn decreases the probability of delinquency. This causal sequence is supported with measures of delinquency based on police contacts and self reports. For each study period the probability of dropout is more than two times higher for those who experienced police contact than for subjects with no police contact. Extensive involvement in delinquent behavior, whether or not it leads to official action, increases the probability of dropout.

The dropouts' out-of-school experiences with respect to marriage and employment are related to their involvement in delinquency. With marriage and employment, the dropout makes the transition from adolescence into conventional adult roles. It is this factor, we suggest, that accounts for the general decline in the dropouts' rates of delinquent behavior. This interpretation is consistent with the finding that marriage is a more significant deterrent for delinquency than employment, as marriage is a less ambiguous indicator of adult status than employment, particularly when sporadic and part-time employment to some extent characterize student roles.

The employment-delinquency relationship is more complex than the association between marriage and delinquency. Unemployed males and unmarried females have consistently higher police contact and self-reported rates of delinquency. For married females, the opposite is true; girls with jobs have higher rates than unemployed females. In part, then, the lower rates of delinquency observed among dropouts may be attributed to changes in marital and employment status which follow dropout. We have concentrated on the relationship between delinquency and dropout rather than the explanation of either phenomenon. The explanation for the high rates of in-school delinquency on the part of dropouts, as well as the explanation of dropout itself, requires examination of the causal sequence postulated in our theoretical formulation.

Notes

1. This inference is consistent with the conclusions regarding differential risks presented in Chapter 4, because dropouts are disproportionately drawn from lower-class and minority-group youth.

2. In Period II (early ninth to mid-tenth grade) 109 subjects dropped out of school. Fifty percent ($N = 55$) of these dropouts failed to complete the fourth annual questionnaire and thus had missing data for the second SRD measure. The means in Table 5-4 for senior high school and the residual gain means in Table 5-5 are based upon an N of 54. A check for possible selectivity in this loss involved comparison of the offense rates in junior high school for those with and without SRD scores for senior high school. Initially, those with both scores reported a mean of 8.81 SRD offenses, and those without a second SRD score reported 8.34 SRD offenses. Neither this difference nor the difference in their serious SRD scores in Period I was statistically significant, and there was no evidence of a selective loss with respect to prior delinquency scores. This loss did not affect the police contact measures, as official records were searched in the appropriate geographical areas for all dropouts and graduates whether or not they completed each of the annual questionnaires; except for 8 cases, the whereabouts of all subjects were known even if interviews were not completed.

3. Recently, it has been argued that adjudication is a form of labeling, which leads to increasing delinquency on the part of those labeled. This finding provides limited support for such an argument.

4. The means for married and "unmarried-married part of the time" males are 2.00 and 8.46, respectively. For females the comparable means are 2.60 and 5.30. However, the N in the married male category is only 2; all other Ns involved in the calculation of means exceed 13.

6

Independent Predictors of Delinquency and Dropout

In this chapter we describe the development of our predictor measures and their independent relationships with the criterion variables, delinquency and dropout.[1] Some of the conditional relationships specified in our theoretical formulation are also considered. We examine the predictive effects of initial scores or origin predictors as well as gain predictors, measures of the direction and magnitude of change in these scores during the course of the study. The origin measures show the static relationship or the predictive utility of the original score on a variable for subsequent delinquent behavior or dropout. The gain predictor relates the direction and amount of change in the measure through time to the dependent variable and thereby reflects the dynamics of the predictor.

An unequivocal causal argument can be made on the basis of the origin predictors, as the temporal order of the independent and dependent variables is always correct. This is also true of gain scores for dropout, because they reflect change from the initial measurement to the beginning of the period in which the student leaves school. Hence, the gain predictors always involve the correct temporal sequence as they measure change prior to the occurrence of dropout. The gain scores for dropouts involve variable lengths of time, whereas the comparable values for graduates measure change throughout the study. For delinquent behavior the gain score reflects the average increase or decrease from the initial level over the next 3 years. It may be recalled that one measure of the dependent variable consists of self reports of delinquent behavior for Periods II through IV. Because the gain predictors are based on information obtained in Periods II, III, and IV, there is overlap in the time period covered by the gain scores and the self reports, and the issue of temporal order cannot be fully resolved. We recognize that contamination is possible, but believe that it is highly unlikely because the residual gain scores represent an average for a three-year period. In any case, we adopt a conservative approach and do not argue for the causal importance of a variable on the basis of gain scores unless the origin measure is also predictive of subsequent delinquent behavior.

Initially we assumed that both the original level and changes through time in a variable might be important determinants of delinquency and dropout, but we had no a priori assumptions about the nature of the relationship between origin and gain scores. The origin and gain measures may have both direct and interaction effects on subsequent rates of delinquency or dropout. For example, increased exposure to delinquent behavior may have no effect on subsequent delinquency for subjects whose initial level of exposure is high, although it may have a substantial effect for persons with a low initial level. Origin and gain scores for a variable are statistically independent because residual gain scores hold origin levels constant. The combined effect of the origin and gain predictors is measured by the multiple correlation coefficient.

Two measures of the criterion variable, delinquency, are used. The first is a frequency score or the number of delinquent acts reported during the study period. The second is a gain score, a measure of the relative gains, either positive or negative, in delinquent behavior during the study with level of involvement in delinquent activity prior to the study controlled. The gain measure reflects the relative change in delinquency attributable to the predictor variable. For comparative purposes the product-moment correlations between prior delinquency and the initial level for a variable are presented. We use the term *prior delinquency* with reference to self-reported delinquency for the junior high school years or prior to our initial data collection. When police contact reports serve as the source of data about delinquency, comparable measures of frequency and gains are employed. In the analysis of dropout, we examine the relationships between the origin and gain predictors and Final Dropout Status, a dichotomy in which intellectually capable dropouts are distinguished from intellectually capable nondropouts. Involuntary and educationally handicapped dropouts are excluded from these analyses because our theoretical propositions are stated with respect to capable dropouts.

Failure and Anticipated Failure

We hypothesized that the causal sequence leading to delinquency and dropout begins with failure or anticipated failure to achieve culturally valued goals. We identified three distinct sets of goals that might serve as instigators for delinquency and dropout in the locus of the community, school, and home. In each annual questionnaire a series of inquiries related to success were made, and we developed "success" or success-failure scales for the community, school, and home contexts. The items in these scales are shown in Appendix B. The community scale reflects the individual's assessment of his chances to achieve his educational and occupational aspirations.[2]

Three measures of success in school were developed. The first scale, a composite of achievement test scores, grade point averages, and teachers' evaluations of academic performance, reflects academic success or achievement in the formal system of the school. Teachers' evaluations were obtained only in the first year. Although comparable data were not available for later years, the teachers' evaluations were included in the first-year scale because these judgments were relevant to academic success, and this scale serves as the origin predictor.[3]

According to the values of the youth culture, involvement in school organizations and activities is an important criterion of success in the informal system of the school. Gordon says that achievement in activities is the most important determinant of a student's status in school [87]. The activity scale is based on two measures of the discrepancy between a student's desired and actual level of participation in school activities.[4] The third measure of success in school reflects status deprivation or informal distinctions in relation to peers. The scale is based on the questions posed by Reiss and Rhodes to measure status deprivation [176].[5] Finally, to measure success in the home we constructed a two-item scale pertaining to parental acceptance.[6]

Only 2 of the 5 success scales are related to social class or minority-group status at any point in time. With one exception, the correlations with the activity, status deprivation, and home scales are close to 0. There is a weak correlation between status deprivation and social class in the first year.[7] However, for the last year this correlation is 0. Although lower-class youth make more unfavorable status comparisons during the ninth grade, this is no longer the case in the twelfth grade. At least with respect to the informal status system of peers, the school appears to be a class-leveling context.

The community and academic scales are associated with social class, and the latter is also related to minority-group status. It is somewhat surprising to find the community scale related to class but not to minority-group status. Nevertheless, the expectation that youth on the lower end of the class hierarchy are more likely to anticipate failure with respect to educational and occupational goals is realized, although the relationship is weak. In comparison with the community scale, the association between class and academic achievement is more consistent from year to year and is stronger; all of the correlations fall in the moderate range, but none are as strong as class-linked theories of delinquency would suggest. In no case does class account for as much as 10 percent of the variance in the success scale scores. Minority-group status appears to be even less important as the correlations are uniformly weaker. There are no sex differences in any of the class or minority status relationships.

Failure and Delinquent Behavior

The static and dynamic relationships between the success-failure scales and subsequent delinquency are presented in Table 6-1. It is apparent that scores on the community scale are not predictive of delinquency for either males or females. Only 4 of the 16 zero-order correlations are statistically significant, and these values are so low that no substantive importance can be attributed to them. Neither the initial perception of opportunities nor the direction and amount of change in these perceptions is related to the amount of change in delinquent behavior. Consequently, these data offer no support for Cloward and Ohlin's original hypothesis. Correlating prior delinquency with subjects' percep-

Table 6-1
Correlations[a] Between Success-Failure Predictors and Measures of Delinquent Behavior[b]

		Males					
				Delinquent Behavior			
Success-Failure Predictors		Total SRD Frequency	Serious SRD Frequency	Total SRD Gain	Serious SRD Gain	Total SRD Prior	Serious SRD Prior
Community:	Origin	.06	.05	.02	.02	.13	.12
	Gain	.07	.05	.03	.03		
	Origin & Gain	.07	.05	.03	.04		
Academic:	Origin	−.13	−.14	−.08	−.10	−.23	−.23
	Gain	−.03	−.01	−.01	−.01		
	Origin & Gain	−.14	−.14	−.08	−.10		
Activity:	Origin	−.08	−.07	−.04	−.05	−.13	−.10
	Gain	−.08	−.08	−.04	−.06		
	Origin & Gain	−.11	−.10	−.04	−.06		
Status Deprivation:	Origin	.06	.06	.08	.06	−.04	−.06
	Gain	.05	.01	.02	−.01		
	Origin & Gain	.06	.06	.08	.06		
Home:	Origin	.12	.08	.04	.04	.28	.20
	Gain	.17	.12	.14	.11		
	Origin & Gain	.21	.14	.15	.12		

		Females					
				Delinquent Behavior			
Success-Failure Predictors		Total SRD Frequency	Serious SRD Frequency	Total SRD Gain	Serious SRD Gain	Total SRD Prior	Serious SRD Prior
Community:	Origin	.05	.05	.02	.04	.11	.08
	Gain	.09	.01	.06	.00		
	Origin & Gain	.09	.05	.06	.04		
Academic:	Origin	−.08	−.03	−.05	−.01	−.13	−.17
	Gain	−.10	.00	−.08	.01		
	Origin & Gain	−.13	−.03	−.08	.00		
Activity:	Origin	−.03	.01	−.01	.01	−.03	−.04
	Gain	−.01	.02	.02	.02		
	Origin & Gain	−.03	.02	.02	.02		
Status Deprivation:	Origin	.03	.01	−.01	.01	−.03	−.04
	Gain	.03	−.01	.00	−.02		
	Origin & Gain	.03	.01	.07	.02		
Home:	Origin	.19	.07	.10	.06	.23	.11
	Gain	.26	.11	.25	.11		
	Origin & Gain	.33	.13	.27	.13		

[a]$r \geqslant .06, p < .05$ $r \geqslant .08, p < .01$ $R \geqslant .08, p < .05$ $R \geqslant .10, p < .01$

[b]The abbreviations, TSR and SSR, refer to Total Self-Reported Delinquent Behavior and Serious Self-Reported Delinquent Behavior, respectively.

tions of educational and occupational opportunities, other researchers have claimed support for the disjunction hypothesis. We observe weak but statistically significant correlations with prior delinquency. Hence, this finding is consistent with earlier studies. However, our data indicate that there is no predictive power in the relationship between anticipated failure to achieve long-range goals and subsequent delinquency. There is less support for Cloward and Ohlin's disjunction hypothesis than for an alternative formulation: involvement in delinquency produces an expectation that one's chances to achieve long-range educational and occupational goals are limited (see Bordua [16]). The data are not presented in tabular form, but these results are duplicated with police contacts as the dependent variable. The correlation between the origin measure on the community scale and prior number of police contacts is .11, but it is .06 with the future number of police contacts and .02 with gains in police contacts. All of these correlations are weak, but the relationship between the origin score on the community scale and prior delinquency is consistently stronger than with subsequent delinquency.

The origin predictor on the academic scale is correlated weakly with the total and serious SRD measures for males. On the other hand, this predictor is related only to the total (serious and nonserious) number of self-reported offenses during the study for females. The pattern is reversed with the gain predictor for academic achievement—gains are not predictive of delinquency for males, but they are predictive of the total SRD frequency and gain scores for females. All of these relationships are weak. We conclude that there is only limited support for the hypothesis that academic achievement is related to subsequent delinquent behavior.

The relationships between the origin levels for academic achievement and prior delinquency are generally stronger than the predictive relationships. Again, there appears to be evidence for the hypothesis that delinquency causes academic failure, particularly with reference to boys. To reiterate, the findings of cross-sectional studies can be misleading—low academic achievement has limited predictive utility. In the case of males, the predictive power of academic performance is considerably less than is suggested by its correlation with prior delinquency. The implication of these findings is that delinquency and poor academic performance are mutually reinforcing, although neither relationship is strong. It is worth noting that the origin predictor for academic success is more highly correlated with subsequent police contacts than frequency of self reports; for males and females these correlations are moderate. The origin scores for academic achievement are also more highly correlated with gain scores for police contact than SRD frequency. In other words, poor academic performance is a better predictor of future police contacts than of subsequent delinquent behavior. This suggests that there may be a relationship between school failure and police contacts independent of the frequency of delinquent acts; for students with some involvement in delinquent behavior, the likelihood of police contact is slightly higher for those who are not doing well in school than for juveniles performing satisfactorily.

There is no support for the hypothesis that failure to achieve activity goals is conducive to delinquent behavior. None of the correlation coefficients for females are statistically significant. Although a number of the correlations for males are significant, they are uniformly in the opposite direction from the one predicted. Male subjects who report some discrepancy between their actual and desired involvement in school activities have slightly *lower* frequencies of self-reported delinquent behavior than boys who report no discrepancy. The negative finding is not the result of delinquency-prone males having both low aspirations and low involvement, which is one way of obtaining low discrepancy scores. Males who report extensive involvement in school activities during the ninth grade have slightly higher SRD scores than boys who report low involvement. In short, limited involvement in school activities is not causally related to delinquent behavior.

The hypothesis that status deprivation leads to delinquent behavior also fails to receive support. All of the correlations are low, and the ones that are statistically significant are in the wrong direction. The correlations with prior SRD scores are in the correct direction, though they are equally low. The latter outcome is consistent with the findings of Reiss and Rhodes [176]. They employed similar questions and found a weak but positive relationship between status deprivation and prior delinquency. However, the measure of status deprivation is not a predictor of future delinquency; our data suggest that there is a weak *negative* relationship between status deprivation and subsequent delinquent behavior.

The hypothesis that parental rejection is conducive to delinquency is supported for females. The relationship between the home scale and the SRD scores is not strong, but it is consistent; further, some of the correlations fall in the moderate range. For males, the origin measure for the home scale is not predictive of SRD gains, although it has weak predictive power with respect to frequency scores. Similarly, there are weak associations between the gain measure for the home scale and SRD frequency and gain scores. All of the multiple correlations are significant and vary from weak to moderate in strength. There is some support for the parental rejection hypothesis for males and females, though the relationships are somewhat stronger for females.

Several general comments about the relationships between the measures of success-failure and delinquent behavior are in order. Only limited academic achievement and parental rejection appear to have any predictive value for subsequent delinquency, and in neither case are the relationships strong. Thus, the only school-context measure that is significantly related to subsequent delinquent behavior assesses formal academic achievement. The measures designed to tap peer culture values do not have predictive power. We are tempted to interpret these negative findings as the result of our failure to measure relevant aspects of the youth culture. However, Toby and Toby found that academic achievement was the only school-related variable predictive of subjects choosing delinquent associates [238]. To assess the importance of the peer culture they employed a popularity rating based upon sociometric choices and a sociometric measure of athletic status. There are, then, empirical grounds for challenging the view that failure to achieve peer culture goals is conducive to delinquency.

The relative importance of academic achievement and parental acceptance differs according to sex. Of the two, parental acceptance clearly is the more powerful predictor for females, whereas academic achievement is the more powerful predictor of subsequent delinquent behavior for males. The hypothesis that delinquency is primarily a response to failure generated in the school receives more support with respect to males than females. This is a tentative conclusion, as we have not considered the conditional variables in this relationship. Choice between these predictor variables is an academic question, for the data suggest that there is a mutually reinforcing process between delinquency and both academic achievement and parental acceptance. Limited parental acceptance is not only conducive to subsequent delinquent behavior, but also appears to be a consequence of prior delinquency. The same may be said of academic achievement. These relationships were anticipated. However, this complicates the task of causal analysis—the obvious inference is that researchers cannot rely on their subjects' prior delinquency to evaluate theoretical claims.

Finally, the findings with respect to success in the community and youth culture challenge some prominent theories of delinquency. Status deprivation is not a predictor of subsequent delinquency; in fact, our data could be interpreted as indicating that status deprivation inhibits involvement in delinquency. Neither failure to achieve activity goals nor anticipated failure to achieve educational or occupational goals are conducive to subsequent delinquent behavior. The latter finding leads us to question whether efforts to increase educational and occupational opportunities in delinquency prevention programs are appropriate.

Failure and Capable Dropout

The point biserial correlations between the success-failure scales and Final Dropout Status are presented in Table 6-2. The correlations between community success and dropout are all in the correct direction, but they are weak. The correlations with the origin and gain predictors are statistically significant for males; however, for females the gain measure is not significantly related to community success. Capable male students who perceive low and decreasing opportunities to achieve their educational and occupational goals are more likely to drop out. The perception of decreasing opportunities through time is not related to dropout for females, though initially low perceptions are. With respect to dropout there is some support for the hypothesis concerning limited opportunity.

Table 6-2
Correlations[a] Between Success-Failure Predictors and Final Dropout Status

Success-Failure Predictors	Final Dropout Status					
	Males			Females		
	Origin	Gain	Origin & Gain	Origin	Gain	Origin & Gain
Community	.12	.10	.16	.13	.03	.13
Academic	−.30	−.16	−.34	−.23	−.15	−.28
Activity	−.01	−.27	−.27	−.03	.31	−.31
Status Deprivation[b]	−.09	−	−	−.04	−	−
Home	.08	.10	.13	.08	.09	.13

[a] $r \geqslant .06, p < .05$ $\qquad$ $R \geqslant .08, p < .05$
$r \geqslant .08, p < .01$ $\qquad$ $R \geqslant .10, p < .01$
[b] There are no gain scores available except for dropouts in Period V.

A separate analysis of educational and occupational aspirations reveals that in the ninth grade the dropouts' aspirations were lower than the aspirations of those who eventually graduated. The dropouts also tended to adjust their aspirations downward prior to leaving school. This trend was particularly evident in educational aspirations. The tendency to lower aspirations in anticipation of leaving school reduces the disjunction between aspirations and perceived opportunities and may account for the low correlations between the gain predictors and dropout.

The correlations in Table 6-2 indicate that academic achievement is related to subsequent dropout. The strength of the origin predictor is moderate for males and females, while the relationships are weak in terms of the gain predictors. The multiple correlation between the origin and gain predictors and Final Dropout Status is moderate for both sexes. Students with initially low academic achievement and respondents who experience decreasing academic success have a greater likelihood of dropping out. These data support the hypothesis that limited academic success is conducive to dropout. Because the analysis is restricted to capable dropouts, who by definition have adequate intellectual ability, this finding cannot be attributed to the dropouts' limited ability.

In terms of the origin predictor the relationship between the activity scale and dropout is not significant for either males or females. Initial failure to achieve activity goals is unrelated to dropout. However, the gain measure is related to dropout. What is significant about this relationship is that a *decreasing* discrepancy between desired and actual involvement in activities is predictive of dropout. A separate analysis of the elements in the two discrepancy scores comprising the scale indicates that a substantial reduction in the desired level of involvement, rather than greater achievement, accounts for the observed relationship. Dropouts' participation in school-related activities is uniformly low throughout their years in school. The downward adjustment in activity goals prior to dropout is paralleled by a similar, though less dramatic, decline in educational and occupational aspirations. The decline in the desired level of involvement in activities is particularly marked in Period IV—apparently this adjustment is linked uniquely to dropout during the senior year. After leaving school, dropouts typically explain that they were unable to participate in the kind or number of school activities they desired. However, our data indicate that potential dropouts and graduates are indistinguishable on this variable in the ninth grade; if they differ at all, dropouts are less likely to report discrepancies in desired and actual participation in school activities at the beginning of the period in which they leave school. The findings that dropouts lower their occupational, educational, and school-activity aspirations prior to leaving school are consistent with the idea that dropout involves an internal explanation of failure. As we noted earlier, persons who attribute blame internally have two possible adaptations, apart from developing greater personal competence: they can lower their aspirations or withdraw from efforts to achieve unattainable goals. In our study population the dropouts use both options. Apparently the downward revision of aspirations serves as an initial step taken by youth before they finally give up entirely on the school and drop out. This may be another way of saying that a process comparable to anticipatory socialization takes place prior to dropout.

There appears to be no significant relationship between status deprivation and dropout for girls. For males there is a weak and barely significant correlation between the origin predictor and dropout. We draw essentially the same conclusion about the measure of success in the home. Although the relationships are in the predicted direction and many of them are statistically significant, perception of limited parental acceptance is a weak predictor of dropout. Of the success-failure measures the academic scale is clearly the most powerful predictor for capable dropouts. There is, then, limited support for the hypothesis that anticipation of failure to achieve educational and occupational aspirations is conducive to dropout.

A General Measure of Success and Failure

We hypothesized that the experience of failure in various social contexts may be cumulative, and if this is the case, pressure for delinquent adaptations should increase. Since only the academic achievement scale for males and the measure of success in the home for females are predictive of future delinquency, it is questionable whether a general measure of success and failure across contexts would be a more powerful predictor of delinquency. On the other hand, the academic achievement and community success scales have some predictive power for dropout; hence, a general measure might produce an improvement in predictability. On the basis of the inter-scale correlations, we concluded that they were relatively independent (see Appendix A). A general success-failure scale was constructed by summing the individual's normalized scores on each of the five original scales; the scores on academic achievement and status deprivation were necessarily reversed so that a low score corresponded to a limited degree of failure, and a high score indicated extensive failure. This procedure has the effect of weighting each scale equally. Three of the 5 scales pertain to the school context, and the summated scale reflects this emphasis on failure in school.

The general scale does not increase predictive utility. For males, the academic scale produces slightly higher product-moment correlations with subsequent delinquency scores than the general scale, and the home scale is more highly correlated with delinquency for females than the general scale. Academic achievement scores are better predictors of dropout than the general scale for males and females. Apparently the weak relationship between community success and dropout is a function of the correlation of community success with academic achievement (see Appendix A). In any event, the idea that a measure of failure in diverse social contexts would be a better predictor of delinquency and dropout proved to be incorrect.

The Explanation of Failure

We suggested that the explanation of failure is an important conditional variable in the relationship between failure and delinquency. Specifically, the relationship was thought to be contingent upon external, rather than internal attribution of blame. The approach employed in this research is similar to Rosenzweig's [186; 187]. Four cartoons were included in the first annual questionnaire. Each portrayed two characters involved in a frustrating situation. One of the characters made a statement; the subjects were instructed to write their response in the blank "balloon" attached to the other character. This is a projective measure in which it is assumed that the subject identifies with the frustrated character, and his response represents his reactions to similar situations. Responses were scored according to the direction of aggression by three independent judges. The Coefficient of Agreement between judges' ratings is .79, an indication of a fairly high degree of consensus [181; 182]. A composite score was derived for the four situations to classify respondents either as persons who attribute blame externally (extrapunitive), attribute blame to themselves (intropunitive), or avoid imputation of blame (impunitive).[8]

The classification of subjects on the measure of punitiveness is presented in Table 6-3. A slightly higher proportion of females than males are classified as extrapunitive, whereas more males than females are classified as impunitive. Lower-class and minority-group youth tend to be slightly more impunitive than middle-class and Anglo youth, but the relationships between punitiveness and

Table 6-3
Punitiveness, by Sex (Percentages)

Punitiveness	Males Percentage	Females Percentage	Total Percentage
Extrapunitive	16.5	21.9	19.2
Impunitive	39.4	31.6	35.6
Intropunitive	37.0	38.6	37.7
No Response or Unclassifiable	7.1	7.9	7.5
Total	100.0	100.0	100.0
N	1338	1279	2617

class and minority-group status are not statistically significant. There is no substantive support for our speculation that lower-class youth might be less extrapunitive than middle-class youth.

Failure, External Attribution
of Blame, and Delinquency

Having proposed that the linkage between failure and delinquency may be contingent upon an external attribution of blame, we examined the conditional relationship by means of three-way analyses of variance. The origin and gain measures of success-failure and the punitiveness classification were employed as the predictor variables with SRD gain scores as the dependent variable. The earlier findings that only academic achievement and home success were predictive of future delinquency are confirmed. Few of the direct or interaction effects for the other success-failure scales are significant. Therefore, we limit our discussion to the relationships involving punitiveness, delinquency, and academic success or parental acceptance. The results of these three-factor analyses of variance on SRD gain scores are presented in Tables 6-4 and 6-5.

The predictive capacity of the origin measure for academic achievement is again demonstrated for changes in total SRD scores (Table 6-4). The gain measure is also predictive of total SRD gains for females. These findings coincide with the results of our earlier correlational analysis. Of more immediate concern is the fact that punitiveness is not directly predictive of delinquency for either males or females. However, the interaction of punitiveness and academic achievement gain scores produces a statistically significant effect on total SRD gains for females, and this interaction effect approaches significance for males.

The greatest positive gains in delinquency occur among extrapunitive boys with low and decreasing academic achievement. There are also slightly greater total SRD gains for extrapunitive males with high academic achievement. Among

Table 6-4

Analysis of Variance F Values for Origin and Gain Scores for Academic Success and Punitiveness on Self-Reported Delinquency Gain Scores

	Males		Females	
Direct Effects	Total SRD Gain	Serious SRD Gain	Total SRD Gain	Serious SRD Gain
(A) Academic Success − Origin	6.00**	.34	7.42**	1.29
(B) Punitiveness	1.26	.71	.16	.17
(C) Academic Success − Gain	1.02	.09	2.99*	.21
Interaction Effects				
A × B	1.59	.47	1.30	.41
A × C	1.17	.07	1.17	.99
B × C	.44	2.05	2.66*	.98
A × B × C	1.65	.74	1.61	1.17

*$p < .05$
**$p < .01$

Table 6-5

Analysis of Variance F Values for Origin and Gain Scores for Home Success and Punitiveness on Self-Reported Delinquency Gain Scores

	Males		Females	
Direct Effects	Total SRD Gain	Serious SRD Gain	Total SRD Gain	Serious SRD Gain
(A) Home Success − Origin	1.36	.95	7.48**	.68
(B) Punitiveness	1.59	.36	.61	.09
(C) Home Success − Gain	15.45**	4.25*	26.49**	3.07
Interaction Effects				
A × B	.93	.22	1.12	2.02
A × C	.48	1.70	.81	1.34
B × C	.91	.40	1.69	.81
A × B × C	.43	.62	.96	.92

*$p < .05$
**$p < .01$

boys with moderate academic achievement, the ones who are impunitive have a higher average positive gain than those who are extrapunitive. The data for males are not completely consistent, but offer some support for the hypothesis about external attribution of blame. The interaction effect is slightly greater for females than males, and examination of their mean total SRD gains reveals a different pattern. The greatest gain in delinquency occurs among extrapunitive females who have moderate academic achievement scores that decrease through time. Given their initial SRD scores, they report an average of two and one-half more offenses than predicted. In contrast, the second greatest gain is observed among impunitive girls whose initial academic achievement is moderate and remains stable throughout the study period. In other words, the major increase in delinquent behavior occurs among females with moderate initial academic achievement that is either stable or decreasing. In general, positive gains in delinquency are associated with extrapunitiveness and decreasing academic success; negative gains are related to intropunitiveness and increasing academic success. However, the greatest relative gains in delinquent behavior occur among females initially classified as moderate in achievement.

There are no significant interaction effects between origin and gain scores on the home scale and punitiveness (Table 6-5). These findings are consistent with the correlational analysis; the origin and gain measures predict total SRD gains for females, but only the gain measure on the home scale is predictive for males. In the relationship between parental acceptance and delinquency, punitiveness does not appear to be a relevant conditional variable.

An examination of the means in this analysis reveals the power of the gain measure on the home scale. All subjects classified as having increasing scores on the home scale have negative delinquency gain scores, and all respondents with decreasing scores have positive delinquency gains. For males, the greatest positive gains in delinquency occur among those in the moderate category in terms of the origin predictor, whereas for females they are found among those with initially low parental acceptance. Interestingly, this pattern is the reverse of the one observed for academic achievement.

There is some support for the idea that external attribution of blame specifies the relationship between decreasing academic achievement and increasing involvement in delinquent behavior. However, there is no indication that punitiveness is directly related to delinquent behavior; further, it fails to produce any significant interactions with the origin measures for the academic and home scales or for the gain measure for home success. In view of these findings, we question whether punitiveness plays as critical a role in the generation of delinquent behavior as we suggested in our theoretical formulation.

Failure, Internal Attribution
of Blame, and Dropout

Because dropout was treated as a dichotomous variable, it was not possible to test for interaction effects with analysis of variance. Therefore, we examined the joint effects of failure and internal attributions of blame by means of transition rates.[9] Although comparable analyses were conducted for each of the success-failure measures, we limit the discussion to the scales predictive of dropout. Overall, there are no significant differences in the transition rates for respondents classified as extrapunitive or intropunitive.

Although correlation coefficients cannot be read in this manner, it is appropriate to interpret transition rates as probability estimates. An average of 3.8 percent of the males and 3.9 percent of the females in school at the beginning of each study period dropped out during that period. Stated differently, the chance is approximately 1 in 25 that a student will drop out in any given period. However, the proportion of dropouts who left school in each period varies; the greatest proportion dropped out in Period IV.

Trichotomizing the origin and gain scores on the community scale, we label the resulting strata as low, moderate, or high disjunction to reflect the extent of discrepancy between aspirations and expectations to achieve educational and occupational goals.[10] The figures in Table 6-6 show the effects of initial and changing disjunction with respect to these long-range goals. Approximately 6 percent of the subjects with high initial educational and occupational disjunction drop out each year compared to 3 percent of those with low disjunction. Subjects with increasing disjunction tend to have higher dropout rates than those with decreasing disjunction. Among males with initially high and increasing disjunction, those classified as extrapunitive have substantially higher dropout rates than the intropunitive boys; in fact, they have the highest dropout rates. The next highest rate is found among extrapunitive boys with initially high and stable disjunction. For each origin level, extrapunitive boys have higher rates of dropout than intropunitive males. This trend persists with gain scores; in only 2 of the 9 substrata is the dropout rate higher among intropunitive than extrapunitive males. Clearly, the data do not support the hypothesis that dropouts are more likely to be intropunitive.

The pattern is somewhat different for females. The highest dropout rate is found among intropunitive girls with initially high and increasing disjunction, which is exactly where we predicted it would be. This provides support for our hypothesis, although girls classified as intropunitive do not have consistently higher rates of dropout. In 6 of the 9 origin and gain substrata, the transition rates are higher for intropunitive than extrapunitive females; dropout, then, is not systematically related either to intropunitiveness or extrapunitiveness. For the hypothesis regarding punitiveness the data are negative for males and inconclusive for females.

The probability of dropout is strongly related to initially low and decreasing academic achievement (Table 6-7). In the substrata of boys with initially low and decreasing achievement, the rate of dropout is approximately 16 percent or four times higher than the average rate; it is fifteen times higher than the rate for boys with initially high and increasing achievement. During the course of the study, approximately 50 percent of the boys with low and decreasing achievement scores dropped out. Again, for males dropout is linked to extrapunitiveness, not intropunitiveness.

Table 6-6
Mean In- to Out-of-School Transition Rates for Periods II to V, by Community Success, Stratified by Punitiveness (Percentages)

| Community Success: | Males[a] Dropouts, Periods III to V | | | | Females[a] Dropouts, Periods III to V | | | |
| | | Gains | | Dropouts II to V Total | | Gains | | Dropouts II to V Total |
Origin	Decreasing	Stable	Increasing		Decreasing	Stable	Increasing	
		percentages				percentages		
Low Disjunction								
Extrapunitive	2.4	3.6	7.9	3.2	2.9	2.1	4.2	3.1
Impunitive	3.0	3.1	5.5	3.0	3.9	4.6	2.4	2.9
Intropunitive	2.1	2.3	9.9	2.9	3.5	4.1	4.8	3.1
Moderate Disjunction								
Extrapunitive	3.7	5.6	3.6	3.4	8.7	0.0	7.7	4.2
Impunitive	2.6	3.3	7.3	3.2	1.9	3.3	5.9	3.0
Intropunitive	4.1	0.7	2.0	1.9	4.2	3.1	6.6	3.8
High Disjunction								
Extrapunitive	8.6	10.3	10.5	7.2	9.4	1.7	4.0	4.9
Impunitive	6.8	6.8	6.7	5.6	4.1	7.2	9.3	6.4
Intropunitive	7.8	4.4	5.7	6.0	4.2	6.0	11.4	6.0

aSubjects who left school during Period II did not have gain scores and are excluded from the calculation of means for this part of the table. They are included in the total column, in which gain scores are ignored.

Table 6-7
Mean In- to Out-of-School Transition Rates for Periods II to V, by Academic Success, Stratified by Punitiveness (Percentages)

Academic Success:	Males Dropouts[a], Periods III to V				Females Dropouts[a], Periods III to V			
		Gains		Dropouts II to V Total		Gains		Dropouts II to V Total
Origin	Decreasing	Stable	Increasing		Decreasing	Stable	Increasing	
High Achievement								
Extrapunitive	5.9	1.4	0.0	1.2	2.1	1.1	1.6	1.8
Impunitive	5.2	5.8	1.5	3.0	3.2	2.0	0.6	1.3
Intropunitive	4.2	1.1	0.8	1.4	5.9	2.6	2.4	2.6
Moderate Achievement								
Extrapunitive	13.6	10.0	4.4	7.5	12.0	5.9	2.8	5.5
Impunitive	6.6	4.4	1.5	3.2	7.0	1.4	5.2	3.8
Intropunitive	4.8	5.8	3.0	3.7	5.6	6.9	2.6	4.3
Low Achievement								
Extrapunitive	17.2	6.2	8.5	7.2	8.5	4.2	6.6	5.7
Impunitive	14.8	4.4	2.3	5.1	11.9	7.4	4.9	6.7
Intropunitive	13.9	6.6	5.3	7.0	14.5	6.5	2.2	5.9

[a]Students who left school during Period II did not have gain scores and are excluded from the calculation of means for this part of the table. They are included in the total column, in which gain scores are ignored.

For females, the pattern of transition rates according to academic achievement parallels the one observed for community success. The highest dropout rate is found among intropunitive girls with initially low and decreasing achievement. In 6 of the 9 substrata intropunitive girls have higher transition rates than extrapunitive females. There is some support for the hypothesis that among females dropout is a response to low academic achievement and intropunitiveness; however, the relationship is neither a strong nor a consistent one.

For home success, the pattern of relationships is similar to the one noted for the community scale (Table 6-8). The direct effect of initially low and decreasing parental acceptance on dropout is not as strong as initially low and decreasing academic achievement. Dropout tends to be more frequent among extrapunitive males. The data are inconclusive for females. In some substrata the dropout rates are higher for extrapunitive than intropunitive girls; in others the rates are in the opposite direction. We expected to find the strongest support for the hypothesis among females with low and decreasing parental acceptance, but the extrapunitive girls have slightly higher rates than those classified as intropunitive.

We find little support for the hypothesis that external or internal attribution of blame specifies the relationship between failure and delinquency or dropout. Dropouts and delinquents do not consistently blame themselves or the system for their failure. Extrapunitive respondents with decreasing academic achievement have unusually high total SRD gain scores. The interaction effect is statistically significant for females, but not for males. There is a tendency for intropunitive females with initially low and decreasing academic achievement to have higher rates of dropout. To the extent that support for the hypothesis is found, it is associated with the academic scale. However, the data in no way suggest that punitiveness is a critical contingency in the relationship between failure and delinquency.

Our measure of punitiveness may be inadequate; perhaps a measure that directly assessed the individual's explanation for the specific types of failure he encountered would have produced better results. Yet, neither personality measures nor measures specific to particular situations have been successful in other investigations (Chapter 2). Hirschi analyzed anticipated occupational failure and explanations attributing it to discrimination or personal inadequacy; he found no relationship between these explanations and delinquency histories [103]. Consequently, there is reason to suspect that punitiveness is not a critical variable in the explanation of delinquency or dropout.

It is also possible that our failure to verify that intropunitiveness is related to dropout may be due to the confounding influence of delinquency. Many dropouts are highly involved in delinquent activity prior to dropping out; some are pushed out because of their rebellious behavior. Such an argument would be more convincing if there were a clear relationship between extrapunitiveness and

Table 6-8
Mean In- to Out-Of-School Transition Rates for Periods II to V, by Home Success, Stratified by Punitiveness (Percentages)

Home Success: Origin	Males Dropouts,[a] Periods III to V				Females Dropouts,[a] Periods III to V			
	Decreasing	Gains Stable	Increasing	Dropouts II to V Total	Decreasing	Gains Stable	Increasing	Dropouts II to V Total
High Acceptance								
Extrapunitive	7.7	8.3	1.8	4.2	4.5	2.1	6.4	5.1
Impunitive	4.6	4.1	2.1	3.2	5.8	4.9	3.5	4.3
Intropunitive	4.0	0.0	2.1	2.2	2.7	2.0	3.2	2.1
Moderate Acceptance								
Extrapunitive	3.5	3.5	4.5	2.0	7.1	3.1	1.7	3.1
Impunitive	7.8	3.0	3.7	3.1	9.3	2.0	3.3	3.1
Intropunitive	7.6	4.3	1.9	3.1	4.2	5.2	4.9	4.0
Low Acceptance								
Extrapunitive	12.9	4.4	7.8	7.5	11.4	0.0	1.9	3.8
Impunitive	7.1	5.8	5.3	4.7	9.8	4.5	5.3	5.3
Intropunitive	7.8	6.9	6.0	6.3	10.6	5.2	6.0	7.2

[a]Students who left school during Period II did not have gain scores and are excluded from the calculation of means for this part of the table. They are included in the total column, in which gain scores are ignored.

delinquency. We restricted the analysis to capable dropouts but did not distinguish between pushouts and voluntary dropouts. Conceivably, such a distinction might reduce some of the inconsistency in the association between punitiveness and dropout.

The relationships between failure and delinquency and dropout are considerably weaker than expected; our measure of punitiveness does not improve these relationships appreciably. Yet, our theory does not require strong relationships between failure and delinquency or dropout, because there are two other critical intervening variables, alienation and exposure. We did not postulate that failure alone was sufficient to generate these outcomes. Failure is seen as an instigating condition for delinquency, although it is not likely to eventuate in this form of behavior unless the individual also experiences normlessness and exposure to appropriate learning and performance structures. Likewise, it is only when failure is combined with social isolation and exposure to dropout influences that a student is likely to leave school. At this point in the analysis, the weak relationships between failure and the dependent variables do not constitute negative evidence for our general theory. Nevertheless, the relations are weaker than expected, and they challenge the view that failure to achieve valued goals is a sufficient explanation for either delinquency or dropout.

Alienation, Delinquent Behavior, and Dropout

We proposed that normlessness and social isolation should be related to specific contexts or institutional settings. Institutions are viewed as normative systems focused on a particular type of human activity. Normlessness or social isolation with reference to one context need not imply similar feelings with reference to other contexts. For example, the dropout may not be alienated from the home and community as much as he is from the school. There may be different reactions to the normative structure in diverse settings. The early work on alienation focused on economic institutions and the estrangement of the worker; consequently, the existing measures of normlessness and social isolation do not have an institutional reference, and none are specifically designed for the school and home. We developed normlessness and social isolation scales for the community, school, and home from a pool of approximately 90 items. The normlessness scales focus upon normative consensus, whereas the social isolation scales center upon withdrawal or separation from groups and activities in each social context.[11]

Neither of the measures of alienation in the home are related to social class. Nor is the relationship between normlessness in the school and class statistically significant. There is, however, a weak relationship between class and social isolation in the school and community and community normlessness. For the latter scales, the average correlations through time range from .08 to .15, and the association of alienation with class declines appreciably through time. In the fourth year, only the correlation between class and social isolation in school is statistically significant.

Alienation and Delinquent Behavior

With respect to alienation, we hypothesized that delinquent behavior is primarily a response to normlessness in the school setting. Stated differently, the form of alienation most conducive to delinquency is normlessness, and the critical context is the school. The correlations between delinquent behavior and the origin and gain predictors for the several measures of alienation are presented in Table 6-9. Both the measures of normlessness and social isolation in the home are predictive of delinquency rates and gains. The origin predictors are more highly related to SRD frequency scores, and the gain predictors are more highly associated with SRD gain scores. Alienation in the home appears to be a more powerful predictor of delinquency for females than males, at least with respect to the total SRD scores. The zero-order and multiple correlation values for males are generally weak, whereas the relationships fall in the moderate range for total SRD for females. There is no apparent difference in the predictive power of the two home alienation scales for subsequent delinquency.

There are moderate correlations between the home alienation scales and prior delinquency; this suggests that the causal sequence is not unidirectional. Normlessness and social isolation may be effects of prior delinquency, as well as causes of further delinquency. While there is no clear basis for judging the relative strength of the two sequences with these data, the predictive power of the two scales for future delinquency, as indicated by the SRD gain correlations, is consistently less than the relationship between alienation and prior delinquency. Three conclusions are warranted: (1) the two measures of alienation in the home are predictive of future delinquency; (2) they are more predictive of delinquency among females than males; and (3) normlessness, social isolation, and delinquency are mutually reinforcing through time.

The situation with respect to normlessness and social isolation in school is quite different. Normlessness in the school is predictive of both SRD frequency and gain scores; most of the zero-order and multiple correlations fall in the moderate range. On the other hand, social isolation in the school has only weak predictive utility for SRD frequency scores and is *not* predictive of SRD gain scores. Prior involvement in delinquency is controlled in the gain scores, but not in frequency scores. Thus, the difference between the two sets of correlations reflects the effect of prior delinquency. When prior delinquency is controlled, social isolation in the school has essentially no predictive utility. Normlessness in the school is predictive of the frequency and gains in subsequent delinquent activity, whereas social isolation in the school is a weak predictor of frequency and is not predictive of gains in delinquency. These findings are consistent with the earlier observation that neither the level of participation in school activities nor failure to achieve activity goals is associated with subsequent delinquency. These data challenge the control perspective which suggests that a low level of participation or isolation from school activities is conducive to delinquency.

In terms of predictive power, normlessness in the school is the strongest of the alienation scales; it is also the scale which is most highly related to prior delinquency. The strength of the latter relationship partially accounts for the substantial difference in the correlations of the origin predictor with the frequency and gain scores. The origin predictor for normlessness in the school is moderately related to SRD frequency scores, but has only a weak association with gains. On the other hand, the gain measure is equally predictive of the frequency and gains in delinquent behavior. We believe that these data support a causal argument even though it is evident that the gain predictor accounts for most of the strength of the multiple correlation. If the origin measures were not independently predictive of gains in delinquency, we would have reason to question whether there is a causal relationship.

The measure of social isolation in the community is not predictive of future delinquency. With the exception of the gain predictor for females, none of the correlations approach significance. There is a weak correlation between the gain predictor and both frequency and gains in delinquency for females. In the contexts of the home and community, the correlations are generally higher for females than males; apparently social isolation is a more important variable for girls. For normlessness in the community, the origin predictors are weakly correlated with the SRD frequency measures for males and females, but are not predictive of SRD gains. For all practical purposes, the origin scores do not predict future delinquency. The gain measure is related to the frequency and gains in SRD scores, and the relationships are stronger for males than females. Although there is a weak association between normlessness in the community and future delinquency, the causal implications of this predictor are not perfectly clear. In view of the fact that the origin measures do not predict subsequent delinquency, we question whether there is a causal relationship.

Discussion: The hypothesized relationship between alienation from the school and subsequent delinquency is generally confirmed. In the context of the school, normlessness, not social isolation, is predictive of delinquency. The two measures of alienation in the home are also predictive of subsequent delinquency, but the strongest of the alienation scales in terms of predictive power is normlessness in the school. On the other hand, alienation in the community is not causally related to subsequent delinquent behavior.

A two-way analysis of variance substantiates our earlier findings about the direct effects of particular origin and gain predictors, but there are no significant

Table 6-9
Correlations[a] Between Alienation Predictors and Measures of Delinquent Behavior

| | | Delinquent Behavior[b] | | | | | |
| | | Males | | | | | |
Alienation Predictors		Total SRD Frequency	Serious SRD Frequency	Total SRD Gain	Serious SRD Gain	Total SRD Prior	Serious SRD Prior
Home Normlessness:	Origin	.19	.12	.09	.08	.30	.21
	Gain	.16	.11	.14	.10		
	Origin & Gain	.24	.16	.16	.13		
Home Social Isolation:	Origin	.19	.12	.08	.07	.33	.23
	Gain	.12	.06	.11	.05		
	Origin & Gain	.22	.13	.13	.10		
School Normlessness:	Origin	.34	.23	.13	.12	.63	.52
	Gain	.28	.21	.29	.22		
	Origin & Gain	.44	.31	.31	.25		
School Social Isolation:	Origin	.15	.11	.04	.05	.34	.30
	Gain	.08	.07	.05	.05		
	Origin & Gain	.11	.13	.05	.05		
Community Normlessness:	Origin	.06	.06	.01	.04	.14	.13
	Gain	.20	.21	.16	.19		
	Origin & Gain	.21	.22	.16	.19		
Community Social Isolation:	Origin	.02	.03	−.03	.01	.18	.16
	Gain	.00	.01	−.02	.00		
	Origin & Gain	.02	.03	−.03	.01		

| | | | | Females | | | |
Alienation Predictors		Total SRD Frequency	Serious SRD Frequency	Total SRD Gain	Serious SRD Gain	Total SRD Prior	Serious SRD Prior
Home Normlessness:	Origin	.30	.08	.16	.06	.38	.18
	Gain	.21	.07	.20	.07		
	Origin & Gain	.36	.08	.26	.08		
Home Social Isolation:	Origin	.28	.10	.16	.08	.33	.16
	Gain	.19	.08	.19	.08		
	Origin & Gain	.34	.13	.26	.09		
School Normlessness:	Origin	.29	.13	.06	.08	.59	.40
	Gain	.30	.06	.31	.06		
	Origin & Gain	.41	.14	.31	.08		
School Social Isolation:	Origin	.13	.07	.03	.05	.27	.23
	Gain	.05	.00	.02	.01		
	Origin & Gain	.14	.07	.03	.05		
Community Normlessness:	Origin	.08	.04	.02	.02	.14	.13
	Gain	.10	.05	.09	.05		
	Origin & Gain	.13	.05	.09	.05		
Community Social Isolation:	Origin	−.01	.00	−.03	−.01	.05	.10
	Gain	.15	.08	.12	.07		
	Origin & Gain	.15	.08	.13	.07		

[a] $r \geq .06$, $p < .05$ $R \geq .08$, $p < .05$
 $r \geq .08$, $p < .01$ $R \geq .10$, $p < .01$

[b] The abbreviations, TSR and SSR, refer to Total Self-Reported Delinquent Behavior and Serious Self-Reported Delinquent Behavior, respectively.

interaction effects between the origin and gain predictors. The effects of the origin and gain predictors are additive; persons with initially high and increasing scores typically report the highest frequencies and gains in delinquent behavior. For example, males with initially low and decreasing normlessness in the school report an average of 2 fewer offenses than the number expected, whereas males in the high and increasing category report an average of 3 more offenses than expected.

The magnitude of the zero-order correlations between the alienation scales and prior delinquency is generally greater than the comparable correlations with SRD gain measures. This provides evidence for the proposition that delinquent activity both contributes to and is a consequence of alienation in the home and school. Delinquency research has traditionally focused upon the causal effect of alienation; in this approach the extent to which delinquent behavior may introduce conflict into an adolescent's relationships in the home and school is overlooked. Our data reveal the existence of a significant two-way relationship between alienation and delinquency. The implication is that investigators who correlate alienation with prior delinquency may grossly exaggerate the causal importance of alienation. Comparison of two correlation coefficients provides a vivid illustration of this point. Of the several alienation scales, normlessness in the school is the most powerful predictor; its correlation with prior delinquency is .63, but is only .31 with future delinquency.

Again, we find that the home has greater influence on girls—the measures of alienation in the home are stronger for females than males. In the earlier analysis of failure and delinquency, the home scale was a better predictor of delinquency among females than males, whereas low achievement in academic pursuits was the better predictor for males. There is consistency in the findings. The school is the context in which males are most likely to experience failure and normlessness; both are conducive to delinquency. The situation is more complicated for females. For them, failure and alienation in the home, as well as in school, appears to be conducive to delinquency. As a result, normlessness and social isolation in the home are equally predictive of delinquency among females.

Alienation and Dropout

We proposed that dropout is related to social isolation; further, it is social isolation in school, rather than in the home or community, that leads to dropout. The zero-order correlations between the origin and gain predictors for the alienation scales and Final Dropout Status are presented in Table 6-10. Of the various alienation scales, the measures of normlessness and social isolation in the school are the best predictors of dropout. On these scales the origin measures are slightly stronger for males than females, whereas the reverse obtains for the gain measures. The other scales are either not predictive or only weak predictors

Table 6-10

Correlations[a] Between Origin and Gain Measures for Alienation Predictors and Final Dropout Status

Alienation Predictors	Final Dropout Status					
	Males			Females		
	Origin	Gain	Origin & Gain	Origin	Gain	Origin & Gain
Home Normlessness	.08	.07	.11	.09	.05	.10
Home Social Isolation	.05	.04	.05	.08	.11	.13
School Normlessness	.26	.14	.30	.19	.25	.32
School Social Isolation	.24	.10	.26	.16	.09	.20
Community Normlessness	.13	.11	.16	.16	.03	.16
Community Social Isolation	.09	.02	.09	.04	.06	.06

[a] $r \geqslant .06, p < .05$ $R \geqslant .08, p < .05$
$r \geqslant .08, p < .01$ $R \geqslant .10, p < .01$

of dropout. The data support the hypothesis that alienation in the school is more likely to precipitate dropout than alienation in the home or community. However, normlessness and social isolation in school are equally strong predictors of dropout. In the other two contexts, normlessness is generally a better predictor than social isolation, although the relationships are weak. Thus, the hypothesis that social isolation, rather than normlessness, is conducive to dropout is not supported. Delinquency is related only to normlessness in the school, whereas dropout appears to be a consequence both of normlessness and social isolation in this setting. Perhaps this outcome is a result of the fact that a substantial number of dropouts are highly involved in delinquency at the point of departure from school.

The in- to out-of-school transition rates by origin and gain strata for the school alienation scales are shown in Table 6-11. As noted earlier, transition rates can appropriately be interpreted as probability estimates, and the mean transition rates for each study period are 3.8 percent for males and 3.9 percent for females. For normlessness in the school, males and females with initially high and increasing scores for Periods III through IV have dropout rates more than three times the average and more than eight times the rate for those in the low and decreasing strata. It is apparent that the origin and gain scores predict subsequent dropout—in fact, school normlessness is a rather strong predictor of dropout. Normlessness in the school appears to be a stronger variable in terms of transition rates than on the basis of the correlational analysis. Presumably, this is due to the imbalance in the marginal frequencies on the dichotomous dropout variable.

According to the transition rates, social isolation in the school is also

Table 6-11

Mean In- to Out-of-School Transition Rates for Periods II to V, by School Normlessness and Social Isolation (Percentages)

Origin: School	Males Dropouts,[a] Periods III to V				Females Dropouts,[a] Periods III to V			
	Gains			Dropouts II to V Total	Gains			Dropouts II to V Total
Normlessness	Decreasing	Stable	Increasing		Decreasing	Stable	Increasing	
Low	1.1	2.2	5.0	1.8	1.6	2.3	6.2	2.9
Moderate	3.1	2.8	6.9	3.6	4.3	2.9	5.5	4.6
High	6.9	10.3	12.8	8.0	5.3	7.0	12.9	7.8
School Social Isolation								
Low	2.1	3.0	3.1	2.1	0.7	5.6	3.0	2.8
Moderate	3.9	3.8	6.6	3.5	1.7	4.0	8.1	3.8
High	7.4	8.8	9.4	7.0	5.5	8.3	6.0	6.1

[a]Subjects who left school during Period II did not have gain scores and are excluded from the calculation of means for this part of the table. They are included in the total column, in which gain scores are ignored.

predictive of dropout, though it is not as strongly related to dropout as school normlessness. The likelihood that males in the high and increasing strata will drop out is more than twice the average for the cohort, and it is approximately four times higher than the probability for males in the low and decreasing strata. The relationship is slightly weaker for females. For males and females the origin predictors are stronger than the gain predictors, as the differences among the gain strata are less than those among origin strata.

Discussion: Examination of the transition rates substantiates the findings of the regression analyses; however, the predictive strength of normlessness and social isolation in school appears to be considerably greater than is revealed by the correlation values. School normlessness apparently is the stronger of the two predictors; this is contrary to the hypothesis in which dropout is linked to social isolation. The data confirm that dropout is a response to social isolation in school, but suggest that normlessness is also conducive to dropout, perhaps even more so than social isolation. It is evident in the regression and transition rate analyses that dropout is not significantly related to normlessness and social isolation in the home. The findings support the hypothesis that alienation from the school, rather than the home or the community, is most conducive to dropout. This conclusion challenges the common idea that dropout is a response to difficulties in the juvenile's home [25].

Patterns of Differential Association

Presumably differential exposure to delinquency and dropout may occur in several contexts, and the extent to which specific patterns of exposure are conducive to delinquent behavior and dropout may vary. We argued that unless the individual has access to social environments where he can learn appropriate definitions of delinquency or dropout as well as receive positive social reinforcement, he is not likely to engage extensively in delinquent behavior or drop out. Rather than limiting our attention to the influence of highly structured gangs, we are concerned with the individual's exposure to everyday instances of delinquent behavior and dropout in his environment and to the attitudes, values, and social definitions supportive of such behavior. We accept Sutherland's premise that the most significant influences are found in the individual's primary groups, and our measures of exposure focus upon the groups found primarily in the school and home.

Measures of Exposure to Delinquency

Differential exposure to delinquency in the community is measured by a single item designed to tap the individual's subjective impression about the amount of delinquent activity in his community. This item does not measure primary group associations with delinquent youth. It is assumed that subjects who perceive a great deal of delinquency in the community have more exposure to delinquent influences. This question was asked only in the first and fourth years. Males perceive slightly more delinquency than females, though the average subject, male or female, discerns little delinquency in the community.

Exposure to delinquency in the school is measured in terms of the subject's perception of delinquency among his immediate friends and with an objective measure of delinquent behavior on the part of the persons listed as friends in a sociometric question. The first measure, which we refer to as differential association in the school, is based on three items employed by Short [211; 212; 213] and Voss [248] to tap association with delinquent friends. These items were asked only in the first year; consequently, we do not have gain measures for this scale. As might be expected, males perceive more "trouble with the law" among their friends than do females. The second measure of exposure is based on the involvement in delinquency of the subject's friends, as listed in a sociometric question. To differentiate these measures, this one is referred to as sociometric exposure. The proportion of the subject's friends who either report serious offenses on the SRD or have an official delinquency record constitutes the individual's score.[12] When juveniles are asked to provide a list of their friends, their choices may not be reciprocated. Nevertheless, the one-way choices identify persons who are likely to be influential on the subject, whether or not the individual reciprocates the selection. A respondent's list of friends is viewed as his or her reference group. Choices were not restricted to persons of the same sex, and the number of cross-sex choices increases substantially through time. This was true for both sexes, although girls had fewer delinquent friends.

A measure of exposure to criminal influences in the home was obtained for a representative sample of the study population.[13] The names of siblings and parents were compiled for this sample of 296 respondents. These names were checked against the juvenile and adult records of local police departments as well as appropriate municipal and superior courts. The record check extended to January 1, 1959, when 9 was the modal age of the subjects. The measure of exposure to criminality in the family consists of three indicators: official offense rates, the maximum seriousness of any offense, and the type of legal action involved. The first score is simply the total number of criminal or delinquent acts committed by family members, excluding the subject. Scores for the seriousness of the offense and legal action are based upon the single most serious recorded offense for the family. Each of the three indicators was standardized and then summed to provide a single score for family exposure. This measure was obtained only for Period I.

Social class accounts for relatively little of the variability in any of the measures of exposure to delinquency, and for females none of the exposure measures is related to social class. For males the community measure of differential association and the sociometric scale are associated with class; boys from the lower end of the class distribution perceive slightly more delinquency in their communities and choose a slightly higher proportion of delinquent friends. The latter relationship is fairly constant across time, but the correlations are low (.09 to .12). The correlations between differential association and class are also in this range.

Associational Patterns and Delinquent Behavior

The correlations between the exposure measures and delinquent behavior are presented in Table 6-12. The original level of exposure to delinquency in the community is a weak predictor of the frequency of delinquent behavior, but it is not predictive of gain scores. The gain measure for community exposure is predictive of frequency and gain scores; the correlations are weak for girls and moderate for males. Because the gain, not the origin, measure predicts SRD gains, it is questionable whether the relationship is causal. The perception of delinquency in the community in the ninth grade has little predictive utility; yet, the perception of more delinquency in the community in subsequent years is correlated with an increasing personal involvement in delinquent behavior. We suspect that a subject's perception of delinquency in the community is an effect of his participation in delinquency and is not a genuine causal influence for future delinquency. This interpretation is consistent with the relationship between perceptions of delinquency in the community and prior delinquency— respondents who report higher rates of delinquent behavior prior to the study tend to perceive more delinquency in their community. This also may account for the weak associations between the origin measure for community exposure and SRD frequency scores.

The measure of differential association in the school is moderately correlated with SRD frequency scores, but its relationship with the gain measures is weak. Interestingly, the relationship between differential association and prior delinquency is strong. There is a clear tendency for the correlations to decrease as one moves from prior delinquency to frequency to gain scores (Table 6-12). We can explain the higher correlations for SRD frequency scores in comparison with gain scores in terms of the relationship between differential association and prior delinquency. Stated differently, prior delinquency is not controlled in the SRD frequency scores; consequently, we expected the correlations between differential association in the school and SRD frequency scores to be higher. The decrease in the magnitude of the correlation values is dramatic, and the data suggest that perception of official delinquency among one's friends is largely an effect of prior delinquency rather than a cause of future delinquent behavior. This is not to say that differential association lacks predictive utility; rather, for this measure the "effect" relationship is stronger than the causal one.[14]

Table 6-12

Correlations[a] Between Exposure Predictors and Measures of Delinquent Behavior[b]

		Males					
Exposure Predictors		Total SRD Frequency	Serious SRD Frequency	Total SRD Gain	Serious SRD Gain	Total SRD Prior	Serious SRD Prior
Community:	Origin	.09	.07	.00	.02	.26	.25
	Gain	.29	.25	.27	.24		
	Origin & Gain	.30	.27	.27	.24		
Differential Association:	Origin	.27	.22	.07	.12	.59	.53
Sociometric:	Origin	.18	.11	.09	.08	.30	.30
	Gain	.24	.18	.20	.19		
	Origin & Gain	.30	.22	.22	.18		
Home:[c]	Origin	.02	.05	.02	.04	.02	.03

		Females				
Exposure Predictors	Total SRD Frequency	Serious SRD Frequency	Total SRD Gain	Serious SRD Gain	Total SRD Prior	Serious SRD Prior
Community: Origin	.15	.04	.05	.02	.25	.16
Gain	.21	.10	.17	.09		
Origin & Gain	.26	.11	.18	.09		
Differential Association: Origin	.27	.11	.08	.07	.52	.36
Sociometric: Origin	.17	.08	.09	.08	.29	.21
Gain	.22	.07	.17	.06		
Origin & Gain	.28	.08	.20	.08		
Home:[c] Origin	.03	.03	.02	.03	.04	.02

[a] $r \geq .06, p < .05$ $R \geq .08, p < .05$
   $r \geq .08, p < .01$ $R \geq .01, p < .01$
[b] The abbreviations, TSR and SSR, refer to Total Self-Reported Delinquent Behavior and Serious Self-Reported Delinquent Behavior, respectively.
[c] $N = 148, r = .16, p < .05$

Several researchers have employed similar measures of differential association and found substantial associations with prior delinquency. According to our data, such findings should not be interpreted as strong support for the differential association hypothesis and provide as much or more support for Glueck's "flocking" hypothesis [75]. Consequently, there is reason to assume that the predictive utility of differential association is more limited than previous investigators have suggested.

The same pattern of relationships exists for the origin predictor for the sociometric measure, although neither the relationships with SRD frequency measures or prior delinquency are as strong. However, the sociometric measure has essentially the same predictive power as differential association in the school for SRD gain scores. The sociometric gain predictor for males is moderately correlated with all of the delinquency measures. The comparable relationships for females are weaker. The predictive power of the differential association and sociometric measures of exposure are similar, although the multiple correlation for origin and gain scores on the sociometric measure falls in the moderate range for total SRD gain scores. There is another consideration which favors the sociometric measure. It appears to be less influenced by prior delinquency. In comparison with an objective measurement, the respondents tend to assess inaccurately the extent of their friends' involvement in delinquency. Those who are highly involved in delinquency overestimate, whereas respondents with little involvement tend to underestimate the delinquent behavior of their friends.

The measure of exposure to delinquent or criminal influences in the home is not predictive of delinquent behavior. We do not have a gain measure, but presumably there would be relatively little change in the scores through the study period, because the origin predictor covers a six-year period, and few of the subjects' families had any recorded criminal activity. If there were a significant correlation between gains in home exposure and SRD gains, we could not make a clear causal interpretation of the relationship, in view of the fact that the origin predictor for officially recorded criminal and delinquent behavior in a subject's family is not significantly related to any of the delinquency measures. Insofar as the home is concerned, we fail to find any support for the exposure hypothesis, which may be due to our reliance upon officially recorded behavior. We acknowledge that members of a respondent's family need not have an official criminal record in order to provide attitudes and behavior supportive of delinquent behavior. Unfortunately, it was not possible to obtain the kinds of data required for a more sensitive measure. Nevertheless, we find that officially recorded criminal behavior on the part of family members is not conducive to delinquent behavior.

Discussion: Our measures of exposure do not deal with the more subtle types of reinforcement and social support for delinquency implied in Sutherland's statement of differential association. They directly assess the effects of association with persons actively involved in delinquent or criminal behavior. The data indicate that a juvenile's general impression about the amount of delinquency in the community reflects his past misbehavior; when prior involvement in delinquency is controlled, these perceptions are not predictive of future delinquency. Nor is exposure to persons in the family who are officially known as criminals or delinquents predictive of delinquent behavior. This is an unexpected finding, in view of earlier research. Glueck and Glueck [77] and McCord and McCord [140] found a relationship between parental criminality and delinquency on the part of children. However, we use a different measure. We relate known criminality in the family to rates of self-reported delinquent behavior, rather than a classification of juveniles based upon official records. Our research is directed toward explanation of the behavior of our respondents, not police and court officials, and we believe that self reports are a better measure of juveniles' delinquent behavior than official records. Our findings may well differ from those of earlier investigators strictly as a consequence of the disparity in our measures. In any event, there is no support for the hypothesized relationship between family exposure and delinquent behavior.

The only measures of exposure causally related to delinquency are derived from the context of the school. The joint effect on delinquency gain scores of the origin and gain predictors for the sociometric scale indicates that juveniles with initially high and increasing associations with delinquent peers are more likely to report high rates and positive gains in delinquent behavior. The multiple correlations with total SRD gains fall in the moderate range, and those with serious SRD gains are weak.

Association with Dropouts

Three measures of exposure to dropout were developed—two for the school and one for the home. The former are similar to the measures of exposure to delinquency; they reflect the extent of contact with dropout peers. Scores on this scale are weakly related to social class; the correlations decline slightly through time. The second measure involves the sociometric question described earlier with reference to delinquency among the subject's friends. For each respondent, the proportion of his friends who dropped out in the following study period constitutes his score on the sociometric measure of exposure to dropout. Again, there is a weak correlation with social class. A scale measuring exposure to dropout influences in the home was constructed for Periods I and IV. It pertains to parental support for education and dropout on the part of parents and siblings. Of all the scales mentioned thus far, exposure to dropout in the home is the most strongly related to social class.

Patterns of Association and Dropout

Correlations between the measures of association with dropouts and Final Dropout Status are presented in Table 6-13. They indicate that the three exposure measures are predictive of dropout. The correlations are slightly higher for males than females, but no one scale is obviously stronger than the others. The evidence supports the proposition that association with dropouts, whether in the school or home, is conducive to dropout. The two school-related measures reflect patterns of association, whereas the home measure also includes perceived parental support for education.

The measures of association with dropouts are more highly correlated with social class than the measures of association with delinquents. The fact that there are class differentials in dropout but not delinquent behavior may be explained in part by the differences in patterns of association. Exposure to delinquency is at best weakly associated with class, whereas exposure to dropout, particularly in the home, is strongly associated with class.

Commitment to Peers and Parents

The measures of exposure have relatively weak predictive power. In an effort to tap the dimension of differential association Sutherland referred to as intensity, we developed two measures of attachment. Commitment to peers was measured by a single item that followed the sociometric question and referred directly to the respondent's list of friends. The item asked, "If you found that this group of friends was leading you into trouble, would you still run around with them?" The commitment to parents scale consisted of three items, and answers were dichotomized according to whether parents were checked in the list of categories provided. Neither commitment to parents or peers is related to social class. The

Table 6-13
Correlations[a] Between Origin and Gain Measures for Exposure to Dropout Predictors and Final Dropout Status

Exposure to Dropout Predictors	Final Dropout Status					
	Males			Females		
	Origin	Gain	Origin & Gain	Origin	Gain	Origin & Gain
School	.18	.20	.27	.21	.13	.24
Sociometric	.13	.25	.28	.15	.16	.23
Home	.30	.12	.32	.20	.18	.27

[a]$r \geqslant .06, p < .05$ $R \geqslant .08, p < .05$
$r \geqslant .08, p < .01$ $R \geqslant .10, p < .01$

trend for the subject's commitment to parents is the opposite of the one for commitment to peers. With time the subjects became increasingly committed to peers and decreasingly committed to parents.

Exposure, Commitment, and
Delinquent Behavior

To test the hypothesis that commitment to peers specifies the relationship between delinquent peer exposure and delinquent behavior, we use two- and three-factor analyses of variance. The relationship between commitment to parents in Period I, the sociometric measure of exposure to delinquency in Period I, and the SRD frequency scores is presented in Table 6-14. As the relationship is similar for males and females, the entire cohort is combined in this analysis. As hypothesized, commitment specifies the relationship between exposure to delinquent friends and frequency of delinquent behavior. For every level of exposure, substantial differences exist by degree of commitment. It is apparent that commitment to peers has a strong direct effect on delinquent behavior. Commitment to peers is a stronger predictor of delinquency than the sociometric measure of exposure; our data are consistent with the findings of Erickson and Empey [68]. Further, there is a significant interaction effect between commitment to peers and exposure to delinquency, as measured by the sociometric scale. Respondents with high exposure to delinquency and high commitment to peers report an average of three times more delinquent acts than those with low exposure and low commitment.

Table 6-14
Two-Factor Analysis of Variance: Sociometric Measure of Exposure to Delinquency (I), Commitment to Peers (I), and Total Self-Reported Delinquency Frequency Scores

	Proportion of Delinquent Peers			
Commitment	0-25%	26-50%	51-75%	76-100%
High	6.255	8.571	11.805	10.905
Medium	5.813	6.737	7.159	9.007
Low	3.597	4.413	5.568	6.424

	F Ratios:		
	Exposure	30.3751**	
	Commitment	75.2791**	
	Exposure × Commitment	3.5479**	

$**p < .01$

As prior delinquency is not controlled in the SRD frequency measure, a more conservative test of the relationship between commitment, exposure, and delinquency utilizes the SRD gain measure as the dependent variable. Although the results are not shown in tabular form, in this three-factor analysis of variance, the independent variables are the origin and gain predictors for the sociometric measure of exposure and the origin measure for commitment to peers. The hypothesis is again confirmed. While the two origin predictors are not as strongly related to SRD gains as they are to SRD frequency scores, all of the direct effects are statistically significant. However, there are no significant interaction effects. Respondents with high exposure and high commitment report an average increase of 3 offenses, while those with low commitment and low exposure report an average decrease of 1 offense.

These analyses indicate that the degree of commitment to peers is an independent predictor of delinquency; persons with high commitment tend to have higher subsequent rates of delinquency. Data relevant to the hypothesis that the combined effect of high attachment to peers and low attachment to parents should be even more conducive to delinquency are presented in Table 6-15. For the total SRD frequency and gain scores, the hypothesis is confirmed.

Table 6-15

Two-Factor Analysis of Variance: Origin Predictors for Commitment to Parents and Commitment to Peers on Total Self-Reported Delinquency Frequency and Gain Scores

Commitment to Parents	Mean SRD Frequency Scores Commitment to Peers		
	High	Moderate	Low
High	7.23	5.93	4.48
Moderate	8.57	6.51	5.81
Low	9.98	9.33	6.61
Commitment to Parents	Mean SRD Gain Scores Commitment to Peers		
High	.583	−.146	−1.294
Moderate	.723	−.377	−.474
Low	.941	2.071	−.024

F Ratios	SRD Frequency	SRD Gain
(A) Commitment to Parents − Origin	20.03**	5.19**
(B) Commitment to Peers − Origin	22.65**	5.82**
A × B	.96	1.65

**p < .01

Respondents with low attachment to peers and high attachment to parents have the lowest mean delinquency scores, and those with high peer and low parental attachment have the highest average scores. Again, the relationship is stronger for the total SRD frequency measure. In neither case is there a significant interaction effect. Separate two-factor analyses of variance involving origin and gain predictors for each commitment scale reveal that they are related to the delinquency measures; in both instances the gain measures are considerably stronger than the origin measures. It is clear that the influence of peers is greatly accentuated when a juvenile is highly committed to them.

Exposure, Commitment, and Dropout

In similar analyses we examined the effects of peer and parental attachment on the relationship between exposure and dropout. The mean transition rate for respondents with high and increasing exposure to dropout is dependent upon the degree of commitment to peers. Males with high commitment to peers have an average annual dropout rate of 16 percent in comparison with 8 percent for those with low commitment to peers. The comparable rates for females are 18 and 6 percent; girls with high scores are almost three times as likely to drop out as those with low scores (Table 6-16). All three variables appear to contribute directly to the probability of dropout. The rate of dropout for respondents with the most favorable combination in terms of origin and gain scores for association with dropouts and initial commitment to peers is approximately 1 percent. In contrast, the annual rate is 17 percent for the respondents with the least favorable combination; this results in a cumulative loss of 50 percent over the study period.

We examined the effect of commitment to parents on the relationship between exposure to dropout in the home and dropout in terms of transition rates in Table 6-17. In general, low commitment to parents is associated with a higher dropout rate, but the relationship is not a strong one. In the high exposure strata, approximately 8 percent of the subjects with low commitment to parents drop out, but so do 6 percent of those with high commitment. In the relationship between home exposure and dropout, the effect of commitment to parents is consistent, but it is not nearly as strong as the effect of peer commitment in specifying the association between school exposure and dropout.

Discussion: The hypothesis that the influence of delinquent peers is affected by the individual's degree of commitment is supported by the data. Juveniles who associate with delinquent peers and are highly committed to them have much higher rates of delinquency. Considering their initial levels of involvement in delinquent behavior, they also have sizable positive gains in delinquency. Strong attachment to peers is predictive of delinquency, regardless of the level of

Table 6-16

Mean In- to Out-of-School Transition Rates for Periods II to V, by Exposure to Dropout in the School, Stratified by Commitment to Peers (Percentages)

Origin: Exposure to Dropout and Commitment to Peers	Gains: Exposure to Dropout			Dropouts II to V Total
	Males			
	Dropouts,[a] Periods III to V			
	Decreasing	Stable	Increasing	
Low Exposure				
High Commitment	2.5	1.8	7.1	3.4
Moderate Commitment	0.7	0.7	8.6	2.6
Low Commitment	1.0	5.4	6.9	2.7
High Exposure				
High Commitment	3.4	6.4	16.3	7.3
Moderate Commitment	4.1	8.0	8.4	5.9
Low Commitment	8.1	5.0	8.1	5.7
	Females			
Low Exposure				
High Commitment	2.2	1.9	8.7	4.2
Moderate Commitment	1.9	3.1	3.0	2.3
Low Commitment	1.2	2.1	4.1	1.8
High Exposure				
High Commitment	6.1	6.9	18.3	9.9
Moderate Commitment	5.5	10.0	3.7	5.3
Low Commitment	1.2	7.5	6.4	4.8

[a]Subjects who left school during Period II did not have gain scores and are excluded from the calculation of means for this part of the table. They are included in the total column, in which gains scores are ignored.

exposure. In other words, commitment to peers is conducive to delinquency even under conditions of low exposure to peer delinquency. In contrast, high commitment to parents appears to inhibit delinquency. Subjects with high commitment to parents have lower initial rates and subsequent gains in delinquent behavior. As a consequence, the combination of high peer and low parental commitment is particularly conducive to delinquency. We infer that youth oriented primarily toward peers have the greatest potential for delinquent behavior.

In general, commitment to peers has the same effect on the relationship between exposure and dropout. Juveniles who are exposed to dropout peers and are highly committed to them have extremely high dropout rates—17 percent annually. In contrast, those with low exposure and low commitment rarely drop out. Commitment to peers is also independently related to dropout. This

Table 6-17

Mean Annual Transition Rates for Periods II to V, by Exposure to Dropout in the Home, Stratified by Commitment to Parents (Percentages)

	Males	Females
Low Exposure		
Low Commitment	2.5	2.6
Moderate Commitment	1.9	4.0
High Commitment	2.1	1.0
Moderate Exposure		
Low Commitment	4.5	4.0
Moderate Commitment	3.1	3.7
High Commitment	2.7	3.6
High Exposure		
Low Commitment	8.4	7.6
Moderate Commitment	6.4	7.9
High Commitment	6.4	5.4

provides evidence that dropout, like delinquency, is a group-related event. The decision to drop out is highly dependent upon a student's association with others who have taken this course of action.

To a limited extent commitment to parents specifies the relationship between exposure to dropout in the home and dropout. Youth who are exposed to dropout influences in the home and who have limited parental attachment are somewhat more likely to drop out. Yet commitment to parents is not as critical for dropout as attachment to peers. Commitment to parents appears to be a more important factor in delinquency than dropout, whereas commitment to peers is strongly related to both.

Summary

There is limited support for the hypothesized relationship between failure and delinquency. Only failure academically and in the home are predictive of delinquency, and in both cases the relationships are weak. Our hypothesis that delinquency is primarily a response to failure in school is supported more strongly for males than for females. Limited academic achievement is predictive of delinquency for males, whereas parental rejection is a predictor of female delinquency. There appears to be a mutually reinforcing process between delinquency and both academic failure and parental rejection. The latter are not only conducive to subsequent delinquent behavior, but also appear to be consequences of prior delinquency.

We fail to find any support for Cloward and Ohlin's disjunction hypothesis. According to our data, few youth anticipate failure in their efforts to achieve long-range goals, and the few juveniles who anticipate failure are no more likely to engage in delinquent behavior than youth who anticipate success. These findings support our contention that delinquency is a response to an immediate, not a long-range problem. However, the measures of success and failure in the youth culture are not predictive of delinquency, and failure in this respect also has immediate consequences. The direct predictive power of academic performance is limited; nevertheless, of the dimensions of success and failure we examined, achievement with respect to formal academic goals appears to be the most salient for subsequent delinquency.

Of the success-failure measures, academic achievement is also the best predictor of dropout for both sexes. It is, in fact, a stronger predictor of dropout than delinquency. The measure of success in school activities produces negative evidence—dropouts report a decreasing discrepancy between desired and actual involvement in school-related activities. Future dropouts' participation in school activities is consistently low, and they revise their aspirations downward prior to leaving school. The other measures of success-failure are at best weak predictors of dropout. A general measure of failure in diverse contexts did not improve predictions of delinquency or dropout.

There is little or no support for the hypothesis that a tendency to attribute blame externally or internally increases the likelihood of delinquency or dropout. Delinquents and dropouts do not consistently blame themselves or the system for their failure. To the extent that support for the hypothesis concerning punitiveness is found, it is generated with the measure of academic achievement. However, the relationships are generally weak and inconsistent; punitiveness produces a negligible increase in predictability. The data in no way suggest that attribution of blame is a critical contingency in the relationship between failure and either delinquency or dropout.

There is adequate support for the hypothesized relationship between normlessness in the school and home and delinquency. Of the alienation scales, normlessness in the school is the best predictor of delinquency for both sexes. Social isolation in the school and community are not predictive, and normlessness in the community is at best a weak predictor of delinquency. There is evidence that delinquent activity both contributes to and is a consequence of alienation in the home and school. Again, there is a sex differential in that alienation in the home is more predictive of female than male delinquency. For males, failure and normlessness in the school are conducive to delinquency; for females, the home and school are salient contexts, and failure and alienation in both leads to delinquency.

Of the various alienation scales, normlessness and social isolation in school are predictive of dropout. Examination of transition rates suggests that the former is a stronger predictor; this is at least in part negative evidence for the hypothesis linking dropout to social isolation. However, support is found for the hypothesis that alienation from the school, not the home or community, is conducive to dropout.

Social class accounts for relatively little of the variability in patterns of association with delinquents. The only measures of exposure causally related to delinquent behavior are based on sociometric choices and reports of association with delinquent friends. Delinquent behavior appears to be a direct consequence of high and increasing exposure to delinquent peers. Neither contacts with parents and siblings who have been apprehended for criminal or delinquent behavior nor perceptions of high rates of delinquency in the community are predictive of delinquency.

For the three measures of association with dropouts, high exposure is linked with lower social class position. Each of the measures is equally predictive of dropout. The evidence supports the proposition that association with dropouts, whether in the home or school, is conducive to dropout.

We argued that the influence of patterns of association, whether with delinquents, dropouts, or conventional persons, would vary according to the degree of commitment or attachment to these persons. With time the respondents became more committed to peers and less committed to parents. The hypothesis that the degree of commitment to peers specifies the relationships between exposure and delinquency and dropout is supported. The combined effect of exposure and commitment is strong. The highest rates of delinquent behavior and dropout are observed for juveniles with high exposure and high commitment to peers. Similarly, the lowest rates are found among youth with low exposure and low commitment. Commitment to peers is itself directly predictive of delinquent behavior and dropout. Regardless of the level of peer association, high commitment to peers is conducive to delinquency and dropout. Commitment to parents has the opposite effect on delinquency. For each level of exposure, juveniles with high commitment have low rates of delinquent behavior. However, commitment to parents does not specify the relationship between dropout and exposure to dropout in the home. Commitment to parents inhibits delinquency, but is less effective in deterring dropout.

Of the relationships we examined, the associations between origin measures and prior delinquency are comparable to the ones analyzed in studies based on cross-sectional designs. The similarities between our findings and previous research imply that our findings concerning the predictive power of the variables may be generalized beyond our study population. Comparison of the different sets of relationships we analyzed reveals that the causal significance of our independent variables has been overestimated in previous research.

Notes

1. Examination of these bivariate relationships provides insight into the nature and operation of each of the variables as a prelude to the multivariate analysis. Changes in the predictor measures through time were examined, as were

autocorrelations, the average one-year time-lagged correlations for a given scale. The inter-scale correlations are presented in Appendix A. All of the correlations presented in this volume represent estimates of the relationship between measures rather than "true" values, and the reader is reminded that we have not corrected the correlation values for attenuation.

2. The community scale does not involve any assumptions about levels of aspiration or objective chances to achieve goals.

3. Unless otherwise noted, a scale was developed for each of the four years, and the items in a scale were identical with the exception of minor changes in wording. For the second, third, and fourth years, the academic success scale was based on achievement test scores and grade point averages. Methodologically, we handled the varying number of items across years by normalizing each scale for each year.

4. These questions were borrowed from Coleman [39]. A person who viewed himself as more involved than he wanted to be was assigned a discrepancy score of 0. The range of discrepancies was from 0 to 5; the maximum score indicates that the subject placed himself outside the circle of activities on the first question and in the center of activities on the second, an indication that he wanted to be highly involved in school activities but was not so involved.

5. Reiss and Rhodes used a single set of response categories, whereas we provided separate response categories for clothes and home.

6. With the exception of the measures of academic success, general success, punitiveness, and exposure to criminality in the home, in which the development of the scales is adequately discussed in the text, the items in each of the scales discussed in this chapter are presented in Appendix B. These scales have satisfactory internal consistency and reliability as measured by the Alpha Coefficient and the Homogeneity Ratio. Cronbach's Alpha [43] is a conservative estimate of scale reliability, and Scott's Homogeneity Ratio [202] is a weighted average inter-item correlation. The value of Alpha is dependent upon the length of the scale; if a scale consists of relatively few items, it is likely to be low. The Homogeneity Ratio is not affected by scale length; for short scales it is a better measure of internal consistency.

7. We refer to correlation values between .05 and .19 as weak, those between .20 and .49 as moderate, and those above .50 as strong.

8. The classification is based upon data gathered at the beginning of the study; it is assumed to reflect a general personality trait that is relatively constant through time. The composite score is based on the subject's modal response. In the event that responses were bimodal the following rules were used: if extrapunitive and impunitive, the subject was classified as extrapunitive; if impunitive and intropunitive, the respondent was classified as intropunitive; and if extrapunitive and impunitive, the subject was considered unreliable on this measure and was excluded from the analysis involving punitiveness.

9. We calculated transition probabilities for each period and then averaged the proportions. In averaging the proportions, we checked to determine that significant trends through time were not obscured. The averages are representative of the rates in the separate periods.

10. With one exception, in each instance in which transition rates are analyzed in this chapter the normalized origin and gain scores on the scales were trichotomized with cutting points of ±.43. For the measure of exposure to dropout in the school the cutting point is +0.0.

11. Data for each year were scaled separately. Items that did not remain homogeneous to their scales over the four years were eliminated, as were most items unique to a particular year. The home scale consists of 6 items in the first and fourth years and 5 items in the second and third years. The home social isolation scale consists of 10 items in the first three years and 8 items in the fourth year. The scale for social isolation in school has 7 items in the first year and 5 items in the following years.

12. The number of friends listed ranged from 0 to 18 with a mean of approximately 6 for males and 8 for females. We attempted to establish group boundaries and to classify groups as delinquent or nondelinquent. This measure of group membership is more highly correlated with the SRD frequency and gain scores than the sociometric measure, but only 35 percent of the subjects could be classified as group members.

13. We acknowledge the assistance of Lawrence J. Severy in drawing this sample and developing this measure of exposure. The sample was representative of the population with respect to age, sex, social class, ethnicity, group membership, delinquency, and dropout status [208].

14. Because we do not have gain predictors, we cannot examine the joint effect of initial and changing perceptions of delinquent activity among a subject's friends. Judging from the strength of the other gain predictors, we doubt whether the joint effect would approach the strength of the relationship between differential association and prior delinquency.

7

A Test of the Theory

In this chapter we present a general test of our theoretical formulation. With one exception, we limit the analysis to the variables that had some predictive power for delinquency or dropout in the bivariate analyses. The one exception involves the measure of punitiveness, which is included because of its theoretical significance. The other variables are: academic achievement and home success; normlessness and social isolation in the school and normlessness and social isolation in the home; the sociometric measure of exposure to delinquency, association with school dropouts, and exposure to dropout in the home; and commitment to parents and commitment to peers. For the contexts of the school and home, each of the postulated causal variables is represented with the exception of exposure to delinquency in the home. We did not include the latter measure for two reasons. This measure was only available for a sample of the study population, and our earlier analysis indicated that it was not predictive of delinquent behavior. On the other hand, none of the measures derived from the community context are included because these measures either were not predictive or were weak predictors of the dependent variables, delinquency and dropout. In every case the school- or home-context measures were stronger predictors. Consequently, we restrict comparison of social contexts to the school and home as generating milieu for delinquency and dropout.

Prediction of Delinquent Behavior

Delinquency and the School

The combined effect of failure, punitiveness, normlessness, exposure to delinquency, and commitment to peers or parents is examined through a multiple regression analysis. We selected a stepwise procedure because it provides an estimate of the increase in predictability attributable to the addition of each variable to the multiple regression equation.[1] Stated differently, some information is obtained about the relative contribution of each variable to the overall predictive power of the entire set of variables. The analysis employing school-context predictors is presented in Tables 7-1 and 7-2. The predictor variable, the multiple correlation coefficient, the F value for each step of the analysis, and the beta weight for each variable in the final regression equation are shown in these tables. In Table 7-1 the dependent variable is the total SRD frequency measure,

175

Table 7-1
Stepwise Multiple Regression Analysis: School Context Predictors on Total Self-Reported Delinquency Frequency Scores

Males: $R = .54$, F Value 60.74

Step Number	Variable	R	R^2	F Value to Enter	p	Final Beta Weight
1	School Normlessness – Origin	.34	.1156	174.76	.001	.2585
2	Commitment to Peers – Gain	.46	.2079	155.64	.001	.2535
3	School Normlessness – Gain	.51	.2591	92.23	.001	.2099
4	Sociometric Exposure – Gain	.52	.2752	29.74	.001	.1275
5	Commitment to Peers – Origin	.53	.2869	21.62	.001	.1184
6	Academic Success – Gain	.54	.2890	4.31	.01	.0523
7	Punitiveness – Origin	.54	.2901	2.02	NS	–.0342
8	Sociometric Exposure – Origin	.54	.2911	1.78	NS	.0386
9	Academic Success – Origin	.54	.2916	.92	NS	.0252

Females: $R = .50$, F Value 46.31

Step Number	Variable	R	R^2	F Value to Enter	p	Final Beta Weight
1	School Normlessness – Gain	.30	.0900	126.30	.001	.2348
2	School Normlessness – Origin	.42	.1741	129.93	.001	.2146
3	Commitment to Peers – Gain	.46	.2126	62.38	.001	.1996
4	Commitment to Peers – Origin	.48	.2299	28.75	.001	.1172
5	Sociometric Exposure – Gain	.49	.2418	19.94	.001	.1222
6	Academic Success – Origin	.50	.2452	5.79	.01	.0673
7	Sociometric Exposure – Origin	.50	.2469	2.72	.05	.0418
8	Punitiveness – Origin	.50	.2472	.60	NS	–.0192
9	Academic Success – Gain	.50	.2473	.17	NS	–.0107

Table 7-2
Stepwise Multiple Regression Analysis: School Context Predictors on Total Self-Reported Delinquency Gain Scores

Males: $R = .44$, F Value 35.67

Step Number	Variable	R	R^2	F Value to Enter	p	Final Beta Weight
1	Commitment to Peers – Gain	.33	.1089	163.39	.001	.2663
2	School Normlessness – Gain	.40	.1625	85.50	.001	.2207
3	Sociometric Exposure – Gain	.42	.1793	27.37	.001	.1328
4	School Normlessness – Origin	.43	.1873	13.22	.001	.0902
5	Academic Success – Gain	.44	.1925	8.52	.001	.0768
6	Punitiveness – Origin	.44	.1933	1.29	NS	−.0264
7	Academic Success – Origin	.44	.1939	1.06	NS	.0338
8	Sociometric Exposure – Origin	.44	.1944	.78	NS	.0203
9	Commitment to Peers – Origin	.44	.1946	.40	NS	.0176

Females: $R = .40$, F Value 26.89

Step Number	Variable	R	R^2	F Value to Enter	p	Final Beta Weight
1	School Normlessness – Gain	.31	.0961	135.77	.001	.2433
2	Commitment to Peers – Gain	.38	.1432	70.21	.001	.2127
3	Sociometric Exposure – Gain	.39	.1564	19.91	.001	.1063
4	Commitment to Peers – Origin	.40	.1589	3.85	.01	.0424
5	Sociometric Exposure – Origin	.40	.1596	1.06	NS	.0276
6	Academic Success – Gain	.40	.1601	.71	NS	.0210
7	Academic Success – Origin	.40	.1602	.19	NS	.0127
8	Punitiveness – Origin	.40	.1602	.02	NS	.0041
9	School Normlessness – Origin	.40	.1602	.02	NS	.0042

whereas in Table 7-2 it is the total SRD gain measure. With respect to the frequency of self-reported delinquent behavior, the multiple correlation coefficient is .54 for males and .50 for females. The data provide strong support for our theoretical explanation. In comparison with any single variable the combined set of predictors provides a substantial increase in predictability.

Interesting to note is the fact that the estimates of the predictive power of our theoretical variables for the frequency of delinquent acts are similar for males and females. Females report lower rates of delinquent behavior than males, but it appears that the conditions reflected by this set of variables are equally conducive to delinquency among males and females. In general, 25 to 30 percent of the variance in the number of self-reported delinquent acts is explained by this set of predictors.

The relative strength of particular predictors is also similar for both sexes. The major proportion of the variance is explained by normlessness and commitment to peers; these predictors were the first to enter the regression equation, and they produced the greatest increases in the multiple correlation coefficient in the stepwise analysis. The gain predictor for academic achievement entered the multiple regression equation at a significant F level for males but not for females, whereas the origin score for the sociometric measure of exposure to delinquency entered at a significant level for females but not for males. The origin predictors for academic achievement and punitiveness failed to enter at significant F levels; neither failure in school nor external attribution of blame leads to any significant improvement in the predictive power of the causal variables in the multiple regression equation.

The initial level of association with delinquent friends also entered the regression quite late and contributes little additional explanatory power. The increase in the proportion of delinquent friends contributes significantly to the prediction of delinquency for both sexes; however, as noted in Chapter 6, the causal argument is less clear for the gain measures than for the origin measures. Examination of the table of partial coefficients for the first three steps in the analysis reveals that with the introduction of the origin predictor for school normlessness, there is a significant decline in the origin partial for the sociometric measure of exposure to delinquency. Specifically, the partials decline from .17 to .08 for males and from .15 to .07 for females. With the introduction of the gain predictors for commitment to parents and school normlessness the origin partials decline even further to .03 for both sexes. The failure of the origin predictor for exposure to delinquency to enter the equation at a significant F level is primarily a consequence of the order in which the variables were added, as school normlessness and association with delinquent peers account for some common variance in the number of reported delinquent acts. Thus, the introduction of the origin predictor for association with delinquent peers does not produce a significant increase in the predictive power of the variables already in the equation. This does not mean that high initial exposure to delinquent peers is not causally related to delinquency; rather, it accounts for much of the same variation in total SRD scores as the initial measure of school normlessness.

The overall power of the school predictors on total SRD gain scores is indicated in Table 7-2. The multiple correlations are .44 and .40 for males and females, respectively. The comparable correlations for the total number of delinquent acts are .54 and .50 (Table 7-1). The school predictors are somewhat more effective in explaining the frequency than the changes in the total number of delinquent acts. This trend was also observed in the zero-order relationships. Prior rates of delinquency are not controlled in the total SRD frequency scores, and the greater predictability for this measure may be a direct consequence of the association between the predictors and prior delinquency. If this is the case, then the regression analysis on the total SRD gain scores reflects the predictive power of these variables more accurately.

Delinquency and the Home

The multiple regression analyses for the home context are presented in Tables 7-3 and 7-4. These tables show the regressions of the predictors on total SRD frequency and gain scores. The multiple correlation of the home-context predictors with total SRD frequency scores is .35 for males and .44 for females. While sex differences with respect to school-context predictors were limited, the home-context measures appear to be better predictors of delinquency among females than males. Further, for females the home predictors are nearly as strong as the school measures; the former account for about 20 percent of the variance in total SRD frequency scores, and the latter explain approximately 25 percent. In contrast, the school predictors account for approximately 30 percent of the variance in male delinquency, whereas the home predictors explain only 12 percent. The sex differential in the predictive power of the measures derived from the context of the home is greatly reduced when a more conservative measure, the total SRD gain score is used; the multiple correlation is .27 for males in comparison with .34 for females. Predictors derived from the home account for approximately 10 percent of the variance in delinquency gain scores. In short, the level of explanation is considerably lower for home than school predictors for males and females.

There are some sex differences in the relative contribution of each predictor to the overall explanation of total SRD frequency scores. First, normlessness in the home appears to be a more powerful predictor for females than males. The origin predictor for home normlessness adds little explanatory power for males, whereas it is one of the most powerful predictors for females. However, this difference is not observed when the total SRD gains are examined, because normlessness in the home adds little independent explanatory power for either sex. In both analyses punitiveness enters the regression equation at a significant

Table 7-3

Stepwise Multiple Regression Analysis: Home Context Predictors on Total Self-Reported Delinquency Frequency Scores

Step Number	Variable	R	R^2	F Value to Enter	p	Final Beta Weight
	Males: $R = .35$, F Value 26.76					
1	Commitment to Parents – Gain	.25	.0625	89.13	.001	-.2010
2	Commitment to Parents – Origin	.33	.1066	65.95	.001	-.1643
3	Home Success – Gain	.34	.1135	10.45	.001	.0658
4	Punitiveness – Origin	.34	.1179	6.67	.001	-.0616
5	Home Normlessness – Origin	.35	.1212	4.90	.001	.0727
6	Home Normlessness – Gain	.35	.1234	3.30	.01	.0534
7	Home Success – Origin	.35	.1234	.02	NS	.0040
	Females: $R = .44$, F Value 43.17					
1	Home Normlessness – Origin	.30	.0900	126.30	.001	.1589
2	Commitment to Parents – Gain	.37	.1404	74.84	.001	-.1712
3	Commitment to Parents – Origin	.41	.1699	45.21	.001	-.1654
4	Home Success – Gain	.43	.1876	27.91	.001	.1264
5	Home Normlessness – Gain	.44	.1914	5.88	.001	.0694
6	Punitiveness – Origin	.44	.1919	.79	NS	-.0230
7	Home Success – Origin	.44	.1921	.31	NS	.0168

Table 7-4
Stepwise Multiple Regression Analysis: Home Context Predictors on Total Self-Reported Delinquency Gain Scores

Step Number	Variable	R	R^2	F Value to Enter	p	Final Beta Weight
		Males: $R = .27$, F Value 14.86				
1	Commitment to Parents – Gain	.23	.0529	74.68	.001	−.2010
2	Commitment to Parents – Origin	.25	.0629	14.25	.001	−.0890
3	Home Success – Gain	.26	.0680	7.26	.001	.0555
4	Punitiveness – Origin	.26	.0701	3.10	.05	−.0447
5	Home Normlessness – Gain	.27	.0717	2.27	.05	.0474
6	Home Success – Origin	.27	.0723	.84	NS	.0319
7	Home Normlessness – Origin	.27	.0725	.30	NS	.0172
		Females: $R = .34$, F Value 23.64				
1	Commitment to Parents – Gain	.26	.0676	92.58	.001	−.1693
2	Home Success – Gain	.31	.0957	39.65	.001	.1435
3	Commitment to Parents – Origin	.33	.1100	20.43	.001	−.0854
4	Home Normlessness – Origin	.33	.1120	2.91	.05	.0606
5	Home Normlessness – Gain	.34	.1149	4.14	.01	.0635
6	Punitiveness – Origin	.34	.1151	.36	NS	.0157
7	Home Success – Origin	.34	.1152	.09	NS	.0093

F level for males but not for females. Inclusion of punitiveness explains some additional variation in total SRD frequency and gain scores but does not lead to a sizable increase in the multiple correlation coefficients.

The Combined Effects of School and Home Predictors

The separate analyses of the predictors derived from the contexts of the home and school indicate that school predictors have greater explanatory power for the frequency of self-reported delinquent acts and the relative change in such behavior during the course of the study. Nevertheless, it is possible that delinquent behavior is not a response to a single context; the effects of failure, alienation, and exposure to pro-delinquent influences may be cumulative across contexts. If this is the case, an analysis simultaneously employing school and home predictors should yield a higher level of explanation. Such analyses are presented in Tables 7-5 and 7-6. In both instances only those predictors which entered at a significant *F* level in previous analyses are included. In no instance did the addition of the other predictors increase the multiple correlation coefficient over the level shown for the last step in the analysis.

The regression of all predictors on total SRD frequency scores yields a multiple correlation of .56 for both sexes. For males, this represents a slight increase in explanatory power in comparison with the school predictors. The latter account for 30 percent of the variance in total SRD frequency scores, whereas the combined school and home predictors explain 31 percent of the variance. The increase in the multiple correlation coefficient is greater for females—the school predictors explain 25 percent of the variance in delinquency rates in comparison with 30 percent for the home and school predictors combined.

For both sexes the strongest individual predictors are derived from the context of the school—school normlessness and commitment to peers. The strongest home predictor appears to be commitment to parents, and it operates to inhibit delinquency. Earlier, in the analyses of commitment, we noted that the effect of strong peer commitment on delinquent behavior was accentuated by weak commitment to parents. This effect was observed in the relationship between exposure to delinquent peers and delinquent behavior; the influence of delinquent friends is maximized when there is little commitment to parents. Examination of the table of partials indicates that there is some reduction in the predictive power of commitment to parents when commitment to peers is introduced into the regression equation. While commitment to parents and commitment to peers account for some common variance, both have a substantial independent effect on delinquent behavior. The only other home predictor producing a substantial increase in the multiple correlation coefficient

Table 7-5

Stepwise Multiple Regression Analysis: All Predictor Variables on Total Self-Reported Delinquency Frequency Scores

Males: $R = .56$, F Value 40.35

Step Number	Variable	R	R^2	F Value to Enter	p	Final Beta Weight
1	School Normlessness – Origin	.34	.1156	174.76	.001	.2273
2	Commitment to Peers – Gain	.46	.2079	155.64	.001	.2397
3	School Normlessness – Gain	.51	.2591	92.23	.001	.1767
4	Sociometric Exposure – Gain	.52	.2752	29.74	.001	.1205
5	Commitment to Parents – Gain	.54	.2873	22.56	.001	-.1146
6	Commitment to Peers – Origin	.55	.2990	22.22	.001	.1136
7	Commitment to Parents – Origin	.55	.3042	10.07	.001	-.0742
8	Home Success – Gain	.55	.3078	6.87	.001	.0804
9	Academic Success – Gain	.56	.3104	5.05	.001	.0576
10	Home Normlessness – Gain	.56	.3117	2.49	.01	.0449
11	Punitiveness – Origin	.56	.3127	1.94	.05	-.0334

Females: $R = .56$, F Value 38.06

Step Number	Variable	R	R^2	F Value to Enter	p	Final Beta Weight
1	School Normlessness – Gain	.30	.0900	126.30	.001	.1726
2	School Normlessness – Origin	.42	.1741	129.93	.001	.1345
3	Commitment to Peers – Gain	.46	.2126	62.37	.001	.1837
4	Home Success – Gain	.49	.2448	54.31	.001	.1198
5	Commitment to Parents – Origin	.52	.2691	42.30	.001	-.1091
6	Commitment to Parents – Gain	.53	.2852	28.76	.001	-.1174
7	Commitment to Peers – Origin	.55	.2975	22.11	.001	.1040
8	Sociometric Exposure – Gain	.55	.3037	11.34	.001	.0891
9	Home Normlessness – Origin	.56	.3088	9.42	.001	.0771

Table 7-6
Stepwise Multiple Regression Analysis: All Predictor Variables on Total Self-Reported Delinquency Gain Scores

Step Number	Variable	R	R^2	F Value to Enter	p	Final Beta Weight
	Males: $R = .46$, F Value 23.78					
1	Commitment to Peers – Gain	.33	.1089	163.39	.001	.2516
2	School Normlessness – Gain	.40	.1625	85.50	.001	.1938
3	Sociometric Exposure – Gain	.42	.1793	27.37	.001	.1299
4	Commitment to Parents – Gain	.44	.1938	24.00	.001	−.1198
5	School Normlessness – Origin	.45	.1997	9.75	.001	.0786
6	Academic Success – Gain	.45	.2046	8.17	.001	.0818
7	Home Success – Gain	.46	.2071	4.30	.001	.0627
	Females: $R = .46$, F Value 22.51					
1	School Normlessness – Gain	.31	.0961	135.77	.001	.1837
2	Commitment to Peers – Gain	.38	.1432	70.21	.001	.1949
3	Home Success – Gain	.42	.1764	51.41	.001	.1217
4	Commitment to Parents – Gain	.44	.1905	22.16	.001	−.1217
5	Commitment to Parents – Origin	.45	.2003	15.62	.001	−.0675
6	Sociometric Exposure – Gain	.45	.2066	10.00	.001	.0761
7	Commitment to Peers – Origin	.46	.2094	2.05	.05	.0385

was the measure of parental acceptance. It yielded an increase of .0322 for females but only .0036 for males. Again, parental rejection is a more significant cause of female than male delinquency.

The regression of all predictors on the total SRD gain scores produces a multiple correlation of .46 for both sexes (Table 7-6). This represents a slight increase over the explanatory power of the school variables alone. The increase in the multiple correlation coefficient is .0125 for males and .0492 for females. The relative contribution of particular predictors is essentially the same as was observed with the total SRD frequency scores; the most powerful predictors are school normlessness and commitment to peers. Parental rejection is a stronger predictor for females than males. Again, the major difference between the total SRD frequency and gain measures is the lower level of explanatory power when the relative increases or decreases in delinquent behavior during the course of the study are predicted.

Discussion: In general, the evidence provides adequate support for our theoretical scheme. In the bivariate analyses we found support for most of the causal sequences specified by the theory; the multivariate analysis confirms that the causal effects of our predictors on delinquent behavior are additive. Yet, the overall level of explanation provided by our predictors is not high. The combined effect of the school and home predictors accounts for only 31 percent of the variance in total SRD frequency scores and 21 percent of the variance in total SRD gain scores. Because we are unaware of any other research that attempts the prediction of delinquent behavior, we have no basis for judging this level of explanation. Clearly, a multiple correlation of .56 is not unusually high for retrospective studies. However, we infer on the basis of our data that the actual predictive power of causal variables is seriously overestimated by their correlation with prior delinquency. Given these considerations, we view the level of predictive power provided by our theoretical variables as substantial, and our findings have important substantive implications.

With respect to specific components of our theoretical scheme, the data suggest that anticipation of success or failure generally plays a minor role in the explanation of delinquent behavior. With the exception of the gain measure for parental acceptance for females, the measures of success-failure are relatively weak variables in the multiple regression equation. The gain scores are consistently stronger predictors than the origin measures, and in most of the stepwise regression analyses they enter the equation at significant F levels. However, their predictive power is generally low. Consistent with our other findings is the fact that the females' gain score for the measure of success in the home is the strongest of the several measures of success-failure.

The measure of punitiveness adds nothing to the prediction of delinquency for females, although it makes a weak contribution to the prediction of delinquency for males. The association is in the predicted direction, but the strength of the independent relationship between punitiveness and delinquency is weak; in fact, it is too weak to offer substantive support for the hypothesis that extrapunitiveness is conducive to delinquent behavior. Deletion of this measure from our set of predictors would have essentially no effect on their predictive power.

The original level and changes in school normlessness and increasing commitment to peers are consistently the most powerful predictors of delinquency. In the analyses involving only school-context predictors and in the analyses employing school and home predictors, these three measures account for the major proportion of the variance explained. The parallel measures for the home context are relatively weak. Exposure to delinquent peers is not as strong a variable as anticipated; this is partly the case because it accounts for some common variance with school normlessness and commitment to peers. Association with delinquent peers is a stronger predictor for males than females.

Several generalizations are warranted. First, the school appears to be a more critical social context than the home or community. The measures of academic success, school normlessness, and exposure and commitment to peers produce a level of explanation that is significantly greater than is generated by home-context predictors and is almost identical to the level that results when all predictors are combined. Further, when the home and school predictors are utilized, the latter are the strongest predictors. These data offer strong support for our hypothesis that the conditions conducive to delinquent behavior are primarily alienation from the school, commitment to peers, and association with delinquent friends. We were surprised to find that commitment to peers had such a strong direct influence on delinquency. In the analyses involving all predictors, the gain in commitment to peers consistently had the highest beta weight in the regression equation. This finding is clearly at odds with Hirschi's contention that attachment to peers inhibits delinquent behavior [103]. Further, it is not simply a reflection of differential association, because high attachment to peer groups is conducive to delinquency whether or not the group is characterized as delinquent. For the home, the most significant measure is commitment to parents, and it complements commitment to peers. This variable acts as an inhibitor—commitment to parents is not conducive to delinquency. School normlessness, exposure to delinquent friends, and the combination of high peer and low parental commitment account for virtually all of the explained variance. While the school predictors are stronger than the home predictors for males and females, it is apparent that the home is a more influential context for females than males. Home predictors alone account for little delinquency on the part of males. For females, however, limited parental acceptance and home normlessness are relatively strong predictors.

Second, our theory accounts equally well for delinquency among males and females. The combined set of predictors produce identical multiple correlations for males and females for the SRD frequency and gain measures. Although there are some sex differences with respect to the significance of particular contexts, the same conceptual variables are involved. Our claim for a general theory of delinquency thus receives support from these data.

Third, the gain scores are generally stronger predictors than the origin measures. The only origin predictors consistently yielding an increase in explanatory power are school normlessness, commitment to peers, and commitment to parents. This outcome may be a function of the extensive time lag built into the measures of the dependent variable, delinquency. This raises some question about the appropriate time span for a causal analysis. In particular, failure and patterns of association with delinquent peers, as measured in the ninth grade, were only weakly associated with rates of delinquency over the following three years. On the other hand, measures of alienation and commitment to peers obtained in the ninth grade were good predictors of subsequent delinquency, and it was the changes in these variables that were the strongest gain predictors. Possibly a shorter time span in the dependent variable would have produced even stronger results. However, we know relatively little about the dynamics of the variables commonly employed in delinquency research and almost nothing about the appropriate time lags for maximizing their effects. We have taken a step in this direction and have demonstrated that failure, alienation, exposure to delinquent influences, and commitment to parents and peers account for a substantial proportion of the variation in delinquency rates over a succeeding three-year period.

The Prediction of Dropout

Dropout and the School Context

A multiple regression analysis similar to that employed for delinquent behavior was utilized to estimate the predictive power of the causal variables on dropout. The stepwise multiple regression analysis with predictors derived from the context of the school is presented in Table 7-7. Final Dropout Status serves as the criterion variable; it may be recalled that in this classification dropouts and nondropouts among intellectually capable subjects are distinguished (see Chapter 3). As in the previous analyses, the origin score is the measure obtained at the beginning of the ninth grade, whereas the gain score reflects increases or decreases in a variable to the beginning of the period in which a subject left school. The gain score for DO Vs and graduates is the average gain across the 4 time periods.

Unlike delinquency, dropout is a class-related phenomenon. The zero-order correlation between class and dropout is .15 for males and females. Although the relationship is not a strong one, lower-class youth drop out more frequently than middle-class youth. We believe that one way to assess the adequacy of our

Table 7-7

Stepwise Multiple Regression Analysis: School Context Predictors on Final Dropout Status

Males: $R = .41$, F Value 23.63

Step Number	Variable	R	R^2	F Value to Enter	p	Final Beta Weight
1	Academic Success – Origin	.30	.0900	128.47	.001	–.1808
2	School Normlessness – Origin	.35	.1209	45.55	.001	.1266
3	Academic Success – Gain	.38	.1411	30.58	.001	–.1177
4	School Normlessness – Gain	.39	.1546	20.76	.001	.1134
5	Exposure to Dropout in School – Gain	.40	.1586	6.08	.001	.0766
6	Exposure to Dropout in School – Origin	.40	.1625	6.01	.001	.0617
7	Commitment to Peers – Gain	.41	.1653	4.28	.01	.0514
8	School Social Isolation – Gain	.41	.1664	1.72	NS	.0321
9	Commitment to Peers – Origin	.41	.1670	1.00	NS	.0366
10	School Social Isolation – Origin	.41	.1677	1.03	NS	.0351
11	Punitiveness – Origin	.41	.1678	.21	NS	.0158
12	Class	.42	.1735	8.91	.001	.0805

Females: $R = .41$, F Value 22.94

Step Number	Variable	R	R^2	F Value to Enter	p	Final Beta Weight
1	School Normlessness – Gain	.25	.0625	85.20	.001	.2219
2	Academic Success – Origin	.33	.1069	63.46	.001	-.1488
3	Exposure to Dropout in School – Origin	.36	.1327	37.95	.001	.0941
4	Commitment to Peers – Origin	.38	.1439	16.69	.001	.1025
5	Academic Success – Gain	.39	.1536	14.64	.001	-.1058
6	Commitment to Peers – Gain	.40	.1604	10.26	.001	.0892
7	School Normlessness – Origin	.40	.1626	3.43	.05	.0750
8	School Social Isolation – Gain	.41	.1643	2.46	.05	.0461
9	School Social Isolation – Origin	.41	.1651	1.22	NS	.0311
10	Punitiveness – Origin	.41	.1656	.90	NS	.0236
11	Exposure to Dropout in School – Gain	.41	.1660	.48	NS	.0257
12	Class	.42	.1724	9.83	.001	.0858

theoretical explanation is to determine whether it can account for this class differential in dropout. In Chapter 2 we suggested two ways in which the theoretical variables might explain such a class differential. One possibility was that lower-class youth were more likely to attribute failure to their own inadequacy and hence were more likely to choose dropout as a solution to school-related difficulties. We also proposed that lower-class youth might be differentially exposed to dropout influences, in the sense that they would be more familiar with and have greater social support for this alternative than middle-class youth. Although there is little support for the first hypothesis, we found evidence that school failure and exposure to dropout were related to social class. Therefore, these variables might account for the class differential in dropout rates. To test this hypothesis, we included our measure of class as a predictor in the stepwise multiple regression analysis, but forced all of the theoretical predictors into the equation before class. In this way we could determine whether our theoretical variables accounted for all of the variance in dropout attributable to class or whether class had some additional, independent explanatory power. Further, an examination of the partials at each step would indicate which variables were class-linked and accounted for this relationship.

The multiple correlation coefficient for the predictors derived from the school context is .41, excluding class. The proportion of variance explained is virtually identical for males and females—approximately 17 percent. The strongest predictor for males is the origin measure for academic achievement, whereas for females it is the gain measure for school normlessness. Punitiveness and the origin score for social isolation in school fail to enter either regression equation at significant F levels; they yield essentially no increase in predictability. The origin score for commitment to peers also fails to contribute any independent explanatory power for males. Similarly, the gain score for the measure of association with dropouts in school contributes nothing for females; its weak showing was unexpected. However, an inspection of the table of partials for each step reveals a decline in the partial for this gain measure from .13 to .02 during the first two steps of the analysis. School normlessness and academic achievement account for the same variance in Final Dropout Status as the gain measure for association with dropouts in school.

The fact that class entered the regression equation at a significant F level for both sexes indicates that our school-context predictors do not completely account for the class differential in dropout. The table of partials shows that at each step the origin score for academic achievement accounts for some of the class effect on dropout; the introduction of this measure reduces the class partial from .15 to .09 for females and to .10 for males. The actual increase in the multiple correlation coefficient attributable to class is minimal—.0057 for males and .0064 for females.

Dropout and the Home Context

The multiple correlation of the home-context predictors on Final Dropout Status is .30 for males and females. In combination, all of the home predictors account for only 9 percent of the variance in dropout; this is substantially below the level of explained variance for the school-context predictors. For both sexes, the origin and gain measures of exposure to dropout influences are by far the strongest of the home predictors. The only other predictors to enter the stepwise analysis at significant F levels for females are the origin and gain scores for home social isolation and the gain score for commitment to parents; for males the origin score for commitment to parents as well as the origin and gain scores for home success enter at significant F levels. None of these latter predictors, however, account for much increase in the multiple correlation coefficient after the measure of exposure to dropout influences in the home enters the equation.

The table of partials for the stepwise analysis indicates that the origin measure for exposure to dropout in the home accounts for almost all of the relationship between class and dropout. The zero-order correlation between this measure and class is .49 for males and .50 for females. When the origin score for exposure to dropout in the home entered the regression analysis, the correlation between class and dropout fell from .15 to .03 for males and .05 for females. Class fails to enter the regression at a significant F level for either sex; it contributes to increases in the multiple correlation coefficient of .0001 for males and .0005 for females. It would appear that the effect of class on dropout is primarily a consequence of the greater exposure of lower-class youth to dropout influences in the home; to a lesser extent, dropout is the result of limited academic success in school.

*The Combined Effects of School
and Home Predictors*

The multiple correlation of all predictors and Final Dropout Status is .45 for males and .44 for females. This represents a slight increase in the level of explanation provided by the school-context measures; the school predictors account for 17 percent of the variance, and the combined set of predictors accounts for approximately 20 percent. This increase is produced by the origin and gain measures of exposure to dropout in the home; they are the only home-context predictors that contribute any substantial amount of independent explanatory power. On the basis of the beta weights in the final regression equation, the order of the most powerful predictors for males is: origin score for exposure to dropout in the home (.20677); origin score for academic achievement (−.15206); origin score for school normlessness (.12163); gain score for exposure to dropout in the school (.10437); and gain score for school normlessness (.10123). For females the order is: gain score for school normlessness (.23101); gain score for exposure to dropout in the home (.15916); origin score for academic achievement (−.13997); and origin score for exposure to dropout in the home (.12007). Again, class was forced into the regression equation last and did not contribute significantly to the amount of variance explained.

The level of explanation provided by our predictor variables is not high, particularly in light of the relatively great differences in the transition rates. In view of the fact that the criterion variable is a dichotomy and only 14 percent of the study population are classified as capable dropouts, regression analysis may not be appropriate.

As an alternative, two discriminant function analyses were completed. Having concluded that the school was the more critical context, we limited the analyses to school-context predictors. First we employed only origin predictors and then included both origin and gain predictors. The first analysis involved an attempt to discriminate between all capable dropouts and graduates, and the origin predictors pertaining to the school discriminated between these categories satisfactorily. The classifications for this analysis are presented in Table 7-8. Some 62 percent of the capable dropouts and 75 percent of the graduates were correctly classified by the predictive measures obtained at the beginning of the study. If the classification is treated as a set of predictions and the actual groups as the outcomes, then our predictions are accurate for 74 percent of the cases.

The classifications for the analysis involving school origin and gain measures is also presented in Table 7-8. Since we had no gain measures for DO IIs, this analysis involves only capable dropouts who left school in Periods III through V. The use of gain measures increases the predictive utility (the percentage of dropouts correctly identified) to 67 percent, but it does not improve the accuracy of our prediction of graduates. The overall accuracy increases slightly to 75 percent.

While this level of accuracy appears reasonably high, more accurate predictions could have been made simply by predicting no dropouts. Using origin measures to predict capable dropouts, we made 624 errors; in comparison, only 339 errors would have been made with a prediction of no dropouts.[2] Our failure to improve upon predictions based upon the modal outcome is a common problem whenever the phenomenon being predicted is relatively rare, as is the case here [253]. A more realistic standard against which we can compare our results is the prediction of dropout obtained from junior high school teachers at the beginning of the study. In essence, we can test whether our predictions, based upon a theoretical model, are more or less accurate than the collective judgment of teachers. The procedure we followed to obtain teachers' predictions was discussed in Chapter 4. We refer to the teachers' modal response for each

Table 7-8

Discriminant Function Analysis: Prediction of Dropout

A. School Origin Predictors[a]–Dropout II to V

Discriminant Function		Outcome	
Classification:	Graduate	Dropout	Total
Graduate	1548	127	1675
Dropout	497	212	709
Total	2045	339	2384

F Ratios: Males = 63.91, $p < .001$
Females = 57.37, $p < .001$

B. School Origin and Gain Predictors[b]–Dropout III to V

Discriminant Function		Outcome	
Classification:	Graduate	Dropout	Total
Graduate	1545	95	1640
Dropout	500	195	695
Total	2045	290	2335

F Ratios: Males = 24.56, $p < .001$
Females = 23.75, $p < .001$

[a]The following Origin Predictors are included: Academic Success, School Normlessness, School Social Isolation, Exposure to Dropout in School, and Commitment to Peers.

[b]Only those predictors entering the stepwise regression analysis at a significant F level are included: School Normlessness, Origin and Gain; Academic Success, Origin and Gain; Commitment to Peers, Origin and Gain; and Exposure to Dropout in School, Origin and Gain.

subject as the teachers' predictions.[3] Two response categories represent a prediction of graduation, and two constitute a prediction of dropout. The middle category, "not very sure one way or the other," is ambiguous with respect to outcome (see Appendix B). For the analysis in Table 7-9, we considered the response of "not very sure" as a prediction of graduation. This decision obviously favored a "no dropout" prediction, and it had the effect of minimizing the potential number of errors in teachers' predictions. Three separate prediction outcomes are presented in Table 7-9. The first involves all dropouts, regardless of type; the second includes only capable dropouts, since this is the type of dropout upon which we focused; and the third involves only capable dropouts who left school during Periods III, IV, and V. The second and third outcomes parallel the predictions of dropout derived from the discriminant function analysis (Table 7-8).

The overall accuracy of the teachers' predictions of dropout, as shown in Part A of Table 7-9, is 84 percent, which is substantially higher than the 74 percent

Table 7-9
Teachers' Predictions of Dropout[a]

A. All Dropouts

Teachers' Predictions		Observed	
	Graduates	Dropouts	Total
Graduates	1705	317	2022
Dropouts	39	108	147
Total	1744	425	2169

B. All Intellectually Capable Dropouts

Teachers' Predictions		Observed	
	Graduates	Dropouts	Total
Graduates	1705	247	1952
Dropouts	39	46	85
Total	1744	293	2037

C. Intellectually Capable Dropouts in Periods III to V

Teachers' Predictions		Observed	
	Graduates	Dropouts	Total
Graduates	1705	217	1922
Dropouts	39	30	69
Total	1744	247	1991

[a]Four hundred and forty subjects are excluded from this analysis; 41 were neither dropouts or graduates, 8 were lost, and 391 had no modal teachers' predictions.

accuracy achieved through use of our theoretical predictors (Table 7-9, Part A). In the prediction of all dropouts, the teachers made 356 errors. This represents a reduction of 16 percent in the errors resulting from a prediction of no dropouts. However, only 25 percent of the actual dropouts were correctly identified as potential dropouts; it is obvious that teachers grossly underpredict dropout.[4]

Limiting the analysis to capable dropouts, we find that the teachers are less successful in identifying this particular type of dropout (Table 7-9, Part B). Only 16 percent of the capable dropouts were identified by the teachers as potential dropouts. The reduction in error or efficiency of these predictions is also low (2.8 percent); it nevertheless is an improvement over a prediction of no dropouts. The overall accuracy of these predictions, 86 percent, is relatively high.

Teachers were more successful in identifying potential dropouts whom we categorized as educationally handicapped than those classified as capable. In fact, the teachers were "very sure" that 20 percent of the capable dropouts would graduate and were "fairly sure" that an additional 31 percent would graduate. In comparison, for only 2 percent of the educationally handicapped dropouts were the teachers "very sure" they would graduate, and they were "fairly sure" about an additional 10 percent. Overall, 46 percent of the educationally handicapped dropouts were identified as potential dropouts by teachers in comparison with only 16 percent of the capable dropouts. Essentially the same picture emerges when the teachers' predictions are restricted to capable dropouts who left after entering high school (Periods III through V). According to the data in Table 7-9, Part C, the teachers' accuracy increases slightly to 87 percent, but the utility of the predictions is 12 percent or slightly lower than in the prediction of all capable dropouts.

The overall accuracy of the teachers' predictions is higher than the predictions on the basis of the school origin measures. The teachers' predictions are also more efficient. However, relatively few of the capable dropouts are identified by the teachers, whereas almost two-thirds are identified by our theoretical variables. The utility of our predictions is, then, considerably higher. While teachers underestimate the proportion of capable dropouts, our predictors overestimate this proportion. These conclusions also apply when the predictions of capable dropouts who leave after entering high school are compared. In the latter case we used both origin and gain predictors. If we had treated the "not sure" category as a prediction of dropout, the teachers' consensus would still have underestimated the occurrence of dropout among capable students and would have failed to identify more than 50 percent of these dropouts.

From our perspective, a good predictive device is one with maximum utility and minimal cost (proportion of graduates incorrectly identified). Such a predictive instrument would maximize the proportion of dropouts identified as potential dropouts and would minimize the proportion of graduates incorrectly identified as potential dropouts [11; 253]. According to these criteria, the prediction of no dropouts would not be satisfactory because such a prediction has no utility, although it also involves no cost. Similarly, a prediction that everyone would drop out would result in 100 percent utility, but it would not be a good prediction because of the high cost or the sizable number of incorrect predictions of dropout for prospective graduates. A useful indicator of predictive effectiveness is utility minus cost [253]. By this definition the predictive effectiveness of our theoretical variables, as measured only in terms of origin scores, is 38.2 percent in comparison with 13.5 percent for the comparable teachers' predictions. For the combined origin and gain predictors the effectiveness is 39.1 percent in comparison with 9.9 percent for the teachers' predictions of dropout during Periods III through V. In terms of this criterion, our theoretical predictors are more effective than the collective judgment of junior high school teachers.

In view of the correlation between academic achievement and dropout it might be surprising that so few capable dropouts were identified by the teachers. Academic achievement was clearly predictive of subsequent dropout. However, few of the capable dropouts were actually failing or even in danger of failing; consequently, they were not particularly visible to teachers. Stated differently, the grade point averages of the capable dropouts were typically in the C to C— range. The capable dropouts had a lower mean GPA than the graduates, but the difference was not great.

Discussion: The evidence from the bivariate and multivariate analyses provides strong support for our general theoretical position. Failure, alienation, and exposure to dropout are all causally linked to dropout; together they account for a substantial proportion of the variance in dropout. However, the level of explanation is not high: the multiple correlation of all the predictors with dropout is .45 for males and .44 for females. Thus, the theoretical measures account for more of the variation in delinquent behavior than in dropout.

Several alterations and qualifications must be made with reference to specific components of the general theory. First, there was some support for the hypothesis that dropouts are intropunitive, both in the bivariate analyses and in the consistent direction of the relationships in the multivariate analysis, but for all practical purposes punitiveness contributed nothing to the explanation of dropout. Elimination of this measure from our set of predictors would have no effect on their predictive power. In the bivariate analysis social isolation and normlessness were predictive of dropout. In the multiple regression analysis, school normlessness was clearly the stronger predictor; normlessness in the context of the home and social isolation in the home and school were relatively weak predictors. Taken together, the initial measures of academic achievement and school normlessness account for virtually all of the predictive power of social isolation in school. In other words, social isolation contributes little independent explanatory power for dropout in the multiple regression analysis. The finding that dropouts tend to score high on the measure of normlessness in school as well as on the measure of social isolation raises a question about our conceptualization of dropout as a retreatist adaptation. Further analysis is required with nondelinquent and delinquent dropouts separated to control for the confounding effect of delinquency, which is causally linked to normlessness.

Failure in school appears to be a stronger factor in dropout than in delinquency. The beta weights for the measure of academic success are considerably larger in the analysis of dropout than delinquency; this is particularly true for males. The measures of exposure to dropout in the school and home are relatively strong predictors of dropout; exposure to dropout in the home interprets the relationship between social class and dropout.

Several generalizations about dropouts may be drawn from these findings. First, the school appears to be the more critical social context. Our measures of failure and alienation in the home are relatively weak predictors of dropout in comparison with similar measures for the context of the school. The predictors derived from the setting of the school account for a substantially greater proportion of the variance in dropout, and in the multivariate analysis they are the more powerful predictors. The one exception involves exposure to dropout in the home. In the general analysis, this is the strongest predictor for males and one of the stronger predictors for females. Dropout appears to be a response to failure and alienation from the school, commitment to peers, and exposure to dropout influences in the school and home.

Second, the level of predictability appears to be quite similar for males and females. There are no sex differences in the level of explanation provided with either home- or school-context measures. Exposure to dropout in the home, school normlessness, academic achievement, and association with dropouts in school are consistently the strongest predictors for both sexes.

Finally, it is apparent that capable dropouts are not as easily identified by teachers as is often assumed. The discriminant function analyses indicate that the prediction of dropout on the basis of our theoretical scheme is more effective in identifying potential dropouts with adequate intellectual ability than teachers' predictions. As might be expected with a relatively rare outcome such as dropout, the overall accuracy and efficiency of our predictions are not particularly impressive. Nevertheless, 67 percent of the dropouts were identified correctly with less than 25 percent of the graduates incorrectly identified as dropouts. Most of our errors are due to an incorrect classification of graduates as potential dropouts; relatively few dropouts are incorrectly classified as graduates by our predictors.

Notes

1. At each step, the variable with the highest partial correlation value enters the multiple regression equation. This procedure is followed until all variables have entered the equation.

2. The efficiency of a predictive device is defined as the percentage reduction in the percentage of error, and the latter term refers to the errors produced by use of modal predictions. In Table 7-8 our efficiency is −84 percent for Part A and −105 percent for Part B of the table.

3. There were no modal predictions for 391 subjects, and these respondents are not included in the analyses presented in Table 7-9. The overall dropout rate among those with no modal prediction was 30 percent in comparison with 18 percent among capable students. Nevertheless, this rate of dropout is lower than the rate for students with a "not very sure" modal prediction.

4. This is in part a consequence of our decision to treat the "not sure" category as a prediction of graduation. Had we considered this modal response as a prediction of dropout, the overall accuracy of the teachers' predictions would have dropped to 80 percent, the efficiency (reduction in error) would have declined to −15 percent and the utility (percentage of dropouts correctly identified) would have increased to approximately 50 percent.

8

Summary and Implications

In this volume we have tested a theoretical explanation of delinquency and dropout which constitutes a modification and elaboration of the formulation set forth by Cloward and Ohlin in *Delinquency and Opportunity* [33]. Although Cloward and Ohlin had different objectives, we developed from their formulation an explanation of delinquent behavior in terms of four variables: (1) aspiration-opportunity disjunction, (2) internal-external attribution of blame, (3) alienation or normlessness, and (4) access and exposure to delinquent groups. We suggested that the critical conditions for delinquency are real or anticipated failure, extrapunitiveness, normlessness, and extensive exposure to delinquent persons or groups. A similar set of variables and causal sequences provided a parallel explanation of high school dropouts: dropout involves failure to achieve valued goals, intropunitiveness, social isolation, and exposure to dropout. This investigation reflects an attempt to relate these conditions as they are found in the community, school, and home to delinquent behavior and dropout.

Our research should not be construed as a test of Cloward and Ohlin's formulation. Whereas they explicitly limited the scope of their theory to gang delinquency among urban, lower-class males, we attempted to account for the involvement in delinquency of both males and females from all social classes. On the basis of critical analyses of Cloward and Ohlin's position and relevant empirical research, we questioned the salience of perceived failure to achieve long-range goals as well as their limitation of the theory of differential opportunity to lower-class males. We assumed that the conditions leading to delinquent behavior and dropout may be found among youth of both sexes and from all classes. The major purpose of this investigation was to evaluate the adequacy of this theoretical scheme. If our objective had been to estimate precisely the delinquency and dropout rates in a community, a probability sample would have been mandatory. Convinced that variable representation is more important than proportionate representation, we employed purposive sampling to obtain the combinations of variable values required to evaluate our theory. The effect of this decision is that generalization of the relationships observed in this study to other populations cannot be made with a known degree of accuracy.

In this research a type of cluster sample was used in which the basic sampling unit was a school, rather than a person. We sampled only in the purposive selection of eight schools to guarantee inclusion of students with a wide range of social, economic, and racial or ethnic characteristics. All of the schools were located in metropolitan areas. Seven of the schools were located in southern California; the other school was in the northern part of the state. All students who entered these schools as ninth graders in September 1963 comprised the target population. With the exclusion of 5 student and 41 parental refusals, the study population consisted of 2,617 students.

We employed a longitudinal design, and data were gathered in the period from September 1963 to September 1967. Initial observations were obtained when the study population entered the ninth grade, and additional data were collected annually until the usual date of graduation from high school for the cohort. The first observations were calculated to precede dropout and extensive involvement in delinquent behavior in order to permit assessment of postulated cause-effect relationships.

Two types of predictor variables were derived from the repeated measures of each independent variable. The initial measure was treated as an origin predictor. The origin predictors were based on raw scores that were converted into standard scores. Gain predictors were also developed to assess the amount and direction of change through time for each independent variable. The gain predictors were residual gain scores, and these were calculated for each of the four years of the study.

In this investigation a dropout was defined as a person who left school for a period of at least 30 consecutive days for a reason other than death. There were 2 deaths in the cohort during the study, and for convenience they were classified as involuntary dropouts. In terms of this operational definition, 558 persons were classified as dropouts during the course of the study; these respondents left school 674 times. This definition adequately conveys the extent to which students interrupt their high school education, but does not indicate their final educational status. At the end of the study, 79 percent of the cohort were graduates, 19 percent were nongraduates, and 2 percent were still enrolled in school. Two percent of the study population are of particular interest in view of the considerable public concern regarding dropout. These respondents, who comprise 10 percent of the dropouts, were dropout graduates; that is, they graduated, even though at one point they dropped out of school.

Three types of dropouts—involuntary, educationally handicapped, and capable—were identified. Only 2 percent of the dropouts left school involuntarily; 32 percent were classified as educationally handicapped, and 66 percent were capable of completing high school. Within the category of capable dropouts, approximately one-fifth were forced to leave school by administrative order; the remainder left voluntarily. Two implications of these findings deserve mention. First, few students, at least in the setting in which our research was conducted, leave school because of financial pressure or serious illness. Second, dropout among intellectually capable youth is not always voluntary. While troublesome behavior undoubtedly triggered the administrative response, a sizable proportion of the capable dropouts were forced to leave school.

As conceptualized in this study, delinquency refers, first of all, to a class of behavior. In our analysis the fundamental measure of delinquency provided an estimate of the number of delinquent acts committed by a respondent during particular time periods. In addition, the relative seriousness of particular acts and the specific nature of each act or type of offense was considered. A self-report instrument, a modification of the Nye-Short delinquency checklist, was included in the questionnaire administered to the study population during the ninth and twelfth grades. The response categories of the SRD items were transformed into frequencies on the basis of a conservative scoring procedure. Classification of offenses with respect to seriousness was accomplished by adoption and extrapolation of the distinction between felonies and misdemeanors in the California Penal Code.

Only 10 delinquent acts are included in the SRD measure; obviously, a number of other acts would have met our definition of delinquent behavior. Nevertheless, the study population reported a considerable volume of delinquent behavior. For the 3 years of junior high school, the 2,617 subjects reported an estimated 10,073 delinquent acts, whereas their responses in senior high school reflect involvement in 13,141 offenses. Over the six-year period, the study population reported 23,214 delinquent acts or an average of 9.63 infractions for each subject. The males reported almost twice as many offenses as the females—12.24 in comparison with 6.90 for females.

A major question regarding self-report analyses has concerned the reliability and validity of the data. The estimates obtained on the basis of the SRD have face validity, and we made a number of external and internal validity checks. While primarily of methodological interest, some underreporting was discovered; the amount of error in the direction of underreporting was substantially greater for serious than nonserious offenses. Nevertheless, the comparisons suggested that responses to the SRD are valid indicators of the nature and extent of involvement in delinquent activities.

For the study population, 1,486 police contacts were recorded. The self-report and official data permitted estimation of the amount of hidden delinquency, the probability of police contact according to the frequency of delinquent behavior, and conditional probabilities of police contact in terms of the sex, ethnic ancestry, and social class of the offender as well as the seriousness of the delinquent act committed. These divergent sources reveal that there are approximately 5 police contacts for every 100 self-reported offenses, indicating that there is a substantial amount of hidden delinquency in this population. Further, police contact rates vary by sex, ethnicity, and social class; males, members of minority groups, and lower-class juveniles have a relatively greater risk of police contact for each delinquent act they commit. The implication is clear: exclusive reliance on official records in tests of etiological propositions is unwarranted.

A few general observations about the findings we derived using a longitudinal design are in order. When we related our origin predictors to prior delinquency, we approximated the associations examined in studies employing a cross-sectional design. In this part of our analysis, our results were highly consistent with earlier research. The implication is that our study population is not atypical, which gives us greater confidence that our predictive findings may be generalized beyond our sample.

Of greater importance are the methodological implications of our findings. We discovered that the relationships between origin measures and prior delinquency are consistently stronger than the predictive relationships, that is, the associations between origin scores and subsequent delinquency. This has an important implication: the strength of all of our predictors is overestimated by their correlations with prior delinquency. A tendency to overestimate the causal significance of independent variables may be inherent in research utilizing a cross-sectional design. Another implication is that the relationships between independent and dependent variables are not unidirectional. Specifically, normlessness and exposure to delinquency appear to be not only consequences of prior delinquency but also causes of subsequent delinquency. As normlessness and exposure to delinquency are predictive of SRD gain scores, their predictive power is *independent* of their relationships with prior delinquency; however, in almost every case the predictive relationships are weaker than the associations with prior delinquency. The pattern is consistent: the strongest relationships are with prior delinquency, the next strongest are with the SRD frequency scores, and the weakest are with the SRD gain measure. In the first instance the temporal order is incorrect, and in the second set of relationships the effects of prior delinquency are not controlled. Prior delinquency is controlled in the SRD gain score; hence, the strongest causal argument can be made with the SRD gain measure. We conclude that the genuine predictive power of all of our variables is lower than has been inferred from analyses which ignore temporal order or fail to control for the effects of prior delinquency.

Further, we find little evidence of interaction effects between the origin and gain predictors. In other words, the effect of a positive or negative gain is similar for respondents with high and low origin scores on a particular measure. For example, increasing exposure to delinquency is predictive of a gain in delinquency even when initial levels of exposure are controlled.

The guiding proposition for this study was that delinquent behavior and dropout are alternative responses to failure and alienation and are influenced by selective exposure to such behavior. Hypothesizing that the school was the most critical social context, we examined the causal relationship between these variables and delinquency and dropout in each of three social contexts—the home, the school, and the community. We proposed that the explanation of failure would specify the alternative selected. Our findings confirmed our central hypothesis, and the predictors derived from the context of the school produced the highest levels of predictability. However, our hypothesis regarding punitiveness was not confirmed. Analyzing the relationship between delinquency and dropout, we discovered that delinquency is causally involved in dropout, and dropout in turn leads to *decreasing* involvement in delinquency. This finding lends additional support to our position that the school is the critical generating milieu for delinquency.

Alienation, association with delinquent friends, and delinquent behavior appear to be bound together in a mutually reinforcing process. This linkage forces us to recognize that delinquent activity is itself a *cause* of conflict and alienation in the home and school and leads delinquent youth to seek other delinquent juveniles as associates. Our findings indicate that we must seriously consider the extent to which conventional delinquency treatment programs facilitate further delinquency by isolating youth from conventional peer associations. Efforts should be made to integrate youthful offenders in conventional activities with nondelinquent peers. Similar processes occur in the school where "troublemakers" and "failures" are grouped in some kind of tracking system. These responses on the part of school authorities increase the juvenile's alienation, exposure to pro-delinquent influences, and further involvement in delinquency.

The weakest link in our causal chain appears to be in the instigation variables. Cloward and Ohlin's original hypothesis is not supported, nor is our hypothesis regarding failure to achieve the goals of the youth culture. Neither delinquency nor dropout appears to be a consequence of failure to achieve peer culture goals. Because failure was the first variable in the causal sequence and was, therefore, the most distant from delinquency and dropout, we expected the relationships between failure and delinquency and dropout to be weaker than the others. Yet, the predictive power of our measures of failure for delinquency is even more limited than expected. The relationship between failure and dropout is stronger, and the types of failure predictive of dropout are identical to the ones predictive of delinquency.

Support for particular causal relationships varied greatly. Our findings with respect to the relationship between failure, the explanation of failure, and delinquency were particularly weak and cast doubt on the significance of perceived failure or limited access to valued goals as an important motivational stimulus for delinquency. Our inability to obtain more consistent support for this postulated relationship may be a consequence of inadequate measurement. We would be inclined to accept this interpretation except for the fact that other researchers have also failed to find empirical support for this relationship. There is accumulating evidence that failure, particularly anticipated failure to achieve long-range educational and occupational goals, is not a highly significant factor in delinquent behavior.

This has serious implications for current delinquency prevention programs that are oriented toward increasing educational and occupational opportunities for youth. Our data lead us to question whether such programs will have any effect on future rates of delinquency. While our findings clearly support the relationship between feelings of normlessness and delinquency, there is little evidence that the perception of limited opportunity to achieve long-range goals is a major cause of normlessness; further, the data show that there is not a direct causal relationship between this type of failure and delinquency.

The only measures for which we established a causal connection between failure and delinquency pertain to academic achievement and parental acceptance. These involve immediate rather than long-range goals. It is difficult to conceive of delinquency as an alternative means to academic success or parental love and acceptance. A more reasonable interpretation seems to be that delinquency is a way of dealing with the immediate social and psychological consequences of failure in school and difficulties in the home; it may be a way of handling degradation and rejection experienced in these contexts. Since failure in school is more visible and has a wider range of immediate as well as long-term social consequences, we would expect it to be more conducive to delinquency than failure within one's home. In any event, we view delinquent behavior as a way of coping with social stigma and loss of self-esteem associated with failure, rather than as an alternative means to achieve academic or familial goals.

While these measures of failure are weak predictors of delinquency, academic success is a relatively strong predictor of dropout, and parental acceptance is a relatively weak predictor. The weakest link in the causal chain leading to dropout is the postulated relationship between internal explanations of failure, social isolation, and dropout. We argued that intropunitive explanations of failure would lead to social isolation and then to dropout. In this sense, dropout was conceived to be a retreatist adaptation rather than one involving rebellion or innovation. Our findings offer only limited support for this postulated sequence. In the setting of the school, normlessness and social isolation are conducive to dropout, but dropouts are only slightly more intropunitive than graduates. Unfortunately, we did not distinguish between delinquent and nondelinquent dropouts. Consequently, our analysis of the variables that should have differentiated delinquents from dropouts was confounded. This may explain the weak showing of intropunitiveness and social isolation as predictors of dropout.

The data generally support our hypothesis that the school is the critical social context for the generation of delinquent behavior. For males, the most powerful predictors of delinquency are limited academic achievement, school normlessness, association with delinquent classmates, and commitment to peers. For females, the best predictors are parental rejection, school normlessness, association with delinquent classmates, and commitment to peers. However, academic failure as well as normlessness and social isolation in the home are also predictive of female delinquency. Clearly, the home is a more important setting for females than for males—failure, alienation, and exposure in the school and home are conducive to female delinquency. In contrast, none of the measures for the home context are strongly predictive of male delinquency.

The strongest predictors of dropout are academic failure, school normlessness and social isolation, exposure to dropout in the home, and commitment to peers; there are no significant sex differences. The fact that exposure to dropout in the home and commitment to school peers are both predictive of dropout is not inconsistent, as association with juveniles who dropped out of school is also predictive of dropout. The data do not support the contention that dropout is precipitated by problems in the home. Rather, the major instigating forces in dropout are to be found in academic failure and alienation from the school. Exposure to dropout, whether it occurs in the school or home, is generally conducive to dropout.

Finally, our data provide an explanation for the fact that dropout is related to class while delinquency is not. A number of our findings, taken together, make it possible to account for the class differential in dropout. Social class is unrelated to school normlessness but is associated with social isolation in school. It is also the case that exposure to delinquent friends is only weakly associated with class, but exposure to dropout in the home is strongly related to class. Lower-class youth are more likely to experience isolation in school, and they have more exposure to dropout influences in the home. Both of these conditions are conducive to dropout. On the other hand, the conditions most conducive to delinquency are either unrelated or weakly related to class. We would, therefore, not expect a class differential in delinquent behavior.

One other finding deserves special comment. The fact that a strong commitment to one's peers was conducive to delinquency, regardless of the extent of delinquency in that group, suggests that the peer culture itself is conducive to delinquency. Respondents with the highest rates of delinquency were youth who had strong commitment to peers and weak commitment to parents. We infer that they were over-committed to their peers. It is not necessary to argue that the general peer culture is involved in direct socialization for delinquency or even that it offers positive sanctions for delinquent acts. There is ample evidence that the peer culture is oppositional, and it is reasonable to assume that a strong attachment to peers would attenuate the power of the conventional norms in the same way that strong attachment to parents would strengthen them. If our interpretation is correct, it accounts for the independent causal effects of commitment to peers and association with delinquent peers.

Our analysis of the particular conditions conducive to delinquency and dropout challenges the conventional stereotypes of delinquents and dropouts. First, we found little support for the view that dropout was motivated by difficulties at home; at the point of leaving school, dropouts were no more likely than graduates to experience rejection or alienation from their parents. In most instances, the immediate stimulus for voluntary dropout was some difficulty or crisis in school. Typically, this involved conflict with a teacher resulting in a temporary suspension from which the student never returned. Since approximately one-fifth of the dropouts were pushed out of school, the phenomenon of dropout cannot be viewed strictly in terms of personal decisions on the part of youth to terminate their education. Although a substantial number of dropouts were in fact pushouts, formal expulsion was rare. Pushout resulted from the enforcement of rules prohibiting pregnant girls, married students, and troublesome 18-year old students from attending the regular day-school program. Few students dropped out of school because they were attracted to work or had to work to help support their families. Thus, there was little evidence that dropouts rejected the benefits of a high school diploma. Second, although dropouts had limited involvement in extracurricular activities, this was not predictive of dropout. The vast majority of high school students in our cohort had little involvement in these activities. An obvious inference is that further involvement in activities will not reduce the dropout rate. Further, the dropouts did not express serious dissatisfaction with their degree of participation in these activities prior to leaving school, though retrospectively they did express some dissatisfaction. Some of them perceived that with greater involvement they might have remained in school. Third, dropout tended to be a group adaptation to school problems. In several instances whole groups dropped out together. Association with dropout peers and limited support for education in the home were both causally related to dropout. Finally, insofar as delinquency is concerned, there is reason to question whether dropouts necessarily suffer all of the negative consequences usually ascribed to dropout. There was considerable evidence that the dropout's involvement in delinquency began while the subject was in school and was primarily a response to experiences in the school. Departure from school reduced the dropouts' rate of delinquent behavior and the likelihood of official police contact.

Our data challenge similar assumptions about the causes of delinquency. First, delinquent behavior does not appear to be related to social class or ethnic origins. Status deprivation—the perception that others have nicer clothes and homes—is related to social class and ethnicity but is not predictive of delinquency. On the other hand, the rate of police contact is related to social class, ethnicity, and perceptions of status deprivation. Second, the level of participation in the school's extracurricular activities is not predictive of delinquency. In fact, youth who are highly involved in school activities report rates of delinquency slightly higher than those with limited involvement. Delinquent behavior is not restricted to those labeled "hoods" or "outsiders" by the peer culture, but appears to be a more general feature of adolescent culture. Third, delinquency among males is less of a response to rejection and alienation from the home than female delinquency. While the school is the most critical social context for both sexes, it is particularly influential with respect to male delinquency. Finally, our analysis suggests that the relationships between failure, normlessness, association with delinquent peers, and delinquent behavior are mutually reinforcing. Failure, normlessness, and association with delinquent friends are both causes and consequences of involvement in delinquent behavior.

Delinquency increases the likelihood that youth will do poorly in school and perceive themselves as rejected by their parents. Involvement in delinquent behavior has a particularly strong influence on feelings of normlessness in school as well as friendship choices.

In view of these findings, the current anti-dropout campaign and attempts to raise the age of compulsory attendance might well be reconsidered. To force a youth to remain in school for a longer period of time is not always beneficial for the individual. There is, nevertheless, a widespread policy among probation officers, court officials, and even state legislators to encourage delinquent dropouts to return to school. This policy is based on the assumption that the school functions as a positive form of social control and is conducive to better life adjustment. Our findings are at odds with this assumption and imply that the school often aggravates a youth's problems rather than alleviating them.

It is not a coincidence that the rate of delinquency is inversely related to the rate of dropout. As the holding power of our schools has increased, so has the rate of delinquency. Compulsory school attendance facilitates delinquency by forcing youth to remain in what is sometimes a frustrating situation in which they are stigmatized as failures. It is not surprising that these youth, trapped in our schools, rebel or attempt to escape. In the final analysis, escape either through dropout or graduation appears to be the only satisfactory resolution of this problem. For the dropout and the graduate, rates of delinquency decline upon leaving the compulsory school setting. Delinquency, on the other hand, is not an adequate solution, but serves only to set into motion reciprocal processes of rejection and alienation and thereby increases the probabilities of failure.

It does not necessarily follow from these observations that all students who are alienated and frustrated by their experiences in school or who perceive the school as meaningless should be encouraged to drop out of high school. In some cases this may be an appropriate course of action and one which should not be restricted by law. A more important strategy would be to change the structure of the school—to explore new types of learning environments in which competition is minimized and in which failure ceases to be a functional prerequisite of the educational system.

Appendixes

Appendix A:
Correlation Matrices

Table A-1
Correlation Matrix: Home and School Predictors and Total Self-Reported Delinquent Behavior

Males

	2	3	4	5	6	7	8	9	10	11	12	13	14	15	16	17
1. Academic Success: O[a]	.00	-.05	-.01	.06	-.31	-.08	-.02	-.01	-.32	-.15	-.23	-.06	.01	-.01	-.13	-.06
2. Academic Success: G		-.02	-.08	-.01	-.10	-.03	-.01	.00	-.12	-.16	-.10	-.06	.06	.01	-.03	.02
3. Home Success: O			.00	-.06	.30	.08	.44	.05	.08	.08	.10	-.01	-.35	-.14	.12	.04
4. Home Success: G				.01	.06	.15	.15	.41	.05	.08	.02	.09	-.12	-.26	.17	.14
5. Punitiveness: O					-.11	-.04	-.08	-.05	-.04	.01	-.07	-.05	.09	.03	-.09	-.06
6. School Normlessness: O						.00	.30	.15	.32	.15	.40	.08	-.35	-.12	.34	.13
7. School Normlessness: G							.15	.27	.10	.15	.03	.19	-.08	-.28	.28	.29
8. Home Normlessness: O								.00	.13	.10	.13	.05	-.39	-.20	.19	.09
9. Home Normlessness: G									.05	.10	.03	.13	-.10	-.30	.16	.14
10. Sociometric Exposure: O										.00	.32	.12	-.11	-.02	.18	.09
11. Sociometric Exposure: G											.20	.13	-.12	-.08	.24	.20
12. Commitment to Peers: O												.00	-.17	-.05	.25	.08
13. Commitment to Peers: G													-.04	-.16	.33	.33
14. Commitment to Parents: O														.00	-.21	-.10
15. Commitment to Parents: G															-.25	-.23
16. Total SRD Frequency																.94
17. Total SRD Gain																

Females

	2	3	4	5	6	7	8	9	10	11	12	13	14	15	16	17
1. Academic Success: O[a]	.00	−.04	−.01	.02	−.32	−.08	−.09	−.01	−.22	−.15	−.17	−.06	.02	−.01	−.08	−.05
2. Academic Success: G		−.02	−.09	−.01	−.10	−.10	−.01	−.08	−.12	−.15	−.10	−.05	.06	.05	−.10	−.08
3. Home Success: O			.00	−.01	.26	.08	.52	.05	.10	.08	.08	.00	−.38	−.14	.19	.10
4. Home Success: G				.01	.06	.17	.15	.41	.05	.13	.02	.12	−.12	−.36	.26	.25
5. Punitiveness: O					−.09	−.04	−.06	−.05	−.07	.01	−.10	.05	.06	.03	−.05	.00
6. School Normlessness: O						.00	.36	.15	.28	.15	.41	.08	−.28	−.12	.29	.06
7. School Normlessness: G							.15	.28	.10	.14	.03	.22	−.08	−.24	.30	.31
8. Home Normlessness: O								.00	.12	.10	.22	.05	−.47	−.20	.30	.16
9. Home Normlessness: G									.05	.09	.03	.12	−.10	−.41	.21	.20
10. Sociometric Exposure: O										.00	.28	.12	−.19	−.02	.17	.09
11. Sociometric Exposure: G											.20	.09	−.12	−.13	.22	.17
12. Commitment to Peers: O												.00	−.24	−.05	.24	.08
13. Commitment to Peers: G													−.04	−.14	.28	.28
14. Commitment to Parents: O														.00	.28	.28
15. Commitment to Parents: G															−.27	−.14
16. Total SRD Frequency																−.28
17. Total SRD Gain																.92

[a]O = Origin; G = Gain

Table A-2
Correlation Matrix: Home and School Predictors and Final Dropout Status

	Males						
	2	3	4	5	6	7	8
1. Exposure to Dropout in the Home: O[a]	.00	−.33	−.20	.05	.08	−.07	.21
2. Exposure to Dropout in the Home: G		−.19	−.16	.07	.14	.00	.08
3. Academic Success: O			.00	−.05	−.01	.06	−.31
4. Academic Success: G				−.02	−.08	−.01	−.10
5. Home Success: O					.00	−.06	.30
6. Home Success: G						.01	.06
7. Punitiveness: O							.11
8. School Normlessness: O							
9. School Normlessness: G							
10. School Social Isolation: O							
11. School Social Isolation: G							
12. Home Social Isolation: O							
13. Home Social Isolation: G							
14. Exposure to Dropout in School: O							
15. Exposure to Dropout in School: G							
16. Commitment to Peers: O							
17. Commitment to Peers: G							
18. Commitment to Parents: O							
19. Commitment to Parents: G							
20. Final Dropout Status							
21. Class							

						Males						
9	10	11	12	13	14	15	16	17	18	19	20	21
.10	.26	.23	.08	.03	.15	.05	.15	.06	−.02	−.05	.30	.49
.05	.25	.25	.02	.06	.07	.10	.07	.01	−.04	−.07	.12	.16
−.08	−.42	−.21	.00	−.05	−.26	−.25	−.23	−.06	.01	−.01	−.30	−.29
−.03	−.11	−.28	−.04	.04	−.14	−.13	−.10	−.06	.06	.01	−.16	−.15
.08	.26	.08	.47	.36	.12	.11	.10	−.01	−.35	−.14	.08	.00
.15	.05	.10	.34	.37	−.01	.13	.02	.09	−.12	−.26	.10	−.03
−.04	−.05	−.02	−.10	−.04	−.08	−.05	−.07	−.05	.09	.03	.00	−.07
.00	.47	.14	.37	.26	.28	.23	.40	.08	−.35	−.12	.26	.08
	.14	.12	.25	.26	.00	.21	.03	.19	−.08	−.28	.14	.01
		.00	.27	.12	.18	.21	.14	.01	−.17	−.07	.24	.12
			.13	.02	.12	.10	.10	−.02	−.05	−.04	.10	.13
				.00	.10	.15	.14	.18	−.58	−.53	.05	.01
					.13	.06	.20	.03	−.45	−.40	.04	.00
						.00	.26	.05	.08	−.03	.18	.14
							.19	.21	−.12	−.17	.20	.13
								.00	−.17	−.05	.18	.06
									−.04	−.16	.02	.03
									.00	.00	−.05	.01
											−.07	.18

Table A-2 (cont.)

	Females						
	2	3	4	5	6	7	8
1. Exposure to Dropout in the Home: O[a]	.00	−.30	−.20	.10	.08	.01	.14
2. Exposure to Dropout in the Home: G		−.19	−.23	.07	.01	.00	.08
3. Academic Success: O			.00	−.04	−.01	.02	−.32
4. Academic Success: G				−.02	−.09	−.01	−.10
5. Home Success: O					.00	−.01	.26
6. Home Success: G						.01	.06
7. Punitiveness: O							−.09
8. School Normlessness: O							
9. School Normlessness: G							
10. School Social Isolation: O							
11. School Social Isolation: G							
12. Home Social Isolation: O							
13. Home Social Isolation: G							
14. Exposure to Dropout in School: O							
15. Exposure to Dropout in School: G							
16. Commitment to Peers: O							
17. Commitment to Peers: G							
18. Commitment to Parents: O							
19. Commitment to Parents: G							
20. Final Dropout Status							
21. Class							

[a]O = Origin; G = Gain

					Females							
9	10	11	12	13	14	15	16	17	18	19	20	21
.10	.28	.23	.04	.03	.19	.05	.06	.06	−.03	−.05	.20	.50
.05	.25	.34	.02	.05	.07	.08	.07	.15	−.04	−.09	.18	.06
−.08	−.49	−.21	−.03	−.05	−.26	−.25	−.17	−.06	.02	−.01	−.23	−.28
−.10	−.11	−.38	−.04	−.04	−.14	−.18	−.10	−.05	.06	.05	−.15	−.14
.08	.19	.08	.50	.36	.14	.11	.08	.00	−.38	−.14	.08	.00
.17	.05	.05	.34	.38	−.01	.20	.02	.12	−.12	−.36	.09	−.01
−.04	−.01	−.02	−.07	−.04	−.03	−.05	−.10	.05	.06	.03	.00	.00
.00	.45	.14	.33	.26	.32	.23	.41	.08	−.28	−.12	.19	.07
	.14	.16	.25	.27	.00	.24	.03	.22	−.08	.24	.25	.02
		.00	.20	.12	.21	.21	.16	.01	−.12	−.07	.16	.12
			.13	.05	.12	.18	.10	.07	−.05	−.09	.10	.07
			.00	.00	.19	.15	.21	.18	−.63	−.53	.08	.01
					.13	.14	.20	.10	−.45	−.50	.11	.00
						.00	.33	.05	−.19	−.03	.21	.15
							.19	.18	−.12	−.24	.13	.11
								.00	−.24	−.05	.19	.00
									−.04	−.14	.15	−.07
										.00	−.07	.05
											−.08	−.03
												.15

Appendix B: Scales

Success-Failure Scales

Community [a]

1. If you could have any job you wanted, what job would you like to have as an adult?
   Describe _____
   What do you think are your chances of ever getting that kind of job?
   _____ 1. Very good
   _____ 2. Good
   _____ 3. Fair
   _____ 4. Poor
   _____ 5. Very poor

2. If you couldn't get this job, what job would you like as a second choice?
   Describe _____
   What do you think are your chances of ever getting that kind of job?
   _____ 1. Very good
   _____ 2. Good
   _____ 3. Fair
   _____ 4. Poor
   _____ 5. Very poor

3. Let's think for a minute about school plans. How far would you like to go in school?
   _____ 1. Quit as soon as I can
   _____ 2. Finish ninth grade [b]
   _____ 3. Finish tenth grade
   _____ 4. Finish eleventh grade
   _____ 5. Graduate from high school
   _____ 6. Go to a business or trade school
   _____ 7. Go to a university or college for a year or two
   _____ 8. Graduate from a college or university

4. How far in school do you think you will actually go?
   (Year 1, 2, and 3)
   _____ 2. Finish ninth grade

---

[a]Mean Alpha Coefficient   = .45
Mean Homogeneity Ratio = .24

[b]This item and item 2 in question 4 was deleted from the questionnaire administered to subjects in the tenth grade. Similarly, in each year, the item for the previous year, which had been completed, was deleted from the scale.

———— 3. Finish tenth grade
———— 4. Finish eleventh grade
———— 5. Graduate from high school
———— 6. Go to a business or trade school
———— 7. Go to a university or college for a year or two
———— 8. Graduate from a college or university

5. As of now, are you planning to go to college or junior college after high school? (Year 4)
———— 6. No
———— 7. Yes, junior college
———— 8. Yes, regular four-year college

6. Realistically speaking, how good do you think are your chances of getting ahead and being successful?
———— 1. Excellent
———— 2. Fair
———— 3. Somewhat limited
———— 4. Not very good

School Activities[c]

1. Suppose the circle below represented the activities that go on here at school. How far out from the center of things are you? (Place a check where you think you are.)

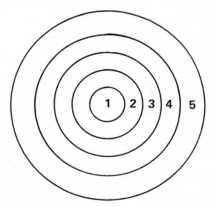

———————————————

[c]This scale is composed of the discrepancy between items 1 and 2 together with the response to item 3.

Mean Alpha Coefficient = .58
Mean Homogeneity Ratio = .42

2. Now, in the circle below, place a check where you would like to be.

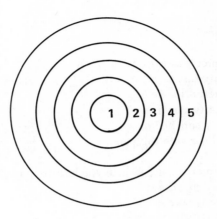

3. Suppose you were chosen to join the club which you most wanted to be in here at school. What club would it be?

_____

Do you already belong to this club?
_____1. Yes
_____2. No

Status Deprivation[d]

1. Would you say that students in your school have nicer clothes than you have?
_____ A lot nicer
_____ A little nicer
_____ About the same
_____ Poorer
_____ I never thought about this before

2. Would you say that students in your school have a nicer home than you have?
_____ A lot nicer
_____ A little nicer

_____

[d]Mean Alpha Coefficient   = .62
Mean Homogeneity Ratio = .40

_____ About the same

_____ Poorer

_____ I never thought about this before

Parental Acceptance[e]

1. Is your father pretty satisfied with you just the way you are?

_____ I'm very sure he *is*

_____ I'm pretty sure he *is*

_____ I'm pretty sure he *isn't*

_____ I'm very sure he *isn't*

_____ I don't live with this parent

2. Is your mother pretty satisfied with you just the way you are?

_____ I'm very sure she *is*

_____ I'm pretty sure she *is*

_____ I'm pretty sure she *isn't*

_____ I'm very sure she *isn't*

_____ I don't live with this parent

Self-Reported Delinquency Scale (SRD)[f]

1. Have you driven a car without a driver's license or permit?
   (Do not include driver training courses.)

_____ 1. Very often

_____ 2. Several times

_____ 3. Once or twice

_____ 4. Never

2. Have you ever taken little things (worth less than $2) that did not belong to you?

_____ 1. No

_____ 2. Once or twice

_____ 3. Several times

_____ 4. Very often

[e]Mean Alpha Coefficient = .87
Mean Homogeneity Ratio = .77

[f]Items 1 and 6 were not included in the scale; item 13 was included only in the fourth year.

3. Have you bought or drunk beer, wine, or liquor?

    _____ 1. Very often

    _____ 2. Several times

    _____ 3. Once or twice

    _____ 4. No

4. Have you purposely damaged or destroyed public or private property that did not belong to you?

    _____ 1. No

    _____ 2. Once or twice

    _____ 3. Several times

    _____ 4. Very often

5. Have you skipped school without a legitimate excuse?

    _____ 1. No

    _____ 2. Once or twice

    _____ 3. Several times

    _____ 4. Very often

6. Have you defied your parents' authority (to their face)?

    _____ 1. Very often

    _____ 2. Several times

    _____ 3. Once or twice

    _____ 4. No

7. Have you "run away" from home?

    _____ 1. No

    _____ 2. Once

    _____ 3. Twice

    _____ 4. Three or more times

8. Have you taken part in "gang fights"?

    _____ 1. Five or more times

    _____ 2. Three or four times

    _____ 3. Once or twice

    _____ 4. No

9. Have you taken things of medium value (between $2 and $50)?

    _____ 1. No

    _____ 2. Once or twice

    _____ 3. Several times

    _____ 4. Very often

10. Have you driven a car without the owner's permission?
    _____1. No
    _____2. Once
    _____3. Twice
    _____ 4. Three or more times

11. Have you taken things of large value (over $50)?
    _____1. Very often
    _____2. Several times
    _____3. Once or twice
    _____4. No

12. Have you used force (strong-arm methods) to get money from another person?
    _____1. No
    _____2. Once or twice
    _____3. Several times
    _____ 4. Very often

13. Have you used marijuana, LSD, or other dangerous drugs?
    _____ 1. No
    _____ 2. Once or twice
    _____3. Several times
    _____4. Very often

Alienation Scales[g]

Home Normlessness

For Boys:
1. How would you like to have your father's job?

For Girls:
1. How would you like to have your mother's job?
    _____ 1. I'd like it.
    _____ 2. I'd neither like nor dislike it.
    _____ 3. I'd dislike it.
    _____ 4. I do not live with an adult male/female
    _____ 7. Don't know.

---

[g]Mean Alpha Coefficient   = .61
Mean Homogeneity Ratio   = .26

2. Have you defied your parents' authority (to their face)?
   (Years 1 and 4 only)
   ———— 1. Very often
   ———— 2. Several times
   ———— 3. Once or twice
   ———— 4. No
   ———— 5. Unreliable response

3. When you grow up and have your own family, how would you feel if you lived the same way your family does now?
   ———— 1. Very satisfied
   ———— 2. Somewhat satisfied
   ———— 3. Neither satisfied or dissatisfied
   ———— 4. Somewhat dissatisfied
   ———— 5. Very dissatisfied

4. When you think of what is right and wrong, do you feel that you and your father and mother agree?
   Father:
   ———— 1. Always agree
   ———— 2. Usually agree
   ———— 3. Sometimes agree
   ———— 4. Never agree
   ———— 9. Don't live with this parent
   ———— 0. No response

   Mother:
   ———— 1. Always agree
   ———— 2. Usually agree
   ———— 3. Sometimes agree
   ———— 4. Never agree
   ———— 9. Don't live with this parent
   ———— 0. No response

5. I have often gone against my parents' wishes.
   ———— 1. True
   ———— 2. False
   ———— 3. No response/Don't know

Home Social Isolation[h]

1. How many of your friends do your parents know?
   _____1. Most of them
   _____2. Some of them
   _____3. Very few of them
   _____4. None of them

2. Generally when something is worrying you or bothering you, does it help you to talk to your father or mother about it?
   Father:
   _____ 1. Always helps
   _____ 2. Usually helps
   _____ 3. Sometimes helps
   _____ 4. Seldom helps
   _____ 5. Never helps
   _____ 9. Don't live with this parent
   _____ 0. No response

   Mother
   _____1. Always helps
   _____2. Usually helps
   _____3. Sometimes helps
   _____4. Seldom helps
   _____5. Never helps
   _____ 9. Don't live with this parent
   _____ 0. No response

4. How many of your problems do you talk over with your father and mother?
   Father:
   _____ 1. All of them
   _____ 2. Most of them
   _____ 3. Some of them
   _____ 4. Few of them
   _____ 5. None of them
   _____ 9. Don't live with this parent
   _____ 0. No response

   Mother:
   _____1. All of them
   _____2. Most of them
   _____3. Some of them
   _____4. Few of them

[h]Mean Alpha Coefficient   = .73
Mean Homogeneity Ratio   = .25

_____5. None of them
_____9. Don't live with this parent
_____0. No response

5. Sometimes I used to feel that I would like to leave home.
_____1. True
_____2. False
_____3. No Response/Don't know

6. My parents never really understood me.
_____1. True
_____2. False
_____3. No Response/Don't know

7. My parents have often disapproved of my friends.
_____1. True
_____2. False
_____3. No Response/Don't know

8. The members of my family were always very close to each other.
_____1. True
_____2. False
_____3. No Response/Don't know

9. I sometimes wanted to run away from home.
_____1. True
_____2. False
_____3. No Response/Don't know

School Normlessness[i]

1. Some people your age like going to school and some don't. How do you like school?
_____1. Like school a lot
_____2. Like school fairly well
_____3. Don't care one way or another
_____4. Dislike school
_____5. Dislike school very much

[i]Mean Alpha Coefficient = .66
Mean Homogeneity Ratio = .22

2. How much time, on the average, do you spend doing homework outside school?

    _____1. None, or almost none

    _____2. About half an hour a day

    _____3. One to two hours a day

    _____4. Three hours or more a day

3. Are there any courses which you think are a waste of time?

    _____1. Yes

    _____2. No

4. Have you ever skipped school without a legitimate excuse?

    _____1. No

    _____2. Once or twice

    _____3. Several times

    _____4. Very often

    _____5. Unreliable response

5. In earlier grades in school, I gave the teachers lots of trouble.

    _____1. True

    _____2. False

    _____3. No Response/Don't know

6. In school, I have sometimes been sent to the principal for acting up.

    _____1. True

    _____2. False

    _____3. No Response/Don't know

7. During my earlier school days I played hooky quite often.

    _____1. True

    _____2. False

    _____3. No Response/Don't know

8. I never cared much for school.

    _____1. True

    _____2. False

    _____3. No Response/Don't know

School Social Isolation[j]

1. Since school started in September, *outside of your regular classes*, how many different *school clubs* have you attended?
   _____1. None
   _____2. One or two
   _____3. Three or four
   _____4. Five or more

2. Not counting clubs, how many different kinds of school activities have you taken part in since September?
   _____1. None
   _____2. One or two
   _____3. Three or four
   _____4. Five or more

3. Suppose the circle below represented the activities that go on here at school. How far out from the center of things are you?

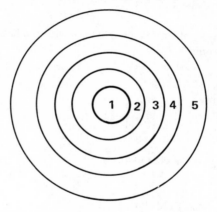

4. Is there any teacher in this school that you feel you could go to if you needed advice on an important question?
   _____1. No
   _____2. Yes

---

[j]Mean Alpha Coefficient = .76
Mean Homogeneity Ratio = .36

5. During an average week, how many hours do you spend taking part in these activities?

  _____1. Less than 1 hour
  _____2. 1 to 2 hours
  _____3. 3 to 4 hours
  _____4. 5 to 6 hours
  _____5. 7 to 8 hours
  _____6. 9+ hours

Community Normlessness[k]

1. What do you think of the following statement? "It's not what you do but who you are that counts with the law."

  _____1. Strongly believe this
  _____2. Believe this
  _____3. Neither believe nor disbelieve this
  _____4. Do not believe this
  _____5. Strongly disbelieve this

2. Do you think that any real trouble people have with the law can be fixed for them by the right people?

  _____1. Always
  _____2. Usually
  _____3. Sometimes
  _____4. Seldom
  _____5. Never

3. I would do almost anything on a dare.

  _____1. True
  _____2. False
  _____3. No Response/Don't know

4. I go out of my way to meet trouble rather than try to escape it.

  _____1. True
  _____2. False
  _____3. No Response/Don't know

---

[k]Mean Alpha Coefficient = .50
 Mean Homogeneity Ratio = .18

5. Would adults in your neighborhood do anything if they saw teenagers fighting?

    _____ 1. Yes

    _____ 2. No

    _____ 3. Don't know

Community Social Isolation[1]

1. A person is better off if he doesn't trust anyone.

    _____ 1. True

    _____ 2. False

    _____ 0. No Response/Don't know

2. Even the idea of giving a talk in public makes me be afraid.

    _____ 1. True

    _____ 2. False

    _____ 0. No Response/Don't know

3. I would rather go without something than ask for a favor.

    _____ 1. True

    _____ 2. False

    _____ 0. No Response/Don't know

4. When I meet a stranger, I often think that he is better than I am.

    _____ 1. True

    _____ 2. False

    _____ 0. No Response/Don't know

5. People often talk about me behind my back.

    _____ 1. True

    _____ 2. False

    _____ 0. No Response/Don't know

---

[1]Mean Alpha Coefficient   = .47

Mean Homogeneity Ratio   = .13

6. I don't think I'm quite as happy as others seem to be.
_____ 1. True
_____ 2. False
_____ 0. No Response/Don't know

Exposure to Delinquency Scales

Community

1. Was there much crime or delinquency committed by young people (in their teens or below) in the community in which you grew up?
_____ 1. A great deal
_____ 2. Quite a bit
_____ 3. Only a little
_____ 4. None

Differential Association in the School (first year only)[m]

1. Think of the friends you have been associated with *most often*. Were any of them ever in trouble with the law?
_____ 1. Most were
_____ 2. Several were
_____ 3. Very few were
_____ 4. None were

2. Think of the friends you have known *for the longest time*. Were any of them ever in trouble with the law?
_____ 1. Most were
_____ 2. Several were
_____ 3. Very few were
_____ 4. None were

3. Have any of your *best friends* ever been in trouble with the law while they were your best friends?
_____ 1. Most were
_____ 2. Several were
_____ 3. Very few were
_____ 4. None were

---

[m]Alpha Coefficient = .84
 Homogeneity Ratio = .64

School–Sociometric[n]

What group of students here in school do you go around with most often? (Give both first and last names)

_____

_____

Exposure to Dropout Scales

School[o]

1. Have any of your *good friends* quit school?
   _____1. None
   _____2. One
   _____3. Two or three
   _____4. Four or more

2. How about your *best friend?* Is he or she still in school?
   _____1. Yes
   _____2. No, quit school before high school graduation
   _____3. No, graduated from high school

School–Sociometric[p]

What group of students here in school do you go around with most often? (Give both first and last names)

_____

_____

Home[q]

1. How far have your older brothers gone in school?
   _____1. Dropout
   _____2. No dropout

2. How far have your older sisters gone in school?
   _____1. Dropout
   _____2. No dropout

---

[n]The scale score consists of the proportion of persons chosen who reported one or more serious offenses (SRD) or had an official police record.

[o]Mean Alpha Coefficient = .30
   Mean Homogeneity Ratio = .26

[p]This scale consists of the proportion of those chosen who dropped out of school in the following study period.

[q]Mean Alpha Coefficient = .60
   Mean Homogeneity Ratio = .17

3. What is the last grade your father attended?*
_____ 1. No formal schooling
_____ 2. Elementary: 1 to 6 years
_____ 3. Elementary: 7 to 8 years
_____ 4. High School: 1 to 3 years
_____ 5. Completed High School (4 years)
_____ 6. Some college (1 to 3 years)
_____ 7. Completed college
_____ 8. Post-College work

4. What is the last grade your mother attended?*
_____ 1. No formal schooling
_____ 2. Elementary: 1 to 6 years
_____ 3. Elementary: 7 to 8 years
_____ 4. High School: 1 to 3 years
_____ 5. Completed High School (4 years)
_____ 6. Some college (1 to 3 years)
_____ 7. Completed college
_____ 8. Post-College work

5. Which of the following best describes your father's attitudes toward continuing school after this year?
_____ 1. Would like me to quit as soon as I can
_____ 2. Would not object to me leaving school before high school graduation
_____ 3. Would think I was foolish to try to go to college
_____ 4. Would think I was foolish if I did *not* try to go to college
_____ 5. Would object strongly to my leaving school before graduation from college

6. Which of the following best describes your mother's attitudes toward continuing school after this year?
_____ 1. Would like me to quit as soon as I can
_____ 2. Would not object to me leaving school before high school graduation
_____ 3. Would think I was foolish to try to go to college
_____ 4. Would think I was foolish if I did *not* try to go to college
_____ 5. Would object strongly to my leaving school before graduation from college

7. How much further in school should _____
   (subject) go before he (she) stops and works full time?[r]
   _____1. Junior high school
   _____2. Some high school
   _____3. Complete high school
   _____4. Some college
   _____5. Complete college and/or more

8. Since things don't always work out the way we would like them to, how much schooling or education do you think _____
   (subject) will actually get?
   _____1. Junior high school
   _____2. Some high school
   _____3. Complete high school
   _____4. Some college
   _____5. Complete college and/or more

9. Let's think about school plans. Suppose you were to decide that you'd like to go to college, how would your family react to this?
   _____1. They would feel happy and encourage me
   _____2. They would think I was doing the wrong thing and would discourage me
   _____3. They wouldn't care much one way or the other

10. Assume that you wanted to go to a regular four-year college after high school to study a subject you liked. Which of the following would best describe your family's ability to pay for your education?[s]
   _____1. My family or relatives would pay all of my college expenses
   _____2. My family or relatives would pay the majority of my college expenses, but not all of them
   _____3. My family or relatives would pay some of my college expenses, but less than half
   _____4. I would get little or no financial help from my parents or relatives to help pay college expenses
   _____5. Money is such a serious problem that I would probably have to start working as soon as I finished high school to help my family

---

[r]This item and item 8 are from the parent interview completed while the subject was in the ninth grade and were included in the origin measure. The first two were also included in the final measure.
[s]These two items replaced the last two parent items (7 and 8) in the final measure.

Commitment Scales

Peers

1. If you found that this group (of friends) was leading you into trouble, would you still run around with them?
   _____1. Yes
   _____2. No
   _____3. Undecided

Parents[t]

1. Who do you confide in when you get into some kind of trouble?
   _____1. Mother
   _____2. Father
   _____3. Teacher
   _____4. Girl (boy) friend
   _____5. Best friend
   _____6. No one
   _____7. Other _____

2. When making the following decisions, whose opinion are you most likely to accept?
   a) Whether a certain action is right or wrong?
   _____1. Parents
   _____2. Friends
   _____3. Teachers
   _____4. No one

3. Which one of these things would be hardest for you to take—your parent's disapproval, your teacher's disapproval, or your friend's disapproval?
   _____1. Parent's disapproval
   _____2. Teacher's disapproval
   _____3. Friend's disapproval

Teachers' Evaluation Items

1. Is this boy (girl) ever disruptive in the classroom?
   _____1. Yes
   _____2. No

---

[t]Mean Alpha Coefficient   = .43
Mean Homogeneity Ratio   = .22

2. Would you describe this student as a problem boy (girl)?

_____ 1. Yes

_____ 2. No

_____ 3. Not sure

3. In your opinion, do you think this student is likely to ever get in trouble with the law?

_____ 1. Very sure he will

_____ 2. Fairly sure he will

_____ 3. Not sure

_____ 4. Fairly sure he will not

_____ 5. Very sure he will not

4. Is this student retarded in his reading ability?

_____ 1. Yes

_____ 2. No

5. How would you rate this student with respect to his classroom performance?

_____ 1. Superior

_____ 2. Above average

_____ 3. Average

_____ 4. Below Average

_____ 5. Poor

6. How would you rate this student with respect to his social adjustment in school?

_____ 1. Superior

_____ 2. Above average

_____ 3. Average

_____ 4. Below Average

_____ 5. Poor

7. Does this student show hostility to teachers and adults?

_____ 1. Often

_____ 2. Sometimes

_____ 3. Seldom

_____ 4. Never

8. In your estimation, will this student complete high school or will he/she drop out prior to high school graduation?

_____ 1. Very sure he/she will complete high school

_____ 2. Fairly sure he/she will complete high school

_____ 3. Not very sure one way or the other

_____ 4. Fairly sure he/she will drop out

_____ 5. Very sure he/she will drop out

Appendix C: Publications and Theses Connected with the Research

Publications

Elliott, Delbert S. "Delinquency, School Attendance and Dropout." *Social Problems* 13 (1966):307-314.

Elliott, Delbert S., Harwin L. Voss and Aubrey Wendling. "Dropout and the Social Milieu of the High School: A Preliminary Analysis." *American Journal of Orthopsychiatry* 36 (1966):808-817.

_____. "Capable Dropouts and the Social Milieu of the High School." *Journal of Educational Research* 60 (1966):180-186.

Voss, Harwin L. "Pitfalls in Social Research: A Case Study." *American Sociologist* 1 (1966):136-140.

Voss, Harwin L., Aubrey Wendling and Delbert S. Elliott. "Some Types of High School Dropouts." *Journal of Educational Research* 59 (1966):363-368.

Wendling, Aubrey and Delbert S. Elliott. "Class and Race Differentials in Parental Aspirations and Expectations." *Pacific Sociological Review* 11 (1968):123-133.

Theses

Bass, Donald. "Status Deprivation and Delinquent Behavior." Unpublished Master's thesis. San Diego State College, 1965.

Cowperthwaite, William S. "Analysis of the Social Structure of the School." Unpublished Master's thesis. San Diego State College, 1966.

Gray, Donald C. "Social Adjustment and Delinquency." Unpublished Master's thesis. Lexington: University of Kentucky, 1971.

Quicker, John C. "Implications of Goal Discrepancy and Punitiveness for Juvenile Delinquency." Unpublished Ph.D. dissertation. Boulder: University of Colorado, 1970.

Severy, Lawrence J. "Exposure to Anti-Social Behavior." Unpublished Ph.D. dissertation. Boulder: University of Colorado, 1970.

Thompson, Ann B. "An Empirical Test of Differential Association: A Replication." Unpublished Master's thesis. San Diego State College, 1966.

References

References

[1]   Akers, Ronald L. "Socio-Economic Status and Delinquent Behavior: A Retest." *Journal of Research in Crime and Delinquency* 1 (1964):38-46.

[2]   Allen, Donald E. and Harjit S. Sandhu. "A Comparative Study of Delinquents and Non-Delinquents: Family Affect, Religion, and Personal Income." *Social Forces* 46 (1967):263-269.

[3]   Amble, Bruce R. "Teacher Evaluation of Student Behavior and School Dropouts." *Journal of Educational Research* 60 (1967):408-410.

[4]   Andersson, Bengt Erik. *Studies in Adolescent Behaviour.* Translated by Albert Read. Stockholm: Almqvist and Wiksell, 1969.

[5]   Andry, Robert G. "Parental Affection and Delinquency." In Marvin E. Wolfgang, Leonard Savitz, and Norman Johnson (eds.), *The Sociology of Crime and Delinquency*, pp. 342-352. New York: Wiley, 1962.

[6]   Bagley, Christopher. "Anomie, Alienation and the Evaluation of Social Structure." *Kansas Journal of Sociology* 3 (1967):110-123.

[7]   Bandura, Albert and Richard H. Walters. "Dependency Conflicts in Aggressive Delinquents." *Journal of Social Issues* 14 (1958):52-65.

[8]   Barron, Milton L. *The Juvenile in Delinquent Society*. New York: Knopf, 1956.

[9]   Becker, Howard S. *Outsiders*. New York: Free Press, 1963.

[10]   Bereiter, Carl. "Some Persisting Dilemmas in the Measurement of Change." In Chester W. Harris (ed.), *Problems in Measuring Change*, pp. 3-20. Madison: University of Wisconsin Press, 1963.

[11]   Berkson, Joseph. " 'Cost-Utility' as a Measure of the Efficiency of a Test." *Journal of the American Statistical Association* 42 (1947):246-255.

[12]   Bernard, Jessie. *Social Problems at Midcentury*. New York: Dryden Press, 1957.

[13]   Berston, H.M. "The School Dropout Problem." *The Clearing House* 35 (1960):207-210.

[14]   Blalock, Hubert M., Jr. *Causal Inferences in Nonexperimental Research*. Chapel Hill: University of North Carolina Press, 1964.

[15]   Bledsoe, Joseph C. "An Investigation of Six Correlates of Student Withdrawal from High School." *Journal of Educational Research* 53 (1959):3-6.

[16]   Bordua, David J. "Delinquent Subcultures: Sociological Interpretations of Gang Delinquency." *Annals of the American Academy of Political and Social Science* 33 (1961):119-136.

[17]   _____. "Some Comments on Theories of Group Delinquency." *Sociological Inquiry* 32 (1962):245-260.

[18]   Burt, Cyril L. *The Young Delinquent*, Fourth Edition. London: University of London Press, 1944.

[19] California Penal Code. *The Penal Code of the State of California.* Los Angeles: Legal Bookstore, 1963.

[20] Call, Donald J. "Delinquency, Frustration and Non-Commitment." Unpublished Ph.D. dissertation. Eugene: University of Oregon, 1965.

[21] Camilleri, Santo F. "Theory, Probability, and Induction in Social Research." *American Sociological Review* 27 (1962):170-178.

[22] Caravello, S.J. "The Drop-out Problem." *High School Journal* 41 (1958):335-340.

[23] Cassel, Russell N. and Jack C. Coleman. "A Critical Examination of the School Dropout, Reluctant Learner, and Abler Non-College Student Problem." *Bulletin of the National Association of Secondary School Principals* 46 (1962):60-65.

[24] Cavan, Ruth S. *Juvenile Delinquency.* Philadelphia: Lippincott, 1962.

[25] Cervantes, Lucius F. *The Dropout.* Ann Arbor: University of Michigan Press, 1965.

[26] Chambliss, William J. and Richard H. Nagasawa. "On the Validity of Offical Statistics: A Comparative Study of White, Black, and Japanese High-School Boys." *Journal of Research in Crime and Delinquency* 6 (1969):71-77.

[27] Christie, Nils. "Reports by Participants." In Robert H. Hardt and George E. Bodine (eds.), *Development of Self-Report Instruments in Delinquency Research*, pp. 1-3. Syracuse: Syracuse University Youth Development Center, 1965.

[28] Cicourel, Aaron V. and John I. Kitsuse. *The Educational Decision-Makers.* Indianapolis: Bobbs-Merrill, 1963.

[29] Clark, John P. "Acceptance of Blame and Alienation among Prisoners." *American Journal of Orthopsychiatry* 33 (1963):557-561.

[30] Clark, John P. and Eugene P. Wenninger. "Socio-Economic Class and Area as Correlates of Illegal Behavior among Juveniles." *American Sociological Review* 27 (1962):826-834.

[31] Clark, John P. and Larry L. Tifft. "Polygraph and Interview Validation of Self-Reported Deviant Behavior." *American Sociological Review* 31 (1966):516-523.

[32] Clinard, Marshall B. *Sociology of Deviant Behavior*, Third Edition. New York: Holt, Rinehart and Winston, 1968.

[33] Cloward, Richard A. and Lloyd E. Ohlin. *Delinquency and Opportunity.* Glencoe, Ill.: Free Press, 1960.

[34] Cohen, Albert K. *Delinquent Boys.* Glencoe, Ill.: Free Press, 1955.

[35] _____. "The Study of Social Disorganization and Deviant Behavior." In Robert K. Merton, Leonard Broom, and Leonard S. Cottrell, Jr. (eds.), *Sociology Today*, pp. 461-484. New York: Basic Books, 1959.

[36] _____. *Deviance and Control.* Englewood Cliffs, N.J.: Prentice-Hall, 1966.

[37] Cohen, Albert K. and James F. Short, Jr. "Juvenile Delinquency." In Robert K. Merton and Robert A. Nisbet (eds.), *Contemporary Social Problems*, Second Edition, pp. 84-135. New York: Harcourt, Brace and World, 1966.

[38] Cohen, Bernard. "The Delinquency of Gangs and Spontaneous Groups." In Thorsten Sellin and Marvin E. Wolfgang (eds.), *Delinquency*, pp. 61-111. New York: Wiley, 1969.

[39] Coleman, James S. *The Adolescent Society*. New York: Free Press, 1961.

[40] _____. *Adolescents and the Schools*. New York: Basic Books, 1965.

[41] Cressey, Donald R. "Application and Verification of the Differential Association Theory." *Journal of Criminal Law, Criminology and Police Science* 43 (1952):43-52.

[42] _____. *Other People's Money*. Glencoe, Ill.: Free Press, 1953.

[43] Cronbach, Lee J. "Coefficient Alpha and the Internal Structure of Tests." *Psychometrika* 16 (1951):297-334.

[44] Davis, James A. *Panel Analysis: Techniques and Concepts in the Interpretation of Repeated Measurements*. Unpublished Monograph. Chicago: University of Chicago National Opinion Research Center, 1963.

[45] Dean, Dwight G. "Alienation: Its Meaning and Measurement." *American Sociological Review* 26 (1961):753-758.

[46] DeFleur, Lois B. "On Polygraph and Interview Validation." *American Sociological Review* 32 (1967):114-115.

[47] DeFleur, Melvin L. and Richard Quinney. "A Reformulation of Sutherland's Differential Association Theory and a Strategy for Empirical Verification." *Journal of Research in Crime and Delinquency* 3 (1966):1-22.

[48] De Grazia, Sebastian. *The Political Community*. Chicago: University of Chicago Press, 1948.

[49] DeLamater, John. "On the Nature of Deviance." *Social Forces* 46 (1968):445-455.

[50] Dentler, Robert A. and Lawrence J. Monroe. "Social Correlates of Early Adolescent Theft." *American Sociological Review* 26 (1961):733-743.

[51] Dillon, Harold J. *Early School Leavers: A Major Educational Problem*. Publication No. 401 (October). New York: National Child Labor Committee, 1949.

[52] Douvan, Elizabeth and Joseph Adelson. *The Adolescent Experience*. New York: Wiley, 1966.

[53] Duggan, Thomas J. and Charles W. Dean. "Common Misinterpretations of Significance Levels in Sociology Journals." *American Sociologist* 3 (1968):45-46.

[54] Dunham, H. Warren and Mary E. Knauer. "The Juvenile Court in its Relationship to Adult Criminality." *Social Forces* 32 (1954):290-296.

[55] Durkheim, Emile. *Suicide*. Translated by John A. Spaulding and George Simpson. Glencoe, Ill.: Free Press, 1951.

[56] Ebel, Robert L. (ed.). *Encyclopedia of Educational Research*, Fourth Edition. New York: Macmillan, 1969.

[57] Elkin, Frederick and William Westley. "The Myth of Adolescent Culture." *American Sociological Review* 20 (1955):680-684.

[58] Elliott, Delbert S. "Delinquency, Opportunity and Patterns of Orientations." Unpublished Ph.D. dissertation. Seattle: University of Washington, 1961.

[59] _____. "Delinquency and Perceived Opportunity." *Sociological Inquiry* 32 (1962):216-227.

[60] _____. "Delinquency, School Attendance and Dropout." *Social Problems* 13 (1966):307-314.

[61] Elliott, Delbert S. and Harwin L. Voss. *Delinquency and Dropout*. A Summary Report to the National Institutes of Mental Health. Grant Numbers MH-170173 and R01 15285 (November). Boulder: University of Colorado Institute of Behavioral Science, 1971.

[62] Elliott, Delbert S., Harwin L. Voss and Aubrey Wendling. "Capable Dropouts and the Social Milieu of the High School." *Journal of Educational Research* 60 (1966):180-186.

[63] Empey, LaMar T. "Social Class and Occupational Aspiration: A Comparison of Absolute and Relative Measurement." *American Sociological Review* 21 (1956):703-709.

[64] Epperson, David C. "A Re-Assessment of Indices of Parental Influence in The Adolescent Society." *American Sociological Review* 29 (1964):93-96.

[65] Epps, Edgar G. "Socioeconomic Status, Race, Level of Aspiration and Juvenile Delinquency: A Limited Empirical Test of Merton's Conception of Deviation." *Phylon* 28 (1967):16-27.

[66] Erickson, Gary E. "Bias in the Processing of Juvenile Delinquents." Unpublished Master's thesis. San Diego: San Diego State College, 1966.

[67] Erickson, Maynard L. and LaMar T. Empey. "Court Records, Undetected Delinquency and Decision-Making." *Journal of Criminal Law, Criminology and Police Science* 54 (1963):456-469.

[68] _____. "Class Position, Peers and Delinquency." *Sociology and Social Research* 49 (1965):268-282.

[69] Fiske, Donald W., Desmond S. Cartwright and William L. Kirtner. "Are Psychotherapeutic Changes Predictable?" *Journal of Abnormal and Social Psychology* 69 (1964):418-426.

[70] Fry, Franklyn D. "A Study of Reactions to Frustration in 236 College Students and in 207 Inmates of State Prisons." *Journal of Psychology* 28 (1949):427-438.

[71] Galtung, Johan. *Theory and Methods of Social Research*. New York: Columbia University Press, 1967.

[72] Gannon, Thomas M. "Dimensions of Current Gang Delinquency." *Journal of Research in Crime and Delinquency* 4 (1967):119-131.

[73] Garabedian, Peter G. and Don C. Gibbons (eds.). *Becoming Delinquent.* Chicago: Aldine, 1970.

[74] Glaser, Daniel. *Social Deviance.* Chicago: Markham, 1971.

[75] Glueck, Sheldon. "Theory and Fact in Criminology." *British Journal of Delinquency* 7 (1956):92-109.

[76] Glueck, Sheldon and Eleanor T. Glueck. *Five Hundred Criminal Careers.* New York: Knopf, 1930.

[77] _____.*Unraveling Juvenile Delinquency.* New York: Commonwealth Fund, 1950.

[78] Gold, David. "Statistical Tests and Substantive Significance." *American Sociologist* 4 (1969):42-46.

[79] Gold, Martin. *Status Forces in Delinquent Boys.* Ann Arbor: University of Michigan, 1963.

[80] _____. "Undetected Delinquent Behavior." *Journal of Research in Crime and Delinquency* 3 (1966):27-46.

[81] _____. "On Social Status and Delinquency." *Social Problems* 15 (1967):114-116.

[82] _____. *Delinquent Behavior in an American City.* Belmont, Calif.: Wadsworth, 1970.

[83] Goldberg, Miriam L. "Factors Affecting Educational Attainment in Depressed Urban Areas." In A. Harry Passow (ed.), *Education in Depressed Areas*, pp. 68-99. New York: Teachers College Press, 1963.

[84] Goldman, Nathan. *The Differential Selection of Juvenile Offenders for Court Appearance.* New York: National Council on Crime and Delinquency, 1963.

[85] Good, Carter V. (ed.). *Dictionary of Education*, Second Edition. New York: McGraw-Hill, 1959.

[86] Goodman, Paul. "The Universal Trap." In Daniel Schreiber (ed.), *Profile of the School Dropout*, pp. 26-39. New York: Random House, 1967.

[87] Gordon, C. Wayne. *The Social System of the High School.* Glencoe, Ill.: Free Press, 1957.

[88] _____. "The Sociology of Education." In George F. Kneller (ed.), *Foundations of Education*, pp. 404-430. New York: Wiley, 1963.

[89] Gottlieb, David and Charles Ramsey. *The American Adolescent.* Homewood, Ill.: Dorsey Press, 1964.

[90] Gould, Leroy C. "Who Defines Delinquency: A Comparison of Self-Reported and Officially-Reported Indices of Delinquency for Three Racial Groups." *Social Problems* 16 (1969):325-336.

[91] Greer, Colin. *The Great School Legend.* New York: Basic Books, 1972.

[92] Hardt, Robert H. and George E. Bodine. *Development of Self-Report Instruments in Delinquency Research.* Syracuse: Syracuse University Youth Development Center, 1965.

[93] Hardt, Robert H. and Sandra J. Peterson. "Neighborhood Status and Delinquency Activity as Indexed by Police Records and a Self Report Survey." *Criminologica* 6 (1968):37-47.

[94] Harris, Chester W. (ed.). *Problems in Measuring Change.* Madison: University of Wisconsin Press, 1963.

[95] Haskell, Martin R. and Lewis Yablonsky. *Crime and Delinquency.* Chicago: Rand McNally, 1970.

[96] Hathaway, Starke R. and Elio D. Monachesi. *Adolescent Personality and Behavior.* Minneapolis: University of Minnesota Press, 1963.

[97] Hathaway, Starke R., Phyllis C. Reynolds and Elio D. Monachesi. "Follow-Up of the Later Careers and Lives of 1,000 Boys Who Dropped Out of High School." *Journal of Consulting and Clinical Psychology* 33 (1969):370-380.

[98] Hausken, Sally A. "Employment Patterns in Littleton High School Dropouts 1960-1963." Unpublished Master of Personnel Service thesis. Boulder: University of Colorado, 1966.

[99] Havighurst, Robert J. "Research on the School Work-Study Program in the Prevention of Juvenile Delinquency." In William R. Carriker (ed.), *Role of the School in Prevention of Juvenile Delinquency*, pp. 27-45. Washington, D.C.: U.S. Government Printing Office, 1963.

[100] Healy, William and Augusta F. Bronner. *Delinquents and Criminals.* New York: Macmillan, 1926.

[101] Heise, David R. "Causal Inference from Panel Data." In Edgar F. Borgatta and George W. Bohrnstedt (eds.), *Sociological Methodology*, pp. 3-27. San Francisco: Jossey-Bass, 1970.

[102] Himmelhoch, Jerome. "Youth Culture and Rural Adolescents." Mimeographed paper. Plainfield, Vt.: Goddard College, 1963.

[103] Hirschi, Travis. *Causes of Delinquency.* Berkeley: University of California Press, 1969.

[104] Hirschi, Travis and Hanan C. Selvin. *Delinquency Research.* New York: Free Press, 1967.

[105] Hollingshead, August B. *Elmtown's Youth.* New York: Wiley, 1949.

[106] Holzberg, Jules D. and Fred Hahn. "The Picture-Frustration Technique as a Measure of Hostility and Guilt Reactions in Adolescent Psychopaths." *American Journal of Orthopsychiatry* 22 (1952):776-795.

[107] Hyman, Herbert. *Survey Design and Analysis.* New York: Free Press, 1955.

[108] Jahoda, Marie and Neil Warren. "The Myths of Youth." *Sociology of Education* 38 (1965):138-149.

[109] Jeffrey, C. Ray and Ina A. Jeffrey. "Delinquents and Dropouts: An Experimental Program in Behaviour Change." *Canadian Journal of Corrections* 12 (1970):47-58.

[110] Jessor, Richard, Theodore D. Graves, Robert C. Hanson and Shirley L. Jessor. *Society, Personality, and Deviant Behavior.* New York: Holt, Rinehart and Winston, 1968.

[111] Kaswan, J., M. Wasman, and L.Z. Freedman. "Aggression and the Picture-Frustration Study." *Journal of Consulting Psychology* 24 (1960):446-452.

[112] Kish, Leslie. "Some Statistical Problems in Research Design." *American Sociological Review* 24 (1959):328-338.

[113] Kitsuse, John I. and Aaron V. Cicourel. "A Note on the Uses of Official Statistics." *Social Problems* 11 (1963):131-139.

[114] Klein, Malcolm W. (ed.). *Juvenile Gangs in Context.* Englewood Cliffs, N.J.: Prentice-Hall, 1967.

[115] Klein, Malcolm W. *Street Gangs and Street Workers.* Englewood Cliffs, N.J.: Prentice-Hall, 1971.

[116] Kobrin, Solomon. "The Conflict of Values in Delinquency Areas." *American Sociological Review* 16 (1951):653-661.

[117] Kobrin, Solomon, Joseph Puntil and Emil Peluso. "Criteria of Status among Street Groups." *Journal of Research in Crime and Delinquency* 4 (1967):98-118.

[118] Kulik, James A., Kenneth B. Stein and Theodore R. Sarbin. "Disclosure of Delinquent Behavior under Conditions of Anonymity and Non-anonymity." *Journal of Consulting and Clinical Psychology* 32 (1968):506-509.

[119] Kupfer, George. "Self-Reported Delinquency in a Canadian City." Paper presented at the Pacific Sociological Society meetings, 1967.

[120] Kvaraceus, William C. *Juvenile Delinquency and the School.* New York: World Book Company, 1945.

[121] Kvaraceus, William C. and Walter B. Miller. *Delinquent Behavior: Culture and the Individual.* Washington, D.C.: National Education Association, 1959.

[122] Labovitz, Sanford. "Criteria for Selecting a Significance Level: A Note on the Sacredness of .05." *American Sociologist* 3 (1968):220-222.

[123] Landis, Judson R., Simon Dinitz and Walter C. Reckless. "Implementing Two Theories of Delinquency: Value Orientation and Awareness of Limited Opportunity." *Sociology and Social Research* 47 (1963):408-416.

[124] Layton, Warren K. *Special Services for the Drop-out and the Potential Drop-out.* Publication No. 408 (October). New York: National Child Labor Committee, 1952.

[125] Lefcourt, Herbert M. and Gordon W. Ladwig. "Alienation in Negro and White Reformatory Inmates." *Journal of Social Psychology* 68 (1966):153-157.

[126] Lefton, Mark. "Race, Expectations and Anomia." *Social Forces* 46 (1968):347-352.

[127] Lerman, Paul. "Individual Values, Peer Values, and Subcultural Delinquency." *American Sociological Review* 33 (1968):219-235.

[128] Lichter, Solomon O., Elsie B. Rapien, Frances M. Seibert and Morris A. Sklansky. *The Drop-Outs.* New York: Free Press, 1962.

[129] Liddle, Gordon P. "Psychological Factors Involved in Dropping Out of School." *High School Journal* 45 (1962):276-280.

[130] Liska, Allen E. "Aspirations, Expectations and Delinquency: Stress and Additive Models." *Sociological Quarterly* 12 (1971):99-107.

[131] Liu, William T. and Frank Fahey. "Delinquency, Self Esteem and Social Control: A Retroductive Analysis." *American Catholic Sociological Review* 24 (1963):3-12.

[132] Livingston, A. Hugh. "High-School Graduates and Dropouts—A New Look at a Persistent Problem." *School Review* 66 (1958):195-203.

[133] Lord, Frederic M. "The Measurement of Growth." *Educational and Psychological Measurement* 16 (1956):421-437.

[134] _____. "Further Problems in the Measurement of Growth." *Educational and Psychological Measurement* 18 (1958):437-451.

[135] _____. "Elementary Models for Measuring Change." In Chester W. Harris (ed.), *Problems in Measuring Change*, pp. 21-38. Madison: University of Wisconsin Press, 1963.

[136] Los Angeles City School District. *Transfers, Entrants, and Dropouts in Los Angeles City Secondary Schools, 1961-62.* Research Report No. 252. Los Angeles, 1963.

[137] Lunden, Walter A. *Statistics on Delinquents and Delinquency.* Springfield, Ill.: Thomas, 1964.

[138] Lystad, Mary H. *Social Aspects of Alienation: An Annotated Bibliography.* Publication No. 1978. Chevy Chase, Md.: Public Health Service, 1969.

[139] Maccoby, Eleanor, Joseph P. Johnson and Russell M. Church. "Community Integration and the Social Control of Juvenile Delinquency." *Journal of Social Issues* 14 (1958):38-51.

[140] McCord, Joan and William McCord. "The Effects of Parental Role Model on Criminality." *Journal of Social Issues* 14 (1958):66-75.

[141] McCord, William and Joan McCord. *Origins of Crime.* New York: Columbia University Press, 1959.

[142] McCreary, William H. and Donald E. Kitch. "Now Hear Youth." *Bulletin of the California State Department of Education* 22 (1953):27-44.

[143] McEachern, A.W. and Riva Bauzer. "Factors Related to Disposition in Juvenile Police Contacts." In Malcolm W. Klein (ed.), *Juvenile Gangs in Context*, pp. 148-160. Englewood Cliffs, N.J.: Prentice-Hall, 1967.

[144] McGinnis, Robert. "Randomization and Inference in Sociological Research." *American Sociological Review* 23 (1958):408-414.

[145] McNemar, Quinn. "On Growth Measurement." *Educational and Psychological Measurement* 18 (1958):47-55.

[146] Manning, Winton H. and Philip H. DuBois. "Correlational Methods in Research on Human Learning." *Perceptual and Motor Skills* 15 (1962):287-321.

[147] Martin, Richard I. and Malcolm W. Klein. "A Comparative Analysis of Four Measures of Delinquency Seriousness." Los Angeles: University of Southern California Youth Studies Center, 1965.

[148] Merton, Robert K. "Social Structure and Anomie." *American Sociological Review* 3 (1938):672-682.

[149] _____. *Social Theory and Social Structure*, Revised edition. Glencoe, Ill.: Free Press, 1957.

[150] _____. "Social Problems and Sociological Theory." In Robert K. Merton and Robert A. Nisbet (eds.), *Contemporary Social Problems*, pp. 697-737. New York: Harcourt, Brace and World, 1961.

[151] Miller, Walter B. "Lower Class Culture as a Generating Milieu of Gang Delinquency." *Journal of Social Issues* 14 (1958):5-19.

[152] _____. "The Impact of a 'Total-Community' Delinquency Control Project." *Social Problems* 10 (1962):168-191.

[153] Mitchell, George A. "The Youth Bureau: A Sociological Study." Unpublished Master's thesis. Detroit: Wayne State University, 1957.

[154] Mizruchi, Ephraim H. *Success and Opportunity*. New York: Free Press, 1964.

[155] Murphy, Fred J., Mary M. Shirley and Helen L. Witmer. "The Incidence of Hidden Delinquency." *American Journal of Orthopsychiatry* 16 (1946):686-696.

[156] Myers, Jerome K. and Bertram H. Roberts. *Family and Class Dynamics in Mental Illness*. New York: Wiley, 1959.

[157] The National Advisory Commission on Civil Disorders. *Report of the National Advisory Commission on Civil Disorders*. New York: Bantam, 1968.

[158] Nelson, Lester W. "The School Dropout—Fugitive from Failure." *Bulletin of the National Association of Secondary School Principals* 46 (1962):233-241.

[159] Norman, Ralph D. and Gerald J. Kleinfeld. "Rosenzweig Picture-Frustration Study Results with Minority Group Juvenile Delinquents." *Journal of Genetic Psychology* 92 (1958):61-67.

[160] Nye, F. Ivan. *Family Relationships and Delinquent Behavior*. New York: Wiley, 1958.

[161] Nye, F. Ivan and James F. Short, Jr. "Scaling Delinquent Behavior." *American Sociological Review* 22 (1957):326-331.

[162] Nye, F. Ivan, James F. Short, Jr. and Virgil J. Olson. "Socioeconomic Status and Delinquent Behavior." *American Journal of Sociology* 63 (1958):381-389.

[163] Parsons, Talcott. "Age and Sex in the Social Structure of the United States." In Talcott Parsons (ed.), *Essays in Sociological Theory*, pp. 89-103. Revised Edition. Glencoe, Ill.: Free Press, 1954.

[164] Perlman, I. Richard. "The Meaning of Juvenile Delinquency Statistics." *Federal Probation* 13 (1949):63-67.

[165] _____. "Antisocial Behavior of the Minor in the United States." *Federal Probation* 28 (1964):23-30.

[166] Piliavin, Irving and Scott Briar. "Police Encounters with Juveniles." *American Journal of Sociology* 70 (1964):206-214.

[167] Polk, Kenneth and David S. Halferty. "Adolescence, Commitment, and Delinquency." *Journal of Research in Crime and Delinquency* 3 (1966):82-96.

[168] Polk, Kenneth and Lynn Richmond. "Those Who Fail." Unpublished paper. Eugene, Oregon: Lane County Youth Project, 1966.

[169] Polk, Kenneth and William Pink. "Youth Culture and the School: A Replication." *British Journal of Sociology* 22 (1971):160-171.

[170] Pollak, Otto. *The Criminality of Women*. Philadelphia: University of Pennsylvania Press, 1950.

[171] Popper, Karl R. *The Logic of Scientific Discovery*. New York: Harper and Row, 1965.

[172] Porterfield, Austin L. *Youth in Trouble*. Fort Worth: Leo Potishman Foundation, 1946.

[173] Putnam, John F. "Information about Dropouts: Terms and Computations." In Office of Education, *The Dropout*, pp. 10-15. Washington, D.C.: U.S. Government Printing Office, 1963.

[174] Reiss, Albert J., Jr. and A. Lewis Rhodes. *A Sociopsychological Study of Conforming and Deviating Behavior among Adolescents*. Iowa City: University of Iowa, 1959.

[175] _____. "The Distribution of Juvenile Delinquency in the Social Class Structure." *American Sociological Review* 26 (1961):720-732.

[176] _____. "Status Deprivation and Delinquent Behavior." *Sociological Quarterly* 4 (1963):135-149.

[177] _____. "An Empirical Test of Differential Association Theory." *Journal of Research in Crime and Delinquency* 1 (1964):5-18.

[178] Rhodes, A. Lewis and Albert J. Reiss, Jr. "Apathy, Truancy and Delinquency as Adaptations to School Failure." *Social Forces* 48 (1969):12-22.

[179] Rivera, Ramon J. and James F. Short, Jr. "Occupational Goals: A Comparative Analysis." In Malcolm W. Klein (ed.), *Juvenile Gangs in Context*, pp. 70-90. Englewood Cliffs, N.J.: Prentice-Hall, 1967.

[180] Robin, Gerald D. "Gang Member Delinquency: Its Extent, Sequence and Typology." *Journal of Criminal Law, Criminology and Police Science* 55 (1964):59-69.

[181] Robinson, W.S. "The Statistical Measurement of Agreement." *American Sociological Review* 22 (1957):17-25.

[182] _____. "The Geometric Interpretation of Agreement." *American Sociological Review* 24 (1959):338-345.

[183] Robison, Sophia M. *Can Delinquency Be Measured?* New York: Columbia University Press, 1936.

[184] Rodman, Hyman and Paul Grams. "Juvenile Delinquency and the Family: A Review and Discussion." In President's Commission on Law Enforcement and Administration of Justice, *Juvenile Delinquency and Youth*

Crime, pp. 188-221. Washington, D.C.: U.S. Government Printing Office, 1967.

[185] Rosenberg, Morris. *Society and the Adolescent Self-Image*. Princeton, N.J.: Princeton University Press, 1965.

[186] Rosenzweig, Saul. "The Experimental Measurement of Types of Reaction to Frustration." In Henry A. Murray (ed.), *Explorations in Personality*, pp. 585-599. New York: Oxford University Press, 1938.

[187] _____. "Validity of the Rosenzweig Picture-Frustration Study with Felons and Delinquents." *Journal of Consulting Psychology* 27 (1963):535-536.

[188] Rothstein, Edward. "Attributes Related to High Social Status: A Comparison of the Perceptions of Delinquent and Non-Delinquent Boys." *Social Problems* 10 (1962):75-83.

[189] Rotter, Julian B. "Generalized Expectancies for Internal versus External Control of Reinforcement." *Psychological Monographs* 80 (1966):1-28.

[190] Rubington, Earl and Martin S. Weinberg (eds.). *Deviance*. New York: Macmillan, 1968.

[191] Runciman, Walter G. *Relative Deprivation and Social Justice*. Berkeley: University of California Press, 1966.

[192] Sandhu, Swaran S. "Perception of Parents as Related to Delinquency in the Gang and Marks in School." Unpublished Ph.D. dissertation. Detroit: Wayne State University, 1966.

[193] San Diego Unified School District. *A Drop-Out History of the Graduating Class of 1955*. San Diego: Department of Research, 1955.

[194] Sando, Rudolph F. "How to Make and Utilize Follow-Up Studies of School Leavers." *Bulletin of the National Association of Secondary School Principals* 36 (1952):66-74.

[195] Schafer, Stephen and Richard D. Knudten. *Juvenile Delinquency*. New York: Random House, 1970.

[196] Schafer, Walter E. "Participation in Interscholastic Athletics and Delinquency: A Preliminary Study." *Social Problems* 17 (1969):40-47.

[197] Schafer, Walter E. and Kenneth Polk. "Delinquency and the Schools." In President's Commission on Law Enforcement and Administration of Justice, *Juvenile Delinquency and Youth Crime*, pp. 222-277. Washington, D.C.: U.S. Government Printing Office, 1967.

[198] Schreiber, Daniel. "The Dropout and the Delinquent." *Phi Delta Kappan* 44 (1963):215-221.

[199] _____. "Juvenile Delinquency and the School Dropout Problem." *Federal Probation* 27 (1963):15-19.

[200] Schwartz, Edward E. "A Community Experiment in the Measurement of Juvenile Delinquency." In Marjorie Bell (ed.), *Social Correctives for Delinquency*, pp. 157-181. New York: National Probation Association, 1945.

[201] Schwartz, Gary and Don Merten. "The Language of Adolescence: An Anthropological Approach to the Youth Culture." *American Journal of Sociology* 72 (1967):453-468.

[202] Scott, William A. "Measures of Test Homogeneity." *Educational and Psychological Measurement* 20 (1960):751-757.

[203] Seeman, Melvin. "On the Meaning of Alienation." *American Sociological Review* 24 (1959):783-791.

[204] Segel, David and Oscar J. Schwarm. *Retention in High Schools in Large Cities*. Office of Education Bulletin No. 15. Washington, D.C.: U.S. Government Printing Office, 1957.

[205] Sellin, Thorsten. "The Basis of a Crime Index." *Journal of Criminal Law and Criminology* 22 (1931):335-356.

[206] Sellin, Thorsten and Marvin E. Wolfgang. *The Measurement of Delinquency*. New York: Wiley, 1964.

[207] Selvin, Hanan C. "A Critique of Tests of Significance in Survey Research." *American Sociological Review* 22 (1957):519-527.

[208] Severy, Lawrence J. "Exposure to Antisocial Behavior." Unpublished Ph.D. dissertation. Boulder: University of Colorado, 1970.

[209] Sherif, Muzafer and Carolyn W. Sherif. *Reference Groups*. New York: Harper and Row, 1964.

[210] Short, James F., Jr. "A Report on the Incidence of Criminal Behavior, Arrests, and Convictions in Selected Groups." *Research Studies of the State College of Washington* 22 (1954):110-118.

[211] _____. "Differential Association and Delinquency." *Social Problems* 4 (1957):233-239.

[212] _____. "Differential Association with Delinquent Friends and Delinquent Behavior." *Pacific Sociological Review* 1 (1958):20-25.

[213] _____. "Differential Association as a Hypothesis: Problems of Empirical Testing." *Social Problems* 8 (1960):14-25.

[214] _____. "Gang Delinquency and Anomie." In Marshall B. Clinard (ed.), *Anomie and Deviant Behavior*, pp. 98-127. New York: Free Press, 1964.

[215] Short, James F., Jr. and F. Ivan Nye. "Reported Behavior as a Criterion of Deviant Behavior." *Social Problems* 5 (1957-58):207-213.

[216] _____. "Extent of Unrecorded Juvenile Delinquency: Tentative Conclusions." *Journal of Criminal Law, Criminology and Police Science* 49 (1958):296-302.

[217] Short, James F., Jr. and Fred L. Strodtbeck. *Group Process and Gang Delinquency*. Chicago: University of Chicago Press, 1965.

[218] Short, James F., Jr., Ray A. Tennyson and Kenneth I. Howard. "Behavior Dimensions of Gang Delinquency." *American Sociological Review* 28 (1963):411-428.

[219] Short, James F., Jr., Ramon Rivera and Ray A. Tennyson. "Perceived Opportunities, Gang Membership, and Delinquency." *American Sociological Review* 30 (1965):56-67.

[220] Simpson, Jon E. and Maurice D. Van Arsdol, Jr. "Residential History and Educational Status of Delinquents and Nondelinquents." *Social Problems* 15 (1967):25-40.

[221] Skipper, James K., Jr., Anthony L. Guenther and Gilbert Nass. "The Sacredness of .05: A Note Concerning the Uses of Statistical Levels of Significance in Social Science." *American Sociologist* 2 (1967):16-18.

[222] Slocum, Walter L. and Carol L. Stone. "Family Culture Patterns and Delinquent-Type Behavior." *Marriage and Family Living* 25 (1963):202-208.

[223] Smith, Ernest A. *American Youth Culture.* New York: Free Press, 1962.

[224] Snepp, Daniel W. "Why They Drop Out: Eight Clues to Greater Holding Power." *The Clearing House* 27 (1953):492-494.

[225] Spergel, Irving. "Deviant Patterns and Opportunities of Pre-Adolescent Negro Boys in Three Chicago Neighborhoods." In Malcolm W. Klein (ed.), *Juvenile Gangs in Context*, pp. 38-54. Englewood Cliffs, N.J.: Prentice-Hall, 1967.

[226] Stinchcombe, Arthur L. *Rebellion in a High School.* Chicago: Quadrangle, 1964.

[227] Sugarman, Barry. "Involvement in Youth Culture, Academic Achievement and Conformity in School." *British Journal of Sociology* 18 (1967):151-164.

[228] Sutherland, Edwin H. *Principles of Criminology*, Fourth Edition. Philadelphia: Lippincott, 1947.

[229] Sutherland, Edwin H. and Donald R. Cressey. *Criminology*, Eighth Edition. Philadelphia: Lippincott, 1970.

[230] Swanson, Richard M. "Sense of Efficacy, Effectiveness, and Control: A Look toward Clarification of Concepts." Unpublished Ph.D. dissertation. Boulder: University of Colorado, 1970.

[231] Sykes, Gresham M. and David Matza. "Techniques of Neutralization: A Theory of Delinquency." *American Sociological Review* 22 (1957):664-670.

[232] Terry, Robert M. "The Screening of Juvenile Offenders." *Journal of Criminal Law, Criminology and Police Science* 58 (1967):173-181.

[233] _____. "Discrimination in the Handling of Juvenile Offenders by Social-Control Agencies." *Journal of Research in Crime and Delinquency* 4 (1967):218-230.

[234] Tesseneer, R.A. and L.M. Tesseneer. "Review of the Literature on School Dropouts." *Bulletin of the National Association of Secondary School Principals* 42 (1958):141-153.

[235] Thomas, Robert J. "An Empirical Study of High School Drop-Outs in Regard to Ten Possibly Related Factors." *Journal of Educational Sociology* 28 (1954):11-18.

[236] Thrasher, Frederic M. *The Gang.* Chicago: University of Chicago Press, 1927.

[237] Toby, Jackson. "The Differential Impact of Family Disorganization." *American Sociological Review* 22 (1957):505-512.

[238] Toby, Jackson and Marcia Toby. *Low School Status as a Predisposing Factor in Subcultural Delinquency.* New Brunswick, N.J.: Rutgers, 1963.

[239] Turner, Ralph H. *The Social Context of Ambition.* San Francisco: Chandler, 1964.

[240] _____ . "Deviance Avowal as Neutralization of Commitment." *Social Problems* 19 (1972):308-321.

[241] U.S. Department of Labor. *School and Early Employment Experience of Youth: A Report on Seven Communities, 1952-57.* Bulletin No. 1277. Washington, D.C.: U.S. Government Printing Office, 1960.

[242] U.S. Senate. *Report of the Committee on the Judiciary.* Report No. 130. Washington, D.C.: U.S. Government Printing Office, 1957.

[243] Van Dyke, L.A. and K.B. Hoyt. *The Drop-Out Problem in Iowa High Schools.* Des Moines: Iowa State Department of Public Instruction, 1958.

[244] Varner, Sherrell E. *School Dropouts.* Washington, D.C.: National Education Association, 1967.

[245] Veblen, Thorstein. *The Theory of the Leisure Class.* New York: New American Library, 1953.

[246] Vinter, Robert D. and Rosemary C. Sarri. "Malperformance in the Public School: A Group Work Approach." *Social Work* 10 (1965):3-13.

[247] Voss, Harwin L. "Ethnic Differentials in Delinquency in Honolulu." *Journal of Criminal Law, Criminology and Police Science* 54 (1963):322-327.

[248] _____ . "Differential Association and Reported Delinquent Behavior: A Replication." *Social Problems* 12 (1964):78-85.

[249] _____ . "Pitfalls in Social Research: A Case Study." *American Sociologist* 1 (1966):136-140.

[250] _____ . "Socio-Economic Status and Reported Delinquent Behavior." *Social Problems* 13 (1966):314-324.

[251] Voss, Harwin L. (ed.). *Society, Delinquency, and Delinquent Behavior.* Boston: Little, Brown, 1970.

[252] Voss, Harwin L., Aubrey Wendling and Delbert S. Elliott. "Some Types of High School Dropouts." *Journal of Educational Research* 59 (1966):363-368.

[253] Voss, Harwin L. and Delbert S. Elliott. "Delinquency, Opportunity and the Prediction of Delinquent Behavior." *Criminologica* 6 (1968):39-50.

[254] Wallerstein, James S. and Clement J. Wyle. "Our Law-Abiding Law-Breakers." *Probation* 25 (1947):107-112, 118.

[255] Weinberg, S. Kirson. "Sociological Process and Factors in Juvenile Delinquency." In Joseph S. Roucek (ed.), *Juvenile Delinquency*, pp. 113-132. New York: Philosophical Library, 1958.

[256] Weinberg, S. Kirson. "Juvenile Delinquency in Ghana: A Comparative

Analysis of Delinquents and Non-Delinquents." *Journal of Criminal Law, Criminology and Police Science* 55 (1964):471-481.

[257] Wendling, Aubrey and Delbert S. Elliott. "Class and Race Differentials in Parental Aspirations and Expectations." *Pacific Sociological Review* 11 (1968):123-133.

[258] Whyte, William F. *Street Corner Society*. Chicago: University of Chicago Press, 1943.

[259] Wilson, Robert A. "Anomie in the Ghetto: A Study of Neighborhood Type, Race, and Anomie." *American Journal of Sociology* 77 (1971):66-88.

[260] Winter, J. Allan and Donald L. Halsted. *Report on the Flint Youth Study*. Ann Arbor: University of Michigan Institute for Social Research, 1961.

[261] Yablonsky, Lewis. *The Violent Gang*. New York: Macmillan, 1962.

Index

Index

261

About the Authors

Delbert S. Elliott is professor of sociology at the University of Colorado and Project Director of the Institute of Behavioral Science, University of Colorado. He received the B.A. from Pomona College and the M.A. and the Ph.D. from the University of Washington. Dr. Elliott has contributed numerous articles to professional journals. He is a member of the American Sociological Association, the Pacific Sociological Association, the National Council on Crime and Delinquency, and the Society for the Study of Social Problems.

Harwin L. Voss is professor of sociology at the University of Kentucky and Director of the Research-Training Program in Deviant Behavior (Drug Abuse) funded by the National Institute of Health. He received the B.A. from North Central College and the M.S. and the Ph.D. from the University of Wisconsin, Madison. Dr. Voss is the editor of *Society, Delinquency, and Delinquent Behavior* (Little, Brown, 1970) and coeditor, with David M. Petersen, of *Ecology, Crime, and Delinquency* (Appleton-Century, 1971); he has contributed numerous articles to professional journals. Dr. Voss is a member of the American Sociological Association, the Pacific Sociological Association, the Society for the Study of Social Problems, the American Society of Criminology, and other professional organizations.